AM
BLACK
ENOUGH FOR YOU?
ANITA HEISS

UNIVERSITY OF HAWAI'I PRESS
HONOLULU

Some pseudonyms have been used in this book and other details altered where necessary to protect the identity and privacy of persons mentioned.

Excerpt from *Demon Guards the School Yard* reproduced with permission from Oxford University Press and Laguna Bay (packager and producer).

Printed in 2014 in the United States of America by
University of Hawai'i Press
2840 Kolowalu Street
Honolulu, HI 96822
www.uhpress.hawaii.edu

19 18 17 16 15 14   6 5 4 3 2 1

First published in Australia by
Random House Australia Pty Ltd
Level 3, 100 Pacific Highway
North Sydney NSW 2060
Australia
www.randomhouse.com.au

This project has been assisted by the Australian Government through the Australia Council's arts funding and advisory body.

Library of Congress Cataloging-in-Publication Data

Heiss, Anita, author.
 Am I black enough for you? / Anita Heiss.
  pages cm
  ISBN 978-0-8248-4027-3 (pbk. : alk. paper)
1. Heiss, Anita. 2. Aboriginal Australians—Biography. 3. Women, Aboriginal Australian—Biography. I. Title.
  PR9619.4.H345Z46 2014
  823'.92—dc23
  [B]
                              2014009346

University of Hawai'i Press books are printed on acid-free paper and meet the guidelines for permanence and durability of the Council on Library Resources.

Printed by Sheridan Books, Inc.

TABLE OF CONTENTS

INTRODUCTION: WHO AM I?   1

THE TRIAL: BEGINNINGS   7

CHAPTER 1

    WHERE I BEGAN . . .   12

CHAPTER 2

    BEING ELSIE'S DAUGHTER   27

    ODE TO MY MOTHER   47

CHAPTER 3

    JOE-THE-CARPENTER   49

    THE TRIAL: THE POSSIBILITY OF A GROUP ACTION   77

CHAPTER 4

    COCO POP, CHOCOLATE DROP . . .   82

CHAPTER 5

    BEING RIDGY-DIDGE   108

    THE KOORI FLAG   127

CHAPTER 6

    EPISTA-WHAT?   130

CHAPTER 7

    ON BEING INVISIBLE   145

    THE TRIAL: WHY GO TO COURT?   167

CHAPTER 8

    WRITING US ONTO THE IDENTITY RADAR   173

CHAPTER 9

    WRITING US INTO AUSTRALIAN HISTORY   193

CHAPTER 10

    ON BEING KOORI BRADSHAW   211

    THE TRIAL: IN THE COURT   226

CHAPTER 11

    SLEEPING UNDER THE STARS   231

CHAPTER 12

    IF YOU ARE A BLACK WOMAN, YOU SHOULD . . .   253

CHAPTER 13

    A BLACKFELLA ABROAD   276

CHAPTER 14

    THE OPRAH INFLUENCE   303

    THE TRIAL: JUDGMENT DAY   327

    GLOSSARY OF TERMS AND ACRONYMS   336

    ACKNOWLEDGEMENTS   345

INTRODUCTION: WHO AM I?

'I AM BLACK OF SKIN AMONG WHITES,
AND I AM PROUD,
PROUD OF RACE AND PROUD OF SKIN.'

KATH WALKER

I'm a Williams; my mob's from Cowra, Brungle Mission, Griffith and Canberra, but I was born in Gadigal country (aka the city of Sydney) and have spent most of my life living on Dharawal land at Matraville, which is strategically placed between the Malabar sewage works, Long Bay gaol and the Orica industrial estate. It's a place where I grew up playing cricket in the street, walked safely to and from school each day, and where neighbours always had a spare key to the house. My home suburb remains the perfect setting for creative inspiration today. I am an urban, beachside Blackfella, a concrete Koori with Westfield Dreaming, and I apologise to no-one.

This is *my* story: it is a story about *not* being from the desert, *not* speaking my traditional language and *not* wearing ochre. I'm not very good at playing the clap sticks either, and I *loathe* sleeping outdoors. But my story is of the journey of being a proud Wiradjuri woman, just not necessarily being the Blackfella – the so-called 'real Aborigine' – some people, perhaps even *you*, expect me to be.

Since my late teens, when I entered tertiary education and began my adult social life, I have been expected by non-Aboriginal people – at university, during school visits, at writers' festivals, at dinner parties, on plane rides and in night clubs – to be all-knowing of Aboriginal culture as well as able to articulate my predefined, exotic and somehow tangible relationship with the land. This has become something I have written and spoken about as I attempt, as an artist and academic, to define myself in the world I have been born, socialised, educated and politicised into – my landscape, my place, my country.

When I talk about my country, I don't mean Australia generally but Wiradjuri country specifically. My country is central New South Wales, around Cowra, Tumut, Brungle, Wagga Wagga, Bathurst, Dubbo and Mudgee. It is this country that I am patriotic to, even though I have spent much of my life working, studying and socialising on Gadigal land. It is because I have lived most of my life in Sydney that I was part of the anthology *Life in Gadigal Country* (2002) which was a statement of recognition of country by its contributors, all visitors to Sydney, but all with connections to

Gadigal country. Similarly, I have published two books with and about the kids at La Perouse because I wanted to recognise that I have physically lived on the land of the Dharawal for much of my life also. And while I can easily call Greater Sydney my home, it is not *my* country. My spirit belongs and will finally rest with those of my ancestors back in Wiradjuri ngurumbang (country).

Connection to country means something more to me than shifting geographic boundaries. Unlike some people I met when I moved to the Gold Coast in 1996, I did not automatically become a Queenslander, for I was never really a Sydneysider (although I have done the Sydney versus Melbourne debate to death!) but a visitor and I have never regarded myself as a New South Welshman (or Welshperson for the so inclined). Wherever I am in Australia or overseas, I am always Wiradjuri. My connection is to my country, my people, the land my mob has always come from. Therefore, my artistic creation has never strayed from being that of the voice of a Wiradjuri woman aware of where she will always belong. It is not to say that state boundaries aren't important to Blackfellas, especially during State of Origin time. And *never* call a Murri (a generic term for an Aboriginal person in Queensland) a Koori (a generic term for an Aboriginal person in most of New South Wales) or vice versa, or expect to feel some backlash, or should I say, Blacklash!

When writing, I am aware of the importance of the words I choose to use. I am always conscious that there weren't any 'Aborigines' in Australia before invasion. There were just *people* who were identified and known by their relationships to each other through familial connections, through connections to country and through language groups. 'Aborigines' were created when the colonisers used a Latin term meaning 'original habitants' to describe the peoples whose land they were stealing. More commonly used today is the term 'Indigenous', another Latin term meaning 'native to'. And while I have used these terms throughout this work because they are standard ways of discussing Australia's First Peoples, they are terms that impact on identity because we have *our* own terms to define who we are and where we are from, and that's another reason I have penned this work, to demonstrate our own forms of self-expression and self-representation.

Many of my mob today don't use or like either word and prefer our own terms: Koori, Goori, Murri, Noongar, Nunga and so on. And we prefer our nation's original name (where known) over a generic 'Aboriginal land' or 'Indigenous land'. In fact, the term Indigenous can be confusing in that its use in Australia includes not only all of the diverse Aboriginal nations that make up Australia, but also Torres Strait Islanders who became Indigenous to Australia when in 1879 the islands of the Torres Strait were annexed to Queensland through an act of Parliament. I have witnessed more and more Aboriginal people preferring the use of First Nations or Aboriginal over Indigenous to clarify the original inhabitants of the land mass now known as Australia. It could be argued that the use of First Nations in the broader community presents problems because it firmly identifies that everyone

4

other than Aboriginal people are 'Second Peoples' . . . and as pointed out by my dear Wiradjuri friend Professor Michael McDaniel, what's there to celebrate in being second?

These kinds of complexities have existed since the point of invasion in 1788, and since then the 'concept of Aboriginality' and what 'an Aborigine is' has been an ongoing construction of the colonisers, an imposed definition. It is also a political issue for Australia's First Nations peoples, who have been forced to live by legislation created around these constructions, answering to variations of it, while at the same time trying to explain to our 'other' (that is, non-Aboriginal Australians) what it actually means to be Aboriginal from *our* perspectives and based on *our* lives in the twenty-first century.

In the 1960s, one of my greatest writing role models, Oodgeroo Noonuccal (then Kath Walker), hit the literary limelight as Australia's first published 'Aboriginal poet'. Since then, Aboriginal writers have been using our literature as a means of publicly defining ourselves and as a tool to defend our right to our identity. We are often inspired by the need to dissect historical government material, exposing how they categorised Aboriginal people into a caste system to put in place a racist assimilation policy. These policies were to ensure Aboriginal people forcibly traded in their own cultural practices and lifestyles for those of white Australian society, but without the rights and benefits white Australians enjoyed. Like other writers today, I aim to use my writing to reclaim pride in our status as First Nations peoples, to explain the diversity of Aboriginal experiences (particularly in urban environments), and to demonstrate the realities and complexities of being Aboriginal in the twenty-first century.

I want to use my published words as a vehicle for asserting my individual and communal identity, to instil pride in others, and to help non-Aboriginal people better understand us. I hope, in turn, that we can all then improve our understanding of ourselves and our collective Australian identity.

I am Anita Heiss. I am a proud Wiradjuri woman. But am I Black enough for *you*?

THE TRIAL: BEGINNINGS

On the morning of 15 April 2009, I rose before 7 am, as I always do. As was my usual routine, I logged on to check emails, Facebook and my blog. The sun was already shining through the north-facing window of my home office. A Google Alert led me to an article headlined 'It's so hip to be black' (produced online as 'White is the new black'). The author was Andrew Bolt, a much-read writer and blogger for the Herald and Weekly Times whose work is syndicated throughout many News Limited publications in Australia. He was known for being an outspoken denier of climate change, the Stolen Generations and now, the right for Aboriginal people to self-identify.

In a rush to get organised for a video recording that morning, I skimmed the article quickly. I was immediately gobsmacked that a poorly researched piece had passed through the editorial process to publication. As well as making ill-informed comments on Aboriginal identity – seemingly based only on personal appearance – Andrew Bolt had written false information about me and people I knew, including my friends

Tara June Winch and Larissa Behrendt. I read misrepresentations about how we had 'chosen' our Aboriginal identity for 'political and career clout', that we were 'white Aborigines' and 'professional Aborigines' who were motivated by political and financial gains. My eyes glazed over as I wondered if what I was reading was real. Was this really in the public domain? And if so, why? What had I done to deserve this rant from someone who had never met me, had clearly never read any of my work, and hadn't bothered to call me to check any of his facts? From just one reading I could tell that Bolt had not conducted interviews with any of those targeted, nor anyone within the Aboriginal community. And yet, his misguided opinions and incorrect 'facts' were now being read internationally.

After challenging the professional reputations of several others, Bolt had this to say about me:

> *Heiss's father was Austrian, and her mother only part-Aboriginal. What's more, she was raised in Sydney and educated at Saint Claire's [sic] Catholic College. She, too, could identify as a member of more than one race, if joining up to any at all was important.*

> *As it happens, her decision to identify as Aboriginal, joining four other 'Austrian Aborigines' she knows, was lucky, given how it's helped her career.*

Upon reading this, I immediately recognised the words of journalist Martin Flanagan, who had written a positive profile piece on me titled 'Wit and wisdom in the concrete Dreamtime' for *The Age* back in 2004. Martin's article, which used the phrase 'Austrian Aborigines', had been manipulated to suggest I may have used those words to describe myself. I've heard the argument about Blackfellas 'choosing' their identity before, heard in every city, every town, here and abroad, all from Anglo-Australians who don't believe racism exists. I was told as a teen that I could 'pass' as something other than Aboriginal: Spanish, Lebanese or even Tahitian. Indeed, I was advised once by an Anglo housewife and neighbour in Matraville that I *should* 'pass' myself off as one of these groups, as it would be better to be anything other than Aboriginal, because Aborigines, according to this woman in particular, 'didn't even know the difference between a feline and canine'. Yes, that is a true conversation I had to endure with someone I babysat for in early 1980.

I have no doubt that woman believed she was liberal-minded and far from racist; she had hired me to look after her children, after all. But in telling me I was stupid for identifying as Aboriginal, and therefore opening myself up to be discriminated against (when I could just as easily *choose to be Spanish* instead), demonstrated how she understood the way racism worked in Australia. In her own mind, she thought it was better to be anything other than Black. She may not have been aware of her own racism, but she was clearly aware of that of others when she recommended I 'pass'.

Usually, such recommendations come from those who don't understand that Aboriginal identity is not something one chooses to be or not be. Aboriginal identity is complex and rarely, if ever, by choice. Identity in my case came from being told by whitefellas as a child that I was Aboriginal (or 'abo', as they most eloquently put it); from only having my Aboriginal family (the Williams) around me because Dad's family were all in Austria; and from always being the darker kid as a child at school, with two fair sisters. Being Aboriginal was always who I was and all I'd ever known growing up. Even if I had been aware of the notion of 'choosing' (or passing) when I was young, there wasn't any possible way that I could. I used to joke as a child that being in Mum and Dad's bed on Sunday morning when we'd all climb in was like a pedestrian crossing – black, white, black, white bodies all lined up.

~

That morning, after reading the article, as I pulled onto Southern Cross Drive, and with my phone set to hands-free, I called Larissa Behrendt just to see if she'd read the article. Of course she had: as had much of the reading public by 11 am that day. Ten minutes later, Mum called. She was distressed. She hadn't seen the article, but she had been called by a contact in the Aboriginal Catholic network who wanted to see if she knew about it. That call had come from Adelaide: the story was national, everyone named was offended and humiliated and so were our families and communities. Mum couldn't understand why it had been written, or why I had been targeted. She was distraught that her own identity had been documented incorrectly. She knew who she was and the struggles she had been through as an Aboriginal woman, but all this had been undermined by the publication of the article. Later, in his witness statement to the court, Andrew Bolt would declare:

> *I wrote in my first article that Anita Heiss's mother was only part-Aboriginal. Annexure O is a copy of a photograph of Anita Heiss's mother which I downloaded from the internet. It appears from the photograph that Anita Heiss's mother has mixed ancestry.*

The photo he referred to came directly from my blog, and included text about what I was grateful for on 7 February 2011 (almost two years after Bolt wrote his article). The misrepresentations continued.

Chapter 1

WHERE I BEGAN . . .

There is a photo of my maternal grandmother – Amy Williams – standing in our old kitchen at the family home in Matraville in 1974. She is with my younger sister, Gisella, who looks rather cute. My grandmother, though, doesn't look happy. And she looks weathered. But when I think of her, it is always this photo that comes to mind.

I was about six when it was taken, only a couple of years before she died in 1976. It's the last time I remember seeing her in the flesh. Her death meant that, unlike most of the other kids at school, I didn't really have a grandmother in my life. I never had school holidays filled with stories or trips to visit her in Tumut. I don't remember getting lots of cuddles from her, but I'm told I loved my grandmother combing and plaiting my hair, because she was gentle. It's what she would do every morning on the rare visits she would make to Sydney. And when I saw her rubbing Vicks into her own chest, I'd push mine out and say, 'Rub my chest too!'

The truth is, I never got to *know* her enough to remember her love. And worse still, I never got to meet my grandfather, James, at all. As a child I felt ripped-off not having grandparents nearby – my Dad's parents were in Austria and Mum's had passed away – but none of the kids in my class had the same harsh and diverse family history as I did. You see, documents held by the New South Wales Department of Aboriginal Affairs show that in 1910 my grandmother, then known as Amy Josephine Talence, was removed by the Aborigines Protection Board from her family in Nyngan, along with her four-year-old sister, Florence. After spending time in Cootamundra Domestic Training Home for Aboriginal Girls, she was moved to a Catholic institution for girls: the Home of the Good Shepherd in Ashfield, Sydney. From the ages of sixteen to eighteen, Amy was still under the control of welfare and went into service for a wealthy English lady my mum says lived at Parsley Bay in Sydney's east, although I have letters addressed to her via a woman in Kambala Road, Bellevue Hill. Amy also spent some time as a domestic servant at Meryula sheep station near Cobar from twenty to twenty-two years of age. She was finally released from her life of servitude around 1927, when she married my grandfather.

It is from this knowledge of the incredibly hard life my grandmother lived – and the one photo that always comes to mind – that I draw my strength, and from where stems my sense of commitment and obligation to do what I do in life. I think about the life she had, the little of it that I know, and how it was a life similarly experienced by thousands of others also removed from their families and taken into state control. I understand that I need to do more than just enjoy the rights that she and the rest of my family went without for so long – I need to also use my position and privilege to help others in the community make the most of the rights our people have fought for.

My maternal grandfather, James Andrew Williams, was born in 1900 and was a labourer from Brungle, near Tumut, New South Wales. He is described as a 'Wiradjuri warrior' by my mother. He was a man who fought hard to keep his family close and to protect my grandmother under appallingly degrading and difficult circumstances. Although Catholic, he was initiated through traditional sacred Aboriginal men's business, and spirituality was a big part of his life. Mum says he was a great storyteller and knew much about the bush life and traditional ways. Mum says most of her cultural identity was given to her by my grandfather.

My maternal grandparents begin the love story of my family as I know it. When my grandmother was eighteen and still in service, she was walking through the Botanic Gardens in Sydney and met another Aboriginal lady, who turned out to be my grandfather's sister. Her name was Tilly Williams and she was also living under the Protection Act. She asked my grandmother, 'Are you Aboriginal?' and that's how they became friends. My great-aunt Tilly later took my grandmother back to Brungle in 1923, where Amy met the love of her life. Brungle was a station but everyone called it and Erambie 'a mission', although they were never Christian-run.

My grandparents maintained a long-distance relationship from Brungle to Bellevue Hill from about 1923 to 1927, surviving mostly on letters and gifts sent by post.

In my possession are letters between James and Amy, and although they suggest there was an equal sharing of pen on paper from both sides, there are far more surviving that are written by my grandfather. Both of my grandparents begin their notes with warm, loving openings, the same each time: 'My dearest Jim' and 'My dearest Amy'. The words so carefully crafted on the page read as if they are yarning over a cup of tea, or even holding each other under the trees along the riverbank where they used to walk. The pages are frail now, but they are strong with compassion, caring, thoughtfulness and longing for each other.

My grandfather's letters to his 'ever loving Amy' provide news to my grandmother of what is happening with her own family especially her mother, and how they are doing. He also provides updates on Tilly, gives a commentary on the weather, who is visiting and who is leaving town, who's shearing, who's fishing and who the Brungle Boys are playing in football. In the letters, 1920s Brungle sounds like a quiet place, though there seemed to be a *lot* of dances and shows going on there and nearby Tumut and Gundagai. The letters are riddled with gossip and promises of keeping such words between themselves. Sometimes they read like cheeky kids in a world of their own, but clearly even trivia is a tool that was essential to them remaining connected to each other when 'real' life kept them so far apart for so long.

The loveliest realisation for me when reading his words is that many of my grandfather's letters came with gifts for my grandmother: 'a simply beautiful watchband', 'a dear little tape measure', some jazz garters (used to hold up her stockings), chocolates, stamps, a tiepin and pressed flowers. I learned from these letters that my grandmother sewed her own dresses – not a skill that is in my genes, but a necessity for women at that time. And while her few remaining letters were written while she was a servant at Meryula Station, they don't talk or complain about her hard life as a domestic. However, it is clear from my grandfather's responses that she must have talked about her domestic chores at some stage. In November 1925, James wrote: 'I wish I was there to help you feed those chickens and do those windows and verandas and a lot more for you.'

In 1927, he wrote:

> *You must have a terrible lot of work to do as ever there. I can just imagine what it must be like having to cook seven meals a day not to mention the washing up and all that. I'm ever so glad to hear that you will be coming home soon dear.*

Every single letter leaves me misty-eyed at the amount of love and kindness and caring on the fragile yellowed pages. In March 1924, three years before they were reunited to be married, my grandfather wrote:

*Don't you worry about me leaving Brungle Amy
dear. I'll be here when you come back again if I
have to wait till the moon turns red, but I hope
that I won't have to wait that long.*

My grandparents signed off all their letters with dozens of
hand-drawn kisses and affirmations of love, and on one
occasion James added a stanza from the popular 1915 song
'Memories'. He also joked once that my grandmother should
destroy all his letters, but I am so glad she didn't.

After a long courtship, my grandparents finally married
in 1927. They had eight children: Roy Lawrence (known to
most as Sandy), William (Billy), John Charles (Bluey), Kevin
(Red), Nellie, Elsie (Dunkie) and Florence and Beatrice, who
both died as young children. Elsie, my mum, grew up as
the youngest of the six remaining children. She was born at
Erambie Aboriginal Station, Cowra, on 11 November 1937.
Her father was thirty-seven and her mother was thirty-two.

The family all lived on Cowra Mission in one of the twenty-
one houses, where the Williams family was related to most:
the Wallaces, Bambletts, Murrays, Ingrams, Broughtons,
Carrolls and Briars among others. Life was tough and con-
trolled at Erambie, and every Thursday the mission manager's
wife, known as the matron, would check the houses were
clean under the instructions of the Welfare Board. Homes
deemed 'unfit' could see children removed under the New
South Wales *Aborigines Protection Act* (1909–1969).

At Erambie, my uncles would catch rabbits with which

my grandmother would make stews. She also cooked fried johnnycakes and damper with syrup, and on occasion they'd have something Mum says was margarine or butter on their damper. The rationed foods provided on the mission were all high in starch: potatoes, porridge and brown sugar. There were certainly no green vegetables or fruit. Mum remembers on special occasions eating sausages and fried bread: 'Uncle Jim Wallace was a drover and he knew the butcher and would bring sausages. Mum would curry them. It was good.' A treat for the kids would be an ice-cream or ice-block or a soft drink, and this would only happen a couple of times a year. A world away from the treats kids in my family enjoy on a daily basis now.

There was a church at Erambie where many weddings and baptisms were held. Mum, however, was baptised at St Raphael's in Cowra proper, while other local Blackfellas got baptised back in Brungle, Tumut or Gundagai. Schooling on the mission was poor. Mum says this is because 'it was a mission school with second-rate teaching. I think they thought it was good enough for Black kids.'

Aside from her parents, my mother's role models as a child were her aunties Florrie, Ruth and Daphne. And in her teens and before she was married, she looked up to Uncle Muddy (Harry Tompkins) and Uncle Donny (Didlo). In an article published in the *Cowra Guardian* promoting my visit to the Erambie Aboriginal Mission in 2009, Dr Lawrence Bamblett writes:

According to Maybe (Mavis Bamblett) Elsie's Uncle Tonks was a musical man who used to run dances at Erambie and charge threepence for the teenagers to get in. Maybe says that her and Josie (Josie Ingram nee Moynihan) were too young to get in so they would watch through the window. People that knew them always talk about the creative abilities of Tonks, Muddy and Ruth so it may be that Anita has inherited her creativity from right here on Erambie Mission. See what our people can do!

In 1946 my grandparents decided to leave the mission and seek a new place to raise their family. They arrived in Griffith by train at around five in the afternoon. Mum was nine at the time, and she remembers the stationmaster at Griffith ran from his office, looking flabbergasted at the family.

'Who owns all this?' he asked.

My grandfather replied, 'Do you mean the kids or the bags? Yes, they belong to me.'

'You can't stay here,' the stationmaster declared. 'What are you doing here anyway?'

My grandfather James responded calmly, 'I'm trying to find a place for my family to settle, work and have a life. But don't worry, just point us to the nearest waterhole and we will be gone.'

Just then the stationmaster had more to deal with because off the train also came my great-uncle Alex and great-aunty

Muriel with their seven kids and eleven chaff bags. And so began life on the Riverina for the Williams mob. Farmers needed fruit pickers, and the Blackfellas were the best and needed the work. The farmers would collect them – men and women – and they'd pick grapes, peaches, pears, apples and even prunes that fell to the ground when ripe. Mum reckons the women were better pickers than the men, based on the efforts of my aunty Zillah (Uncle Kevin's wife) who was one of the best cherry pickers in Young! Lawrence Bamblett reminded me recently that most families in the region have their own legends of fruit picking; those known as 'gun pickers' won competitions, earned the most money and so on.

The kids went to Hanwood Primary, where they were told quite blatantly, 'You play up and you're out on your heads. You are only here thanks to the courtesy of the parents and *citizens.*' It was the reference to 'citizens' that stung the most, making a point of the non-status the Blacks had, not only in town, but around the country. School was a nightmare for the Williams kids. 'What did we know about attending a white school? We were pushed around and treated badly by both teachers and the other children,' Mum says. The classes were segregated, with the Blacks in a corner up the back of the classroom. On the playground they were told not to speak in the pidgin language – which the kids thought was a funny order to be given, since they didn't know it was called 'pidgin' and how could you tell kids not to speak their own language? – and they were not to 'congregate' on the playground.

Mum says the good times came when the family moved

to Darlington Point, on the Murrumbidgee River, where they would bog in for the winter. My grandfather and uncles would build a shack out of any material they could find at the town tip. My grandmother would sew chaff bags together for curtains and to divide the space. 'All the Blackfellas lived the same way,' Mum recalls. She says:

> *Times were good here, there were lots of Aboriginal families camped on the riverbanks. My father and brothers could build our humpy in no time. Who would've thought that this sacred place would be sacrificed to make way for a caravan park and the river cleaned out of fish and lobsters? We all carved our names in the gum trees there. The times I ran through the long fresh grass, believing that wherever we camped was our land but the authorities would move us on. This was called 'progress'.*

At fifteen years old, Mum started work as a ward maid in the Griffith Public Hospital, where her own mother was a cook in the kitchen and her sister and cousins worked also. At sixteen, Mum went to work at Yanco Agricultural College as a scullery maid – a life of pots and pans. She got pneumonia and that was the end of her career there. At seventeen, Mum moved to Sydney to live with her aunty Mary, who was married to Uncle Harry 'Major' Murray (James Williams' cousin), and she worked in a laundromat in North Sydney. Her next job was at Sweet Acres in Rosebery, the home of such famous Australian favourites as Fantales, Minties and Jubes. Mum's favourites were Sunbuds – little chocolate buds, now discontinued. Mum's job was to get chocolates out of their moulds and also to make the boxes for the Fantales. It's amazing that my mother was so scarily thin despite this tempting work, but there's no doubt where I got my chocolate-loving gene from.

In 1957 and 1958, life for Mum in Sydney sounds enjoyable. Other than following Koori footballers around the eastern region and hanging out at Redfern Oval, she had a social life of dancing better than mine in the 1980s. Mum would go to the dances at the Redfern Town Hall and the Australian Hall on Elizabeth Street. Australian Hall was the site of the momentous national civil rights meeting on 26 January 1938 and continues to retain its historical meaning. Mum would head there with her workmates from Sweet Acres – Black and white – and two of her oldest friends, Barbara Nichols (who lived in Caroline Street behind Mum in 1956) and Jeannie Merritt (who grew up with mum in Cowra Mission). Decades later, I'd become friends with Jeannie's niece, Kim, as well as Barbara's daughter, Kerry, who I worked alongside at the Australia Council for the Arts.

The girls would go to a place called The Park Hotel, opposite Hyde Park. Only once was Mum told she couldn't be served because she was Aboriginal. Most of the time she was with non-Aboriginal women from work, and so she thinks they just let her in. The Crown Hotel just down from The Foundation was the main hangout, though, and usually the women would stay there until closing at 10 pm, because none of the men went to the dances until the pub shut.

At the end of 1957, when Mum was twenty years old, she met my father at a birthday party in Pagewood, only a few kilometres from where they both eventually settled with their brood. One of Mum's friends, Leigh, a woman from Graz in Austria, introduced them. Mum says Dad could hardly speak English, and all he got from his attempts to speak to her in German was laughter. On their first date they went to the Lawson Theatre in Redfern, because it was close to where Mum lived with her aunty Mary. Dad at the time was living in Pagewood. Aunty Mary had warned: 'Be careful of those *New Australians*. They carry knives; you don't know what they'll do.' On that date they saw a Greek movie with English subtitles, an odd choice given Dad didn't speak Greek or English. But the cinema *was* close to Mum's home.

It's sad but true that when Mum was dating my father, she went dancing without him while he waited for her outside. He didn't want to have to talk to the other patrons because he was embarrassed about his language skills, although he was forced to improve his English quickly. The other reason he didn't go in was because some of the Koori men in Mum's circle didn't really make him feel welcome. Mum admits: 'Blackfellas hated the fact that a Black woman was going out with a New Australian. It wasn't the done thing.' My mother dating my father was an apparent slight on Black men, but her female friends liked Dad, they just never understood him. It makes me sad to think of my father being ridiculed and laughed at for loving my mother. And he loved her *so much* that after she had finished dancing for the night, he would drive her home and ensure she was safe. He was no doubt making sure she wasn't going home with anyone else, either.

My Aunty Nellie – who looked the spitting image of Mum – moved to Sydney in 1959 and lived with my mother in Edward Street, Redfern. Both sisters then went to work at White Wings cake factory in Chippendale. I've no doubt that's where my mum's passion for making chocolate cakes came from. My parents finally married in St Vincent's Church, Redfern, the same day as my father's birthday, 5 November 1960. We often joke that Mum was Dad's birthday present that day, and every year after. There were no invitations to the wedding: people just turned up, and there were more babies and children than adults. Aunty Nellie and Roy Carroll (Mum's cousin) were the witnesses on the day. Mum's other cousins (on her father's side) Kay Carroll and Deana Murray were bridesmaids and Ernie Wallace and Hanz Moser (one of Dad's Austrian mates) were groomsmen.

As painful as it is to write it here, my grandfather James did not walk my mother down the aisle of St Vincent's that day. Mum was the only one of the six children to not marry, or get 'married up' – living with a partner but not legally married under the law or the church – to a Blackfella, and to make matters worse in my grandfather's eyes, she was marrying a New Australian. My great-uncle Muddy, my grandmother's stepbrother, walked Mum down the aisle while my grandfather stood out the front of the church proclaiming, 'I could never give my baby girl away'. None of my uncles were at my parents' wedding either, mainly owing to distance and their own families, but they also couldn't understand why Mum wasn't marrying a Blackfella. Thankfully, at least my grandmother was excited about the wedding. She proudly welcomed all the guests at the Masonic Temple in Mascot for the reception.

I have six black-and-white photos in my lounge room of my parents' wedding day. It is one of the things I would grab in a fire. The images symbolise for me the absolute truth of unconditional love and that real love knows no boundaries, least of all race. My father ignored the ridicule of local Blacks and his own white friends to be with the woman he loved, while my mother risked the wrath of her family. But once they were married, my father was genuinely welcomed into the extended Williams family and community, and his life was cemented in Sydney forever. My father was particularly close to my uncle Kevin and his wife, Aunty Zilla. When my parents went to Austria in 1964, Uncle Kevin came to Sydney and bought my parents' blue Ford Zephyr and drove it back to Griffith. It meant a lot to Dad that his beloved car was staying in the family.

Mum and Dad lived in Edward Street, Redfern, from 1960 to 1962, then Bondi Junction until 1966. Dad worked at an insulation firm at Arncliffe and Mum worked at White Wings until 1964, when my parents travelled to Austria so Mum could meet the Heiss family. Mum recalls going to the Department of Immigration in Sydney for her passport, where she was asked questions about whether or not she'd been in an institution. She had to show that she had been registered at birth and had been christened. She was granted a passport and my parents went to Austria for six months, where Mum picked up the local lingo within weeks. Without any formal language education, my mum was somehow able to learn the dialect of the Austrian Lungau region. She was loved by my dad's family, even if they didn't understand some of her ways or the fact that my father, although coming from a very gender-biased life to living as a bachelor in Australia for some years, was now used to doing his own ironing.

On Anzac Day 1966, my parents moved into what remains the family home in Matraville where they raised their five children – Monika, Anita, Gisella, Josef and Mark.

While we were growing up in Matraville, Dad worked mostly seven days a week as a carpenter, and Mum worked nights for sixteen years at the Matraville Skyline Drive-Inn. During the day, Mum was busy doing the school tuckshop for twenty-five years, keeping an anally clean and tidy house (a legacy of a life living in fear of the Welfare Board removing children from so-called 'unfit houses'), and baking the odd chocolate cake (which she is now famous for in our family). One of my favourite childhood memories was licking cake beaters.

Chapter 2

BEING ELSIE'S DAUGHTER

Everybody loves my mother. As soon as they hear I am 'Elsie's daughter' they go into a monologue about how they know her, how wonderful she is and how much they adore her. It sometimes sounds like they love her more than I do, which makes me wonder if I ever gush about her like that, and indeed, if I love her enough.

But obviously I love my mother. She and I are friends. There is absolutely nothing I would be embarrassed to tell her. I've read letters I wrote to her when I was backpacking around Europe at twenty-two, and I can't believe the things I told her then. No wonder parents worry about their children all their lives. Actually, my mum used to say to me as a teenager, 'I hope when you have a daughter, she's just like you, and then you'll know what it's like.' I don't think it was a compliment.

Mum and I, we have our own groove. We do things *our* way, not like other mothers and daughters. I'm not one of those daughters who calls her mother every day for a chat.

That would be weird for me; well, for both of us. I live 400 metres from Mum so I see her most days anyway, flying in and out the back door with her mail, to raid her fridge, or both. We don't generally sit and have long yarns, but when we do it's quality.

We began our own tradition over a decade ago: every Boxing Day we go to Westfield Miranda and 'do the sales'. We begin the shopping tour with a coffee, then we try on clothes, buy each other a gift and have lunch in the *same* café, eating the *same* thing every year. We've only missed doing it twice: once when I was in Fremantle for Christmas with my friends Frané and Mark, and once when someone else came along, so the tradition was broken and it made me angry at the time. Then it just made me sad. It was the one thing that my mother and I did alone together, and it was ours. If only for half a day a year, I had some time with Mum that was sacred to me. We're back to normal now, but I'm thinking it's probably time for a new tradition.

I inherited the shopping gene from my mother, but I don't think I got her style gene. I don't mean *Vogue* stylish, more dignified stylish. Style in our home is about how a woman carries herself in public. My mum has style that way. I've never seen her lose her cool in a public forum, and her ability to carry herself with dignity in times of adversity is what I aim to mirror. It's not that she's not passionate – when she's arguing with me she's firing on all cylinders – but she's not the type to grab the mic at a rally and have a go, and she'd never shame anyone in public, even if they deserved it.

In fleeting moments of budget review, Mum and I have tossed around the idea of me moving into her house to save some money. But I don't think it would work. People tell me it's because we are so much alike. We are both competitive: for example, if I say I'm going to Mallorca, Mum will come back saying she's going to Melbourne. If I say I met someone famous, Mum will drag out the two popes that she's met – which, I admit, is pretty impressive and hard to beat.

I'm like Mum in some ways. I 'do' things like she does. I hang the washing like her (socks and knickers on the first inside lines, towels on the outside). I wash the dishes like Mum – although she'll tell me I use too much dishwashing liquid – glasses first, then bread-and-butter plates, dinner plates, cutlery and pots 'n' pans. I clean my home like Mum, orderly and to a schedule: dust, clean mirrors, vacuum then mop. Mum cleans mainly on Fridays, I clean on Saturdays.

I talk a lot, like Mum. I shop a lot, like Mum. I'm social, like Mum. In many ways I am my mother's daughter. But I don't have my mother's patience, and that's where I come undone. I'm big on huffing and puffing with exasperation if I am forced to wait for anyone (especially Mum), and I hate that trait in myself. Just writing this now I am embarrassed because what could be so important that I couldn't wait an extra few minutes for my mother? Or my brother for that matter: Mark is a classic for making me wait. I also get frustrated with Mum when she makes up her own statistics in a conversation. We like to call them 'Elsie's stats'. For example, we may be talking about the environment, and Mum will make up a number about how many people do or don't recycle. Completely from nowhere a figure will appear to support Elsie's argument, whatever it may be. My siblings tend to let it slide but I will always disagree. Why? I don't know. I do know that the house would be a lot happier if I just enabled as well. God knows, I have enough of my own enablers to pay it forward a little, at least to my mother.

I admire my brothers and their relationships with Mum. I watch them at the dinner table at home or when we go out for someone's birthday (usually a Greek restaurant in Brighton or a pizza place in Maroubra) and Mum's eyes will sparkle as she's given their full attention. They'll just sit and chat and catch up and totally indulge her. Mum continues to indulge all of us through acts of motherly kindness. It's normal for Mum to offer to drive to my place with a goodies-bag of chips and a bottle of wine, or to press a dress for me, hang out the washing I've done at her place, box me up some leftover food, or pull something from the freezer that I might like to cook while on the run. Mum also always has an extraordinary number of eggs in her fridge, carton upon carton. Some things are best left unquestioned. For many years I would blame Mum for what I thought was being overweight (in hindsight, I look back now at photos of my youth and I wasn't really fat at all) and for making me feel fat by taking me to Weight Watchers. To Mum's credit, she reminds me that she never shovelled food into my mouth, and that I begged her to take me to be weighed in each week because other girls in my class were doing it.

In December 2009, I went back to my mother's birthplace, at Erambie, Cowra, where my family had lived under the *Aborigines Protection Act*. The act aimed to regulate the life of Aboriginal people: restricting their freedoms to travel, own property and possessions, live and work where they wished, and forcing them to survive without basic human rights. Even after writing some of my mother's story here, I can't imagine what her life was like not even being a citizen in her own country, spending life in a shack with minimal food and having a mother who was one of the Stolen Generations.

In New South Wales there was a government body called the Aborigines Protection Board, set up in 1883. In 1940 they changed their name to the Aborigines Welfare Board, and continued to control Aborigines until 1969 under the authority of the *Aborigines Protection Act* and the government policy of assimilation. There was one of these government bodies in every state and territory of Australia. They operated on the belief that the only way Aboriginal children would have a good life was if they were taken away from their families to be raised in white families or orphanages, even though their real parents didn't want them to go. The policies of protection and assimilation are the reason that so many Aboriginal families, communities and societies suffered almost complete destruction. The children who were taken from their parents became known as the 'Stolen Generations', and survivors number between 15,000 and 20,000 in New South Wales alone.

Erambie became a managed reserve in 1924, meaning there

were compulsory house inspections, the searching of visitors' baggage (to confiscate alcohol), the expulsion of 'troublemakers' and the potential removal of 'neglected' children from their family homes to live in the Protection Board's children's homes. And while they lived under threat the community were far from passive. I'm told that the community leaders resisted the inspections, and some women used to lock their doors to refuse entry.

Erambie was where my mum had spent her childhood, still living in fear of removal by the authorities, and so her life there is part of my own story, and I was eager to visit in December 2009, although I was heading there alone. On the morning I woke up in the Aalana Motor Inn on Kendall Street, Cowra, nearly seven decades after my mum had been a resident of the town, I took a stroll at 6.30 am on the beginning of a stunning December day. As I pounded the pavement down the main drag, I searched out locals, but I didn't see any joggers or anyone doing the walk-of-shame, or any dog walkers. I was surprised at how quiet it was when it was a perfect morning for a walk. Past the shops, I stopped and stood on the bank of the Lachlan River and imagined the harsh conditions of my mum's childhood. But I also imagined how bush life on the river back in the 1940s could also have been fun, a world without handheld computer games and internet chat rooms. I am sure my mum had a much better appreciation of country and land as a child than I can ever hope to have today.

Under the Lachlan River bridge are painted pylons: murals created by Aboriginal artist Kym Freeman, depicting the history of the Wiradjuri people of the Cowra area prior to invasion. Seeing these, I felt sad about the racist country Mum was born into and sad that I was there without her. I had planned to be there with her and some of my siblings, as a pilgrimage of sorts, but logistics and Mum's health at the time meant I went alone. I was rude and short with Mum the morning I left Matraville because I was cranky she wasn't coming with me, but it didn't lessen my desire to go and I was excited as I headed down the Hume Highway.

I was visiting Erambie at the invitation of the chair of the Erambie Advancement Aboriginal Corporation, Dr Lawrence Bamblett, who is also the first person from Erambie to gain a PhD. Lawrence coordinated a 'Read With Me Day' event to promote reading and literacy among the local Koori youth. It's an area I'm passionate about, so I couldn't wait to be part of it. It was a surreal morning – 150-plus Koori kids from local schools all wearing bright yellow T-shirts emblazoned with the Aboriginal flag and the words 'READ WITH ME'.

The enthusiasm of the kids inspired me, made me laugh, made me want to go back and do workshops with them on their own stories. I loved reading to them from the book I'd written with children from a school in La Perouse, creating characters with them, and watching them sit under the marquees and read books themselves. I also had the chance to meet young local Koori women working in education, and to meet up briefly with some of the elders, including Aunty Isabelle Coe, Tent Embassy activist and illustrator of *Windradyne: A Wiradjuri Warrior* (written by Mary Coe). The entire day was a gift to me: it was a reminder of who I am and where I have come from, as well as a reminder of the strong sense of community in Cowra.

I returned to Cowra in 2011 as the guest speaker at the Yarraga Debutante Ball at the local Services' Club. It was nothing like my own deb ball back at Randwick Racecourse in 1985, where we waltzed with our partners and our fathers and were presented to the cardinal. Rather, the gorgeous young Koori debutantes of Cowra danced to the contemporary choreography of Michaela Jeffries, as their partners in black suits and pink ties escorted them with style, presenting them to me as they entered the auditorium. For me, it was important to return to Wiradjuri country, and to celebrate the Williams debutantes in particular. It was an event that acknowledged our youth and their future. I'm most grateful to Beatrice Murray, ball coordinator and teacher at Cowra High School, for the invitation to have a role in the night, because it allowed me to give back to my own mob.

I have also visited Mum's country in Tumut, where my grandmother Amy used to live. In 2009 there was a big Williams reunion at the Tumut RSL for my cousin Naomi's twenty-first birthday. It had been some years since I'd been to the area; I'd last visited when Aunty Nellie was still alive back in 1998, spending a weekend with her during timeout from a writers' residency in Wagga Wagga. Naomi's twenty-first, like other family occasions (sadly mainly funerals), was a great opportunity to meet up with my cousins Buster, Sharon and Amy, and to meet new ones.

The morning after the twenty-first, Mum and I and my brothers headed out to Brungle and the Wiradjuri cemetery with my cousin Denese Williams, CEO at the Tumut/Brungle Local Aboriginal Land Council. Amy and her mum, Carol, came too. We took our time going through the cemetery, and compared to other Land Council cemeteries I've visited, it was well-maintained, with new headstones and benches built and covered in artwork by the local mob. It was an emotional experience visiting the cemetery with so many Williams laid to rest there. And it was a difficult time for Mum as we walked through with Denese, hearing about our family members headstone by headstone. The last time I remember being at that cemetery was when my grandmother Amy was buried in 1976. I was only nine then, and my memories are limited to being in a long convoy of cars on a windy road to the burial.

On that visit I also saw the small Brungle school Mum used to go to, nestled under gum trees with a sign saying 'Gadhang Burri Yalbillinga' (translation: Happy Children Learn) at the front gate. It was surreal to imagine Mum at this two-teacher school on the road between Tumut and Gundagai. When I think of Brungle now, I think of Mum's own history and identity as a Williams woman. In 2001 I gift-wrapped my bound PhD thesis and gave it to my parents as a present, in return for their emotional, mental and financial investment in my education. While they were so proud of me, I was aware that the document represented far more than an academic achievement. For me, it represented the mammoth differences in education between three generations of Aboriginal women in my family. I have had a secure and stable private school and university education, spending five years of my life researching and writing about Aboriginal literature and publishing. However, only two generations ago, my grandmother Amy's education consisted of learning how to scrub, sew, cook and pander to the needs of the white families she would go into service for. At the age of eleven she had already been institutionalised in Coota for six years, whereas I at the same age was in Sydney playing netball, going to McDonald's and Luna Park, having family picnics, playing television games and having tennis lessons.

For her part, Mum was educated in country schools: Brungle Mission, Erambie Public School, Hanwood Primary (in summer), Darlington Point (in winter) and Rockdale Primary. She attended Griffith High School until she left at fifteen years of age. In 1989 Mum went back to study at Randwick TAFE two days a week for two years when Gisella, Josef and Mark were in school full-time and I was in my first year of university. At the end of her study she received the college medal and a certificate that enabled her to be employed as a health worker in the Aboriginal community. She worked in the field for fourteen years, many of them spent running a diabetes program at La Perouse.

When I consider the forms of education my grandmother and mother had, my years of tertiary study seem almost meaningless to me in terms of the struggle of Aboriginal women in the Williams family. As proud as I am of my PhD, the academic challenge it entailed and my ensuing successful career, I feel it all pales in comparison to the fact that at the same age, my grandmother's and mother's lives were very, very different. The past is always with me as a reminder of who I am, where I have come from, why I am here and why I do what I do in my career.

My mum's identity is somewhat different to mine in other ways, though, because Mum is and has always been *very* Catholic, if there is such a definition. 'The church' is the only topic that can find us not speaking at all for days. My dad was Roman Catholic, but he didn't go to church outside of special occasions: weddings, baptisms and the occasional funeral. But when it came to us kids going to church, Dad would give the direction, 'Don't do as I do, do as I say! Your mother wants you to go to church with her, so you're going.' And so we did, moaning and groaning as kids do. I don't recall Mum ever saying anything about Dad not going to church, it was just a given that we would go and he would stay home, just as it was a given that on the Saturday or Sunday night we would head up to what was known as the Pizza Hut church at Malabar.

Despite her religious upbringing, Mum says it wasn't until the early 1990s that she took a good hard look at where she was going and became more involved with the church. That was when she met Father Frank Fletcher, a great land rights and human rights advocate, who had a lot of love and respect for Aboriginal people. It was through this meeting that Mum became involved with the Aboriginal Catholic Ministry (ACM), which was set up to promote reconciliation and mutual understanding between the Aboriginal and broader communities. The ACM takes responsibility for the pastoral care of Catholic Aborigines and supports them in the practising of their faith. The work Mum would go on to do with the ACM included representing the concerns of Aboriginal and Torres Strait Islander peoples and advocating on their behalf in national and international religious forums.

Mum says the ACM she was part of had wonderful masses, baptisms, first holy communions and confirmations, but the breakdown of the ACM in Redfern came around 1997, when a lot of the regular Aboriginal families were relocated from Redfern into housing commissions in the suburbs. The ministry work at the ACM still continued, but not in the same form. Mum's journey was not over yet. 'I needed to continue God's work,' she says. In 1998 she moved to the church at La Perouse, which was then known as Our Lady of Good Counsel. Under Mum's leadership, it was handed over to the Aboriginal community and became known as the Reconciliation Church in 1999. Local Kooris – many non-Catholics – started going to the church and getting their children baptised. Others who were not religious started attending for the healing process that mass could give them, especially in that particular community with its casual atmosphere. Many of the parishioners – Black and white – are locals, some travel there because they are Mum's friends and supporters, and some Blackfellas travel from western and northern suburbs for the monthly service.

For myself, I continued to go to church long after Dad's

directions that I 'had to' as a child. Until I was about fourteen, I would climb the Lawson Street hill every Saturday evening to attend St Andrew's, Malabar – but only because I had my first real crush on an altar boy. There, I've said it. It's true, and although he was the brother of a girl in my class, I'm fairly sure he didn't know I existed. (However, only weeks after first writing this down, he contacted me on Twitter. The universe does have a sense of humour.)

When I was young, I never thought about how my Catholicism might contradict my Aboriginality. I had always thought you could be both, because I *was* both, and so is Mum. I went through all the sacraments: baptism, reconciliation, first communion, irregular confessions and confirmation. My confirmation name is Bernardine, after my sponsor, someone who's known me since birth and I call cousin because her Austrian father and my father were mates when they dated our mothers, who are now best friends. We grew up together and are close like sisters; we hang out together but neither of us goes to church anymore. But as a child, Catholicism was just part of my life, and I did as I was told. I'd never learned about the spiritual practices of my ancestors, and only when I was an undergraduate at university, spending four years with mostly Aboriginal students, did I start to question a lot of things, including my religious faith.

Oddly enough, it was a comment by a non-Aboriginal student from my University of New South Wales History tutorial that got me seriously thinking. At the end of the semester, they wrote in my autograph book: 'My friend Anita, Aboriginal

AND Catholic. I didn't think it was possible.' After this, I stopped going to church and started wondering how indeed it *was* possible to be both. Eventually, I understood that I'd be practising my own culture and spirituality if it weren't for the missionaries who Christianised Aboriginal people. I've never really acknowledged being a Catholic since or practised Catholicism, although I appreciate the moral codes I grew up with in the Catholic education system.

My mum, on the other hand, has managed to marry both her Aboriginal spirituality and history with her Catholic faith. She's met two popes, dined at the Vatican and has been a long-serving member of the National Aboriginal and Torres Strait Islander Catholic Council. In 2010 she was awarded an honorary Doctorate of Arts from the University of Notre Dame, Sydney, for her contribution to the Catholic community. In 2009 she was awarded (jointly with Doris Eaton) NAIDOC Female Elder of the Year, partly because of her work in the church. Mum has so much faith in God she even prays to him asking that one day I'll find a husband! She told me once the students at Nungalinya College in the NT, where she was doing her Diploma of Theology, prayed for me also. But to date, God has not delivered said husband.

Mum says that my grandparents – also fiercely Catholic – believed that spirituality was the basis of our connection to land, identity, culture and community. By this she means that we can have a strong sense of country, place, family and self, while still valuing, appreciating and living by the teachings of the Bible.

As for my father, although he didn't go to church much, he did do a lot of work around the church for Mum. Even if he never knelt down to pray, he would still mend the padded wooden kneelers so that others could be comfortable when *they* prayed. Dad also hung paintings and doors and would do anything else Mum asked him to do. What makes me laugh a little now is that while my father was not a religious or even seemingly spiritual man, he was given the last rites *three times*. That's not bad for someone who rarely went to church. When he went in for his final operation, less than two months before he died of cancer, he was administered the last rites in the hospital straight after his operation, and then twice more at home – once when he went into his coma, and then just before he died. If it weren't such a painfully tragic experience, it'd be almost funny – having three goes seems like we were saying, 'Take him already!' But of course we weren't.

Some people find solace in praying to God during times of sickness and pending death, but I didn't and don't. I'm of the ilk that thinks, 'If God loved me, then he wouldn't have taken my father; he would've taken a lesser father.' I know that sounds harsh, but grief makes you think, feel and say things that would not normally come into your mind or heart. A complete contradiction being that while I don't believe in the Christian God any longer, I still have in my laptop bag a string of rosary beads that have been blessed by the pope. I figure that if the plane I'm on goes down, then every little bit will help. Apropos of that, I've always believed that in the case of any disaster I would survive. I would be the Stuart Diver – the sole survivor of the 1997 Thredbo landslide – because I would have to write the story about it.

I reminded my writerly friend Doug MacLeod of this when we were flying from Darwin to Kununurra back in 2007. The weather had been so bad that planes were being refused landing and sent back to their original destinations. Our flight had not taken on any luggage due to the need for extra fuel in case we were turned back. On the seat to the right of me was a handsome young fella in his early teens from Halls Creek going home to visit family. He was a boarding student in Darwin, and was very nervous. Within minutes of me sitting down, he put his head on my shoulder and asked if he could hold my hand. Doug sat across the aisle, also nervous. I suggested jokingly that we all pray, and so we held hands in preparation. At that point I assured Doug I'd be fine, because I was the Stuart Diver of any possible disaster.

'Who am I then?' Doug asked.

'You're Princess Diana,' I told him.

'But she died!' Doug was not impressed.

'Yes, but she's immortalised.' He was not comforted at all by that.

While not religious now, I believe I experience the essence of spirituality every day of my life, just by walking and appreciating the landscape and life (plants, animals, air) in the suburbs. It is different when I find myself in Wiradjuri country like Wagga Wagga, Bathurst, Mudgee, Orange, Tumut and so on, because when I'm there I look at the landscape differently.

And I feel at peace when I am on my own land, because I know it's home, it's *my* country. I think of the history of the place, and the stories still untold. I try to imagine in my mind what life was like on the land for my ancestors before caravan parks and hotels and massive freeways. What life was like for Amy and James, for Mum and all my aunties and uncles and their kids, my cousins, who still live in Griffith, Brungle, Tumut and Cowra.

In Sydney, my own personal temple or place of thanks, peace, and solitude is Maroubra Beach in the south-east. It's home to the surfie gang known as the 'Bra Boys', and our local member is the former frontman for Midnight Oil, Peter Garrett. Maroubra has been my sacred place since I was a teenager and first found the sea air and the ocean itself a powerful healer, and a place to centre myself during the most challenging times of my life. I cried away a lot of teenage heartache there, and some adult pain as well.

When my father was diagnosed with cancer in November 2004, I began to grieve immediately from the morning that I sat on my parents' bed and Mum told me the prognosis. She was incredibly strong, and I can't begin to imagine how difficult it was for her to be so, considering I spent the next three days straight crying down at the beach. I couldn't work. I couldn't make sense of my everyday life. The only place I found some sense of relief was at South Maroubra. It was November and it was hot, and I sat on the sand and just stared out to sea and wept. Dad passed away the following November. I also grieved at that beach for Paul Travini, a principal of La Perouse Public School who died in January 2005, but I don't spend much time at South Maroubra these days. Although I was keen on waves in my youth, and indeed the surfers that rode them, now that I'm older I'm less inclined to be thrilled by being dumped or riding whitewash into the shore. And so after consecutive summers of grieving, I needed a new place for nourishment.

I now have another special place at Maroubra, and it is where I earth myself often. I have a rock at North Maroubra and it is as close as you can get without sitting in the actual sea. I sit there most weekends in summer, and some days during the week if I am particularly stressed or sad. I remember sitting there the day after I had stepped down from the chair of Gadigal/Koori Radio in September 2008. I felt relieved that I'd handed over the reins of what was becoming an enormously important and sizeable organisation. I was satisfied with what I had been part of during my time there as a volunteer broadcaster, an unpaid board member, editor of the anthology *Life in Gadigal Country* and an organiser of literary events. I needed to sit on that rock and take time to reflect and be grateful for the experience of being part of Gadigal and the extraordinary people I had worked with there along the way, like Cathy Craigie (a founding member of the organisation) and broadcaster / board member Phillipa McDermott.

When I have been away for long periods of time, it takes only an hour of meditation on my rock-of-reflection to bring me home properly. At other times, when on the run, a quick drive past and glimpse of the sea will sustain me. Maroubra Beach is as much a place of peace for me as a place of thanks and 'prayer'. I'm always amused that some whitefellas think we Blackfellas have some inherent sense of spirituality, as if it is unique to us and only us; that there is a certain brand of spirituality only available to Aboriginal people. In fact, all people can find a sense of spirituality, but the truth is we can't give you ours and we can't help you find yours.

And we don't *own* a sense of place either, like it's something tangible we can give to you, or that can come or go with relocation. Although our connections to places are specific to us – mine is obviously Wiradjuri country and Gadigal and Dharawal land because I have spent my life growing up on it – I've had to tell whitefellas that they too can in fact have a sense of place. My experience has been that for many whitefellas it is not feeling a spiritual connection to the land or place itself, but more a connection to the human/manmade aspects: their homes, their friends, their local footy club and so on. Quite often that connection changes when they move from Victoria, for example, to Queensland, and they often then become Queenslanders. To me that ability to shift geographical allegiances is what sets Aboriginal and non-Aboriginal people apart when talking about connection to country.

To return to the topic of churchgoing, I go to mass at La Perouse occasionally. My attendance is more to make Mum happy than anything else, but I always enjoy seeing local elders like Aunty Gloria Martin and Aunty Ali Golding there. The mass and church itself has been 'Aboriginalised', with the Stations of the Cross painted by artist Richard Campbell, Aboriginal-authored hymns sung to the sounds of clap sticks and didges, and vestments containing Aboriginal symbols and meaning. The church also enjoys a long list of high-ranking and respected priests who preside over the monthly services. I make a point of going when Jesuit priest Father Frank Brennan is there because, aside from him being a staunch advocate for human rights, he delivers meaningful contemporary sermons that engage the entire congregation. In recent years I've also convinced myself it's more of a 'gathering' than a mass. Mum's okay that I don't go to mass much, although she shines when the church is filled with her family. A full house would see Joe, Clare and their four children taking up the front row, with Mark, Gis and her boys scattered throughout, with me usually up the back somewhere.

I don't know if Mum's okay with me declaring that I am no longer a 'practising Catholic', but I think we've both reached a stage in our lives where we're content to know the other is genuinely happy. I did go to mass at St Patrick's Cathedral in New York City on Christmas Day 2011 for my mother, and she ordered down the phone: 'Take lots of photos!' Quite frankly, I don't really mind what Mum believes in, as long as it brings her peace. I remember when I was driving both her and Mark to Randwick Racecourse back in 1995, when the pope was visiting, heading along Belmore Road in my ugly blue Commodore. I was being cheeky and disrespectful, suggesting Mark poke his tongue out as far as possible and take communion that way. Mum countered my suggestion by instructing Mark to take communion in his hands so that the pope would touch him. I said something obnoxious, causing Mum to declare that the pope was her 'only hope'! If indeed the Holy Father is Mum's only hope for inner peace, then who am I to suggest otherwise?

ODE TO MY MOTHER

She inspires and never tires
But always conspires –
to motivate
to procreate
to maintain
and sustain
to nurture
and protect
always direct
what is left of Kooridom.
An audience
with the pope,
gives her hope
that the future
will be better
than the past.
Her smile
lights the universe
wrinkled hands

invade her purse
and she gives,
and gives
and gives
and gives.
Black curls
frame a face
full of grace
and dignity.
Forgiveness reigns
in my Mother's heart
too often torn apart
by unnecessary pain.
Her commitment to family
matched by no other
for she is the eternal mother
her role as matriarch
the key to her identity.

Chapter 3

JOE-THE-CARPENTER

I have often been asked how I can be Aboriginal when my father was Austrian. My identity was in part shaped by my father – how could it not be? He was a strong male role model in my life, and supported me in every endeavour I undertook. He respected my mother and showed me how men should treat women, the kind of behaviour I should expect from a man, and what he wanted me to have in a life partner. And he never let himself be influenced by the obvious differences between his and Mum's cultural backgrounds.

What I have always found interesting about me identifying as Aboriginal is that my father never questioned me about it. And really, being my own flesh and blood, he was the only one I felt had any right to do so. He would listen to me yelling at the television when something racist was said. He would drive me to marches and festivals and so forth, but we never talked about identity at all.

Although I have always been a romantic who believed in

the power of absolute love, and was raised in a house by a loving white father, my dad was different to other non-Aboriginal partners I have seen. He didn't ask questions. He didn't butt into political discussions or feel he had a right to comment about community issues just because he was 'married to a Blackfella'. I don't see white men like that today: they don't seem as secure in themselves and have endless questions and justifications for their often unsolicited and unwanted comments. I don't have the patience to deal with them. My father, on the other hand, was extraordinary on that front. Perhaps he didn't have issues with me identifying as Aboriginal because I had also been to Austria a number of times, spent time with his family, and acknowledged in very practical ways that I was also proud to be a Heiss. Indeed, I will never change my name: after all, it means 'hot'!

To his workmates and clients, my father was affectionately known as 'Joe-the-carpenter', and those who didn't know his name knew him as the guy who drove the white kombi van, because he was a legend around the eastern suburbs of Sydney for decades. He was also known as Poppy, Uncle Joe, Big Joe, and to some – Mum and my Austrian family – he was known as Seppi. An Austrian immigrant, Dad was born in 1936 in St Michael, in the Lungau region of Salzburg, Austria. The eldest son of Josef and Maria Heiss, he was one of seven children. He realised as a teen that the little farming village wasn't big enough for him and decided at the age of twenty to migrate to Canada. However, on his last night in Austria with his mates, urban (or is it rural?) myth has it that he drank too much and ended up on the wrong boat the next day, arriving some weeks later in Australia. On his trip over, he learnt only the necessary English to get him through, beginning with the keywords: schooner, apple and chocolate. Those three words remained constant in his everyday vocabulary. I blame my father also for my chocolate addiction!

Dad spent three weeks in a Villawood hostel in 1957 before he was shipped to Tasmania, where he would work to pay off his fare. This was where he met his close friends the Knorr brothers. Once he paid off his assisted passage, he moved to Sydney, stayed in a boarding house in Pagewood with other Austrians and, as we know, met my mother through an Austrian friend, Leigh. Dad fell in love immediately: Mum was beautiful, kind, elegant and could dance. But she was a challenge for any man, not because she was Black, but because of her very strict Catholic upbringing and 'Catholic girls were *good* girls!' But my father was charming and persistent and my mother could not ignore my father, he pretty much stalked her. Admittedly, in those days they called it 'courting'. Mum tells me stories of Dad sitting on the doorstep in the early hours of the morning of her home in Lawson Street in the late 1950s. 'For God's sake, Elsie, go and talk to that wog. He's been driving up and down the street since five o'clock this morning,' my grandparents would say. Racism went both ways in the 1960s, but once Mum had married and made it clear that Dad was the man she was spending the rest of her life with, everything shifted and the family accepted the New Australian.

When my parents started dating, my dad wanted to fatten my poor skinny mother up. Even though she worked at the Sweet Acres chocolate factory, my mum was too, too thin. My dad fed her pasta to bulk her up, a food she'd never eaten before – she actually believed him when he told her that spaghetti grew on trees. He continued to pursue my mother with a stalker-like passion. 'Is that Joe behind us?' Mum's girlfriends would ask, as they pulled away in a taxi after a night of dancing. Dad would be in eager pursuit on his motorbike or in his car.

Although they didn't dance much in their courting days, I remember my dad being a great twister, even if I only witnessed it at the fun street parties in the 1970s where suburban Matraville would come alive for New Year's Eve, Christmas and birthdays. One year, to my absolute mortification, Dad attempted a cricket-ground streak at our neighbours' New Year's Eve party. He ran through the backyard holding his dark-green pants up, laughing. 'Else made me do it!'

Even though I know my father wasn't the man my grandparents would like to have chosen for my mum, for as long as I can remember the Williams family was Dad's family too, his own being so far away. I remember being at my Uncle Kevin's funeral in Griffith in October 1997. At the wake in the hall afterwards, someone called out over the platters of egg sandwiches, 'Hey Elsie, I didn't know Joe was a wog. I always thought he was Koori.' There was something obviously offensive about that statement, and yet it was somehow endearing to my father and made him smile. I knew Dad was grateful for the sense of belonging that Mum's family had given him over the years, even though it hadn't always been that way.

Austria was in Dad's heart, but he rarely went home to visit. His life was with Elsie and his soon-to-be family. Mum and Dad went to Austria in 1964, and my father returned there again in 1977 with me. I was the lucky one who got to go because Josef was a baby and Gisella was too young. I remember the trip vividly, although only nine years old. Photos document me as a chubby brown kid among my leaner and fairer Heiss family members in St Michael. I met my cousin Sabine (my Uncle Gerhard and Aunty Burgi's only child) for the first time on that trip. She remains as close as a sister, even though we hardly see or speak to each other. But when we do talk, it's as if we were together only yesterday, when it may have been years since we saw each other last. When we met as kids we had to use sign language and minimal words to get our messages across, but it worked.

While backpacking around Europe with my girlfriend Patricia, I spent Christmas 1991 with my dad's family in the little village of St Michael. It was my first white Christmas, and a weird experience being part of the Austrian village Weihnachten traditions: midnight mass at 9 pm because it was so cold, lighting candles in the cemetery at dusk, having Christmas dinner with carols and presents on Christmas Eve, before going out to bars and bowling with friends on Christmas Day. It was during this visit that my cousin Sabine told me she had always thought my mum was from Tahiti because of her long black hair. It struck me as odd at the time that she didn't know Mum's actual background, but I guessed my mum's racial identity was of no great interest or concern for Dad's family. Sabine has since told me that back in the 1970s, 'We didn't care about your mother's background, because for us all countries outside of Austria, especially those separated by oceans – like America, Australia or Asia – were really "exotic".'

It was during this same visit, while trying to ski on the Katschberg (but only mastering the art of après ski), that I realised I needed to do something to change the stereotypes of Aboriginal people abroad. But what could I do? And how could I do it when tourism campaigns and documentaries focusing on Aboriginal life and culture in 'traditional set- tings' in the Northern Territory had already managed to instil fairly strong characterisations into the minds of those who knew little about Australia generally?

I met many locals desperate to talk to the 'Australische kusine', the 'Heiss' from Australia. But with my minimal German I could barely order myself 'ein Bier, einen Kaffee und eine Schokolade', and while I knew how to say work, shop and sleep – 'arbeiten, einkaufen und schlafen' – there was little chance of me defining or explaining adequately the notion of Aboriginality in all its diversity to the villagers. More disturbing than my language skills were the two things that most villagers I met knew about Australia: Skippy and Aborigines. In that order. I must admit that watching *Skippy* with a German translation is hilarious although, obviously, the Skippy-speak is the same. Nevertheless, it was the only Australian television Austrians got in the 1970s, 1980s and even the 1990s.

You can imagine the difficulty I had trying to explain in my broken German that I was Aboriginal, without even attempting to break it down to being Wiradjuri or generically Koori. As it was, there was only a remote understanding of Aboriginality in a generic context, if anything. I remember being at a rather fun beer-fest in a village one night, trying to use sign language with a fella holding a beer. He was motioning with his free hand trying to confirm whether I was Aboriginal by miming putting ochre on his face. I said, 'No, I wear Clinique,' as I waved my hand across my cheek. The joke was lost on him though.

'Do you have a kangaroo?' another fella asked (and no, ladies, he was not wearing lederhosen!). 'Yes, I ride it to work,' I answered, not being able to help myself, but only causing another frown. Humour gets lost in attempted foreign translation. Having said that, I did use the same joke on a radio show in Canada with Tom King, who laughed and followed up with, 'Is the roo an automatic or stick-shift?' 'Depends whether the roo is female or male, of course.' And the corniness continued.

Back to the beer-fest: I remember thinking at that very moment that the tourism industry had a lot to answer for in terms of exploiting one aspect of Aboriginal culture in order to lure international visitors to our shores. They were selling the chance to see the exotic other in lap-laps, dancing around fires, singing in a strange language and eating bush tucker they'd hunted and cooked themselves. I realised that it would be near impossible to explain the diversity of Aboriginality in Australia in a contemporary context when I couldn't even explain it in English that well back home.

Three years later, in 1995, I started to question for the first time why my father identified himself as an Australian more than he did as an Austrian. I was in Killington, Vermont, with my cousin Sabine. We were staying with our fathers' cousin Poldi and his family. Poldi flew to the US after being scouted out in the Alps of Austria by another Austrian who had also been to Killington. He loved his voice and decided he would be great in the Killington ski school as an entertainer. Once there, Poldi met his wife, Dale from Massachusetts, on the ski fields. He then settled in the area, which ironically mirrors a typical Austrian village: the architecture, flower boxes, street names and of course, the skiing. Although St Michael is at the base of the Katschberg Mountain, Dad couldn't ski at all. He did joke though that he was good at handball, another Austrian sport.

My visit to Killington was during a week's break between working at *The Eastern Door* newspaper on the Mohawk Reserve in Kahnawake and *Windspeaker* in Edmonton, Canada. Sabine was working at The Summit Hotel on the mountain in Killington, enjoying everything American. That week, we took a driving trip to Cape Cod to work on one of Poldi's friends' houses. Poldi's a plumber, and I climbed into his truck while Sabine climbed into the vehicle behind with another plumber. During the drive, Poldi and I talked for hours about life in Austria, Australia and the US. He told me he had never become an American citizen because he could never pledge allegiance to another flag. It made me consider my father's adoption of Australia as a home.

I wouldn't say my father was heavily patriotic to either Austria or Australia. He loved Austria but became so acclimatised to Sydney that he'd comment that Austria was now too cold. Dad easily made a home in Sydney with Mum, but in some ways he would have been classified under that ridiculous category of 'un-Australian' because he didn't watch or play any code of footy. He didn't watch the cricket or enjoy the surf. In fact, my dad couldn't swim, something I only learned in my early teens when he nearly drowned in front of me at Little Hartley Farm near the Blue Mountains, where we went for family holidays between 1976 and 1982. My dad didn't eat Vegemite either, preferring jam and thickly spread butter or smoked speck on black bread. He didn't mind a Foster's though, and that should immediately make him authentically Australian.

On 26 January each year, Dad flew the Australian flag at our family home, for he *was* very proud and grateful to be Australian, but he would also raise the Aboriginal flag on that day, for his wife and children and out of respect for the history he knew of this country. Then, on 26 October each year, he flew the Austrian flag to acknowledge Austrian National Day. We raised the red-and-white flag at half-mast to let the neighbours know he'd passed away on 6 November

2005. And we still fly it each October for Dad, and for us.

On the political front, while Dad never marched with Mark and I, he made the pole for us to fly the Aboriginal flag on when we went in the Sydney leg of the global peace march opposing the Iraq war with 200,000 others in 2003. Dad would also drive me into the city to participate in rallies, like the one against Black deaths in custody in the 1990s, for example. The only thing he'd say as he dropped me off was, 'Don't get arrested.' I always replied with a laugh, 'Have your chequebook ready to bail me out.' He would not even laugh. Mum and Dad always supported us in standing up for what we believed in, but neither wanted us to have criminal records.

When my parents were first married, Mum and Dad lived in Edward Street, Redfern, then Bondi Junction, before moving to suburban Matraville. My parents had a very traditional kind of marriage for most of their lives. The man goes out during the day to his job, and the wife works at home, makes all the meals and tends to the children. But my mum always worked outside the home as well: there were the sixteen years working as a cashier at the drive-in, then she worked as a health worker with South Eastern Area Health Service and Home Care before starting at the church. All the while she kept an immaculate house, fed us all and fussed over my father. But my dad was a man who appreciated everything my mum did, and knew that her duties should never include dragging a bin up the driveway when there was a capable man around. He was right, and I loved him for that.

The reason Mum and Dad worked so hard was in order to

put us all through Catholic schools. My parents were determined that we would have the education neither of them had access to. Three of us went on to university and made the most of the educational opportunities afforded us through our parents' hard work.

It's funny how two people who both came from poor families behaved so differently to each other. My dad was a saver, not a spender, and would recycle other people's lights, furniture and doors from trash-'n'-treasure sales and sometimes the tip. On the odd occasion, he'd score something being thrown out from a job he was working on. In fact, I think some cabinet doors of mine are made out of the old Waverley Council mayoral doors, and I have two chests of drawers previously discarded by neighbours during the council clean-up.

Our screen door from the tip used to always get stuck on the back of people's heels as they entered the house. It was painful to the victim and somehow funny to everyone else watching when the victim would then complain about how crappy the door was. But one man's trash and all that was Dad's motto. Dad saved hard and complained when he thought we were being wasteful. When I worked for the Australian International Development Assistance Bureau (AIDAB) as a cadet in Canberra in 1990, and lived in Queanbeyan, the winter was harsh. I'd call home and complain about being cold. Dad once suggested that I wrap my electric blanket around me while watching television on a cold winter's night, to save the cost of heating.

On the other end of the spectrum, Mum, who came from

poverty in Cowra and never had money to spend when she was young, now loves to shop. She buys a new outfit for every church event she attends. She has handbags to meet popes, special camisoles for cardinals (to hide, not enhance) and new shoes for meetings and conferences. And I can't tell you how many suitcases she has. For a long time before Gisella and my nephews Matt and Ben moved into the family home, Mum's cases had a room all to themselves. My dad never stopped my mum from buying anything and in 2002 I found out why. I was walking with Mum along the upper concourse at the Sydney Opera House, on our way to the launch of the anthology *Life in Gadigal Country*, and we were talking about cosmetics and other girly things. I commented that I couldn't afford the lipstick I wanted and that Dad would freak if Mum bought the expensive one. Mum responded, 'You buy the lipstick you want. And don't be standing at the altar next to a man who won't let you buy the lipstick. Love won't last very long in that case.' Thankfully for my dad, Mum wore Holiday Magic and Avon, which are both quite affordable, so there wasn't much to argue over. However, my choice of lipstick could indeed cause an argument with a less emotionally intelligent or capable fella.

My dad was a good provider. It was his job as husband and father to look after his family. When he was diagnosed in November 2004 with the cancer that would eventually kill him (he'd had earlier bouts of prostate cancer in 2000), he went straight into preparation mode, getting the house – our home – in order for Mum. I was only working three days a week at Macquarie University at the time, for which I remain grateful because I couldn't have done any more once I had begun grieving for my father, who was still alive. While Dad was being practical and logical, I was being emotional, thinking of all the things he wouldn't see in my lifetime. He wouldn't be there to walk me down the aisle, and I couldn't give him grandchildren unless I got very busy very quickly. I couldn't stop crying and that was the one thing my father hated most: crying. He didn't know what to do when someone he loved cried. He'd get fidgety and want to change the subject immediately. Once, when I was sitting on the black leather lounge in Dad's TV room, crying, Dad said, 'I don't like it when you cry. I don't know what to do.' I said, 'Dad, sometimes you don't have to *do* anything, you just need to sit there.' Nevertheless, 'Don't be such a sook,' or 'Don't turn on the waterworks,' were common things he said, at least to me. I was and still am a sook.

Over the next twelve months of his illness, my father began to shed a lifetime of tears. It still breaks my heart to think about him that way, since he was always so bravely unemotional before. I am glad, though, that he was eventually capable of showing his distress. Crying with him was something that brought us closer. I need to say here that we are not a family of bawlers. I am the only sook, and maybe one or two of my nephews, but my excuse for crying is that I am an emotional artist, okay? That's my story and, despite the cliché, I'm sticking to it!

One day, six months after the initial diagnosis, I stood at

Dad's garage door – where he spent most of his time at home – and asked him what he was doing. 'I'm fixing the screens for Mum,' he said, holding some mesh. He was mending fly screens on windows that didn't need mending. The next six months played out the same way as he fixed up the house that he'd mostly built himself and would no longer be there to maintain. 'Who will look after Mum?' he said sadly, more than once. Even in his final hours before he slipped into a coma from which he would never return, he was worried about Mum driving, maintenance on the house or how Mum would manage financially.

'I will Dad, I will look after Mum,' I said to appease him. Although I knew that I could easily take care of her, my siblings, especially Mark and Gisella, would probably do much of it.

'And who will look after you?' he would ask, concerned.

'I can look after myself, Dad.' My father was always worried about me finding (or rather *not* finding) a husband. More than Mum worried, more than even *I* worried. Not because he wanted to pay for a huge wedding, Dad was thrifty remember, but because he believed that every woman should have a man to look after her. Turn away right now you feminists reading this, because while I don't think any woman *needs* a bloke to take care of her, I do, at the age of forty-three, believe that life would be easier if you had someone to take the garbage out, change the light bulbs, empty the vacuum cleaner and kill spiders. Quite frankly, I'm over it, and I do happen to believe in blue jobs and pink jobs.

But a man that does all the 'male' chores leaves a woman without certain necessary city-based survival skills. The fact that Elsie can't put petrol in the car is a demonstration of Dad's determination to be the man of the house, but also shows how dependent Mum was on her husband. Being the chauvinist he was, Dad made sure that there was another man responsible for Mum's wellbeing when he was gone. My brother Mark was charged with being the man of the Heiss house, paying the bills, checking the fly screens, doing all the gardening and putting petrol in the car. This was apparently preferable to Elsie learning how to do it herself, a fact which didn't faze Mum at all. It's been interesting to watch my mum these past few years because I had always viewed her as highly independent when Dad was alive. I had always thought that the way they managed home life was completely normal, but in reality they were truly co-dependent: Dad emotionally and Mum practically.

One of the reasons I really wanted to give my dad grandkids was because he loved kids. And not just those in his family: he would even stop and talk to kids at Westfield Eastgardens, sometimes dropping two dollars into the slot of those ride-on machines outside Kmart when a child just happened to be sitting there. I don't remember him doing that for us, though; we rarely went shopping with Dad. He was always working long hours and shopping was 'the woman's domain'. But he did take us to the carnivals that would park themselves on Bunnerong Road, Hillsdale, or at Brighton-Le-Sands, back in the early 1970s. It was a weekend activity that added to our early morning bike rides around Centennial Park on Sundays.

My father didn't go shopping much because he was really a man of very simple means; labels meant nothing to him. He wore the same tracksuit for about a decade. It had the word 'TRAINING' emblazoned across the top, sitting above his ever-growing and obviously untrained gut, and it nearly drove me to despair. He briefly replaced it with a 'PLANET HOLLYWOOD, HONOLULU' sloppyjoe I bought him, before opting for a Saucony one. I still have the Planet Hollywood top; I can't throw it out. It's a piece of Dad that I can't let go of. I gave him other sweats and T-shirts, but they still had the tags on them when he died – 'The other one isn't worn out yet,' he'd say.

I was pleased when Dad became less frugal in his old age and finally enjoyed his too many years of hard labour. I take some pride in teaching my father how to spend his hard-earned cash. My view is that there's no point in all the effort if you can't enjoy it. There's no fun lying on your deathbed wishing you'd done something other than watch the numbers tally up in your bank account. I don't watch numbers tally: they go up, they go down, and they disappear at regular intervals. 'I might be dead tomorrow,' I often said when Dad would comment on a new pair of shoes I'd bought. 'And you might not,' he'd say. 'And you've only got one pair of feet. How many pairs of shoes do you need for two feet?'

'Like my new ring?' I asked while showing him a cheap topaz and gold band I bought when I won the New South Wales Premier's History Prize for the Barani website (which is a stepping stone to some key Aboriginal events and people in the history of the city of Sydney). 'How many rings do you need? You've only got ten fingers.' Dad was right, as fathers often are. I didn't need that many shoes, and I hardly ever wore that ring. When Dad died, I received a black onyx ring from his belongings that I'd never seen him wear. I had it melted down along with my topaz ring and made into a pendant. It now gets worn so I have Dad with me on special occasions.

Although Dad didn't like to shop, he did love a bargain, and if he could save two dollars on a case of light beer by driving six kilometres from Matraville to Coogee, then he would drive there and buy two cases. Speaking of beer, one of Dad's favourite comments to me was, 'You've got champagne tastes on a beer budget.' I often enjoyed gee-ing up my father by telling him I was going out to buy a bottle of bubbly, even when I wasn't. Over three consecutive weeks in the later part of his illness in 2005, we would banter about money as I'd fly in and out, just checking up on him.

'You live beyond your means,' he said during the first week of me teasing him about champers.

'Ah, but I don't live beyond *your* means, Dad,' I joked back.

'You live beyond your means,' he said during the second week when I told him I was going out for dinner with the girls again.

'I'm just living, Dad,' I said with a cheeky grin.

In the third week, I flew in and announced I was going out again. 'You're living beyond . . . ' and then he stopped and said, 'I know, you're just living.'

My dad was a perfectionist with a strong work ethic. And he was a craftsman who preferred to work alone, whistling as he chiselled and functioning according to the clock. But my mum was often on Koori time. (For the uninitiated, 'Koori time is anytime': the scheduled event will happen whenever it happens.) So, it was normal for my dad to be halfway down the street in the car while Mum was still putting lipstick on, even if they were already fifteen minutes late for something. Dad hated tardiness. Mum is far more relaxed. I think I got living by the clock and my anal scheduling from my father. Timing was something he took so seriously: if you said you were going somewhere at 6 pm, then at 5.45 pm Dad was in the car, it had already been warmed up, and it was creeping out the driveway. Whenever my brother Mark was getting a lift somewhere, he had learned to reply, 'Soon,' when Dad asked him when he would be ready. This frustrated Dad as it wasn't as specific as he would have liked. And the same 'Soon,' response drives me equally nuts.

My dad had his eating habits set to the clock also: breakfast of tea and biscuits standing at the kitchen sink at 6 am, smoko at 9 am, lunch at work at 12 noon *sharp*, afternoon tea at 3.30 pm and dinner at 6 pm. This worked on weekdays when Dad would take off to his job, where he would build significant 'cultural' objects and spaces locally: the first skateboard ramp at Bondi Beach, the squash courts at Bronte Surf Club, the renovated Bondi Tram and numerous pieces of furniture for the houses that our family could never afford to live in. But when Dad came into the kitchen at midday on the weekend looking for lunch, if Mum wasn't organised there would be panic, exasperated sighs and, on the odd occasion, a banging door. Dad was a door slammer. We didn't see him get angry often but, when he did, the hinges on all the doors would panic wondering which one might wear Dad's wrath. But my parents would never have screaming matches in front of us kids. I don't think they had them away from us either. They didn't argue often, and Dad would joke that when Mum was cranky she would send him to work with his standard lunch of fruit, cake, sandwich and yoghurt – but no spoon to eat it with. That was her only way to show any displeasure.

Like Dad, Saturday lunchtimes were very important to me when I was growing up. Even in my teens it was always like a childhood birthday gathering: party pies and sausage rolls with tomato sauce. Whoever was home at the time sat at the round laminated kitchen table held up by chrome legs recycled from someone else's dining room. We still have the same ugly mustard-coloured vinyl chairs that came with it. Dad loved the colour brown. It was a running joke in our family when choosing anything new for the house: a chair, some paint, carpet. It wasn't *What colour will it be?* But rather *What shade of brown will it be?* Even when the upholstery of his mustard-coloured vinyl Jason recliner wore down he replaced it with dark-chocolate velvet. It remains a chair we all gain comfort from at different times. The patterned wallpaper throughout the front of the house and in my parents' bedroom was also some indescribable collage of browns. It's since been removed, and the hall is a mocha colour. The lino on the kitchen floor was also various shades of brown over time. Dad was often heard saying, 'There's nothing wrong with mission brown.' Not surprisingly, Elsie, having been born on a mission, wasn't really convinced of that!

My dad was the ultimate woodworker. A cabinetmaker as opposed to a carpenter, he created much of the furniture in our family home and my Matraville apartment. The one time I bought a wooden bedhead from IKEA, it caused a huge argument between Dad and I. 'Why did you buy something I could make?' he asked angrily. 'You must have a lot of money.' I said, 'I thought the cost of the bedhead was less than the cost of you and me arguing over what I wanted.' I regret now having bought it because my father loved so much to fill our homes with his handiwork. It was also something that made him feel needed. I have realised too late in life that there seems to be some 'need gene' that men have that requires them to always feel some sense of dependence from the women in their lives. I am practising being more needy, but it doesn't come easy. When I look at a tile missing in my bathroom and the door hanging slightly off its hinge in the kitchen and the light globe that just will not shift out of its socket so I can replace it, I am reminded of how easily and gladly Dad would have repaired everything within hours of being told of it. And now, things go for months and years untouched.

I wasn't the only one Dad did odd jobs for. He framed paintings for friends, hung blackboards in our classrooms, and made my tidda Kerry Reed-Gilbert bookcases back in

the 1990s. I remember delivering them to her Enmore home
in Dad's kombi van. We both thanked him for making what
appeared to be very strong, good-looking bookcases. Dad
replied, 'I don't make bookcases, I make pieces of furniture.'
At one point in the late 1990s Dad made letterboxes for a
couple of acquaintances and painted the Aboriginal flag on
their lids. I had this great idea to turn it into a business. I was
full of entrepreneurial ideas back then, but Dad needed to
put food on the table for his family and couldn't spend time
making things that people didn't want to pay for.

As I said before, my dad had a strong work ethic and in
many ways both my parents were workaholics, neither capable of sitting down in the middle of the day to rest even when
their bodies told them to. Mum is getting better at it now
after a lot of nagging, and so did Dad before he passed away. I
know I got my own work ethic and nervous energy from them
both, but I'm pleased to say that I've learned how to relax as
well. As a carpenter, Dad worked a full day, leaving home at
6.30 am. When I was in primary school I would nearly always
see him off. If I wasn't already up sitting in the dark watching
Gene Autry, the singing cowboy, then I would peer under the
venetians when the noise of Dad's kombi woke me so I could
wave goodbye through the window as he pulled out of the
driveway. I think I did that until I was six or seven. I don't
know what Dad made of it – I suppose if you're a parent you
think it's cute. (On the Gene Autry front, it's family legend
that I had my first childhood crush on a certain black-and-
white television star who rode a horse named Champion and

had a best mate called Frog Millhouse.) When Dad used to come home, we'd hear his kombi the minute it turned into our street, and the neighbours' dogs would run alongside the van. Dad would have his afternoon tea, including Mum's chocolate cake, and work in his garage.

Then at around 6 pm most nights, one of us kids would sing out the back door towards the garage metres away, 'Daaaaaaad! Dinner's readeeeeee!' Dinnertime was story time when I was a kid. Stories about your day and 'remembering when'. We're all good at doing the 'remembering when', especially since Dad has passed away. We remember Dad as someone who would thump the table when he was angry, but my memories of dinnertime are mostly happy ones. We always ate dinner together when we were growing up: no television, no-one in their rooms. Everyone around the brown table. One meal, one choice, too many voices at once. There were often laughs, sometimes arguments (usually Mum and I) and, on occasion, a really bad joke (usually Dad).

I love that we still eat around the table in the Heiss house. Same as the old days: lots of laughs, some arguments and the odd bad joke. I used to sit in Dad's seat, until Gis moved in, now she sits there. These days there's always more than one option of what to eat, and there's nearly always a television on in the kitchen. How times change. Still, on the odd occasion, like my nephew Matthew's tenth birthday, there's one of Mum's famous homemade chocolate cakes to remind us of the old days. But largely they have disappeared. I'm not sure when Mum stopped making cakes, I just know they were noticeably absent by high school and replaced by Herbert Adams frozen donuts. Nowhere near as good as Mum's creations.

Like I said, Dad would work in his garage for a few hours each day after an already physically gruelling work effort else-where. He'd churn out desks for Rockdale Office Furniture, often lifting the heavy loads by himself, moving them from the garage to the van. As a child I was my father's shadow, sit-ting by his side in his kombi as he went to Rockdale to deliver the desks. Sometimes he would even drop me off in Target, where I would roam the store, try on clothes, and always come out with a block of Cadbury Caramello for him (well, also for me). In hindsight, it was something parents should and would not do today – letting a child roam a department store unsupervised – but in the 1970s it seemed completely normal. And always with Mum's blessing. When cash pay-ments became a tax issue, the desks dried up. I was glad to see Dad finally work a forty-hour week and eventually go from being a contractor to an employee of Waverley Council after twenty-five years of being his own boss. It was hard for him to go through the standard job application process, take a major cut in pay and work in a team, but he was thrilled to get sick days, holidays, a uniform and a pair of boots.

I think my dad worked too hard, but he loved what he did. Carpentry – I mean, cabinetmaking – was his hobby, and while it took its toll on his body, I know my dad got joy from every final product and took pride in his achievements. I never inherited any of my dad's woodworking talent although both my brothers did. Dad was proud, however, and so too was I, when I painted the tiles in my kitchen and put new knobs on the doors and drawers as an alternative to getting a new kitchen. Now, though, my flat has wobbly kitchen doors, another door needing a new handle, and sliding wardrobe doors that don't in fact slide that well. Ah, the things Dad would've fixed immediately!

When I was in my early twenties, Dad stood in the lounge room he built mostly himself – from the carved triangular lights to the polished floorboards he laid and all the brown furniture in between – and said to me, 'Anita, you should do what makes you happy. Lots of people get up around the world every day and go to a job that they hate . . . If you can afford to do what you really want, what your heart wants you to do, then you should do that.' I never forgot those words, and Dad lived them. I don't recall him *ever* complaining about his day. He got paid, it seemed, to do his hobby, and I took heed of that. In 2004 when I left my job coordinating the Aboriginal projects at Streetwize Comics after two years there because I wanted to write a book, Dad was mortified. 'But you said to do what makes me happy,' I repeated his words back to him. 'Yes,' he said as we drove along Anzac Parade. 'But you still need to have a wage.' *Oh!* I thought to myself.

Throughout his career, whether as a leader at working bees at St Andrew's School, Malabar, or as the neighbour who built aviaries, hung doors and generally took on any task that required a hammer and nail, Dad remained a perfection-ist. He was a true believer in doing it right the first time or not doing it at all. And anything that he built was built to last. Later in life he put effort into creating a rose garden, and while I angst over keeping the flowers in some kind of respectable state now, I never inherited his green thumb. On the contrary, I have the capacity to easily kill a cactus!

As well as being a dedicated worker, Dad was also a dedicated kombi driver. Dad's old green kombi would do the neighbourhood run from our street to the Malabar tip in the early 1970s, until the van was upgraded in 1977. That year he bought a white ex-Waverley Library kombi – a luxury to him at the time. The white kombi was a fixture in the Heiss family for the next twenty years, and Dad made it work just as hard as he did. We'd all pile in and drive it to our timeshare holiday retreat at Little Hartley Farm, or up to Yamba on the New South Wales north coast for our family holidays just before Christmas. Dad would occasionally turn sideways and threaten to pull over to wale those who were brawling in the back. The term 'wale' is one that I never heard anyone other than my parents use, but we knew it meant whoever was in trouble would be getting a hiding. It never happened to me, because I quite liked the kombi drives, and I think it means something that I spent so much time in a van that used to transport books between library branches in the eastern suburbs. I must have inhaled some book fumes as a child.

Although Dad was always happy to help his neighbours, my parents could not have been more different socially. Mum is the true social butterfly and sometimes I wonder how they ever dated, since Dad was very reserved, quiet and hated going out. In some instances he had no social etiquette at all: he was famous for going to bed in the middle of his own parties. It was normal for someone to screech, 'Where's Joe?' only to find him snoring while Mum was still entertaining. I am a little like Dad in that way. He was early to bed and early to rise, and so am I. 'Good guests are gone by ten on a school night,' I have been known to say more than once at my own dinner table. But I'm like Mum in the social butterfly sense, always out for dinner and catching up with friends. But Dad's disappearing acts didn't mean he didn't love his neighbours. From his deathbed he was ordering Mark to mow Don's lawn next door, to give Gerry across the road the water pump, and to see if Jim wanted the forty-four-gallon drums along the side of the house.

But what was always clear to all, the big passion in Dad's life was Mum. He was grumpy and unbearable when Mum was away for any length of time, and as she got more involved with the church there were more engagements and events to attend. Naturally, he was proud to see Mum on the telly when she was the only Aboriginal representative at the Synod of Oceania in Rome in 1998, but he really liked Mum to be home, near him and, especially, cooking his meals. Elsie, like lots of women of her generation, would often be cooking up a storm before going away because she felt guilty about leaving him. In return, my father was chivalrous with his 'Else', doing almost *everything* for her. From brushing her hair, to building a new cupboard or side table whenever she asked him to, to maintaining *her* car. I am not exaggerating when I say that rather than throw something out and cause an argument with Mum, Dad would effortlessly knock up a new piece of furniture to house more Tupperware or another pair of shoes.

My dad was chivalrous in general, probably because he was from a small village where everyone knew everyone and everyone had old-school manners. Such manners were wasted on some Australians he met here. One of the funniest stories my dad ever told me was about when he first arrived and was walking down the street and saw an old woman struggling with her bags of groceries. As was normal in his world, he went to relieve her of the weight and effort, only to have her abuse him. She thought he was trying to steal the bags. He said he never offered to help someone again, but I don't believe that for a minute.

I know that I am who I am as Anita Marianne Heiss because of the home life I had as a child, teenager and grown woman. I had two parents and a strong male role model: a man who loved his family, and realised how blessed he was to have them. A man that made the world as we know it a better place to be because he was in it. Writing about my father here was the hardest part of putting this memoir together. He passed away on 6 November 2005, and my heart still aches. I'll always be grateful for growing up in a house full of love: a place where my parents showed me that true, respectful and lasting love knows no boundaries, least of all race; where Aboriginality was just a way of life, not an obstacle to it.

Some people might think it strange that my father never talked about identity with me, and I need to say that he wasn't at all silenced from having an opinion. It's because, in his home, the sharing of values and living an honest life were more important than considering differences in cultural background.

THE TRIAL: THE POSSIBILITY
OF A GROUP ACTION

The morning after the publication of 'It's so hip to be black', I woke up and the emails were still coming in. One was from Kirstie Parker, editor of the *Koori Mail*. She wanted to know if I'd make a comment. I called her and asked why we'd give such an ill-considered article any space in our media. She explained that the *Koori Mail* had been receiving calls and comments from around the country and would have to do something. I gave a comment.

On 20 April, five days after the publication of the article, I was contacted by Aislinn Martin, the coordinator of Tarwirri, the Indigenous Law Students and Lawyers Association of Victoria. Past Tarwirri president Abbie Burchill – niece of fellow plaintiffs Graham and Wayne Atkinson – asserted that something needed to be done about the article, and the rest of the Tarwirri committee agreed that they should use their networks to take action. A number of fairer-skinned

Tarwirri members had complained in the past about their Aboriginality constantly being questioned, so the committee felt it was in the broader interests of their membership and the wider Aboriginal community that a stand be taken, and that Aboriginal people lead the debate on identity, not non-Aboriginal newspaper columnists. Aislinn asked if I was interested in being part of a group action against the Herald and Weekly Times. This had become far bigger than I had ever imagined, and yet it would be nothing compared to the media circus and personal trauma that lay ahead.

I'd never been part of a court case before, let alone been at the centre of one. I had no real idea how the legal system worked, even though my closest friends are lawyers and I share an office with a lawyer. I did know that the justice system had long failed to provide justice to Blackfellas, at least in terms of Black deaths in custody, so why would it be any different with this case?

Meanwhile, the online version of Bolt's article, which had been published on his News Limited blog, was going crazy with hurtful, angry and violent comments from his readers. They accused those mentioned by Bolt, and Aboriginal people generally, of trying to 'rort the system'. The main thrust of the article was that so-called 'fair-skinned' Aborigines should not be allowed to regard themselves as Blackfellas, and that our 'choice' of identity was somehow more for 'professional' than personal reasons.

In his article, Andrew Bolt had written:

Heiss not only took out the Scanlon Prize for Indigenous Poetry, but won plum jobs reserved for Aborigines at Koori Radio, the Aboriginal and Torres Strait Islander Arts Board and Macquarie University's Warawara Department of Indigenous Studies . . . this self-identification as Aboriginal strikes me as self-obsessed, and driven more by politics than by any racial reality.

As a direct result of the article, I have been accused by people I don't know – commenters on the blog and via emails sent to me after the case – of only getting on in life because of 'a leg-up' from my Aboriginality. This suggestion that I'd made a decision to identify as Aboriginal for the benefit of employment fails to consider that I am an established writer and highly qualified for the jobs I have held, given that I have a PhD in Media and Communication from the University of Western Sydney. Furthermore, *none* of the jobs Bolt mentioned were actually 'reserved' or identified as strictly Aboriginal positions. And the Koori Radio role was voluntary and unpaid. The only Aboriginal-specific position I've ever had was at Streetwize Comics, and I had a Bachelor of Arts with honours from the University of New South Wales when I applied for that job.

Bolt also stated: 'I think it is sad if we harp on about difference and rights based on trivial inflections of race.' Therein lies the major issue I have with the article. There seems to be no understanding whatsoever of the personal nature Aboriginal identity has for individuals, the way that it connects us to our communities. My identity is not simply about race: it's about my family history, it's about the history of Aboriginal Australia generally, it's about the way I have been shaped as a human being since birth. It's not about blood quantum or the colour of my skin, or whether or not I work in an 'Aboriginal position', although *all* my work (paid and unpaid) is for the betterment of the Aboriginal community in some way.

One of the most surprising impacts the article has had is that only since its publication have I been referred to as a 'light-skinned Aborigine' or a 'white Aborigine'. I was always the dark one when compared to whitefellas. Now whitefellas are not comparing me to themselves but to other Blackfellas, and all of a sudden I'm 'light-skinned'. Does that mean they now accept me as one of their own? Will they be moving the boundaries again anytime soon in an attempt to remove me altogether from any connection to my family and history? I'm wondering if this new terminology of what it means to be Aboriginal will become so much a part of the Australian vernacular that it will appear in the next revision of the *Macquarie Dictionary*.

It's not a coincidence that all those mentioned in the article have succeeded in their chosen fields. Is it possible that this is because of an underlying notion that high achievers can only do well if they are white and not Black? That if you are educated, professional, savvy and smart, then you can't possibly be Aboriginal?

As a Koori living in the city I am not unlike many others

today; 32 per cent of Indigenous Australians live in urban centres and enjoy all the experiences and changes that city life brings. And yet, I feel that we as Blackfellas are still expected by many to remain static as Aboriginal people. That in order to be 'authentically Aboriginal', we must not evolve as a community, even after being moved from homelands and shafted onto missions and reserves under acts of protection and assimilation. I feel we are often still regarded by many in the broader community (propelled by the media) as only being *really* Aboriginal, or *really* Black, if we are desert-dwellers, poor, uneducated, at risk and dark-skinned. So myself and the other people mentioned in the Bolt article must therefore be whites taking Black jobs. Our reality, though, is that we are all educated Blackfellas wanting to give back to our communities by working in roles that allow us to do just that.

I have been asked why I didn't just write a letter to the editor in response to the Bolt article. Aside from a letter not being able to adequately answer all the issues and untruths, there is really no amount of words that will address the deep offence his words caused. My mother was offended by being called 'part-Aboriginal' by someone who knew nothing about her identity or the identity of Aboriginal people in general. His article was a slight on my ancestry and heritage and my family.

CHAPTER 4

COCO POP, CHOCOLATE DROP . . .

am barefoot in my red-and-white sports uniform and I am pacing myself as I take the first bend in the 400-metre girls race at Hensley Oval. I'm coming up from about fifth place and gaining speed as we take the second bend, then I sprint hard as I take the last 100 metres. It's the 1980 St Andrew's, Malabar, athletics carnival and people are cheering; I'm not sure if it's for me, but I pretend it is. At least the kids in the Gold House are cheering for me: they want the points to go to our tally. I cross the line first, a little like Cathy Freeman, but without the lycra body suit or the international acclaim. This is an important 'happy' memory for me in primary school, winning that race.

It's not just about the win, though, it's about the fact I beat the girl named Gold House captain for the carnival. I wanted to be captain, I thought I deserved to be captain, I was almost certain I *would* be captain. Don't get me wrong, I liked my rival back then, and the last time I saw her twelve years ago

I still liked her. But I've never recovered from her also being chosen as overall school captain, because that also stung. So that was why, at our athletics carnival, I *had* to win the race: I *had* to beat her at something. She was a lightning-bolt runner and brilliant in the classroom *and* she was nice – *really* nice. I couldn't beat her at Maths, and I couldn't possibly be as nice as she was, so I had to be better at the sprint. I know this makes me sound competitive, but my dad always said if you were going to do something, do it the best you can. I did my best, but I wasn't made captain, of the house or the school. For the record, though, my brother Mark and nephew Benjamin both went on to become school captains of St Andrew's, so that appeased me in some ways.

Another happy school memory that pops up occasionally is me wearing my mum's wedding gown for a fancy dress parade in fourth class. I won third prize for what Mum had turned into a princess outfit for me: her long-sleeved lace and tulle dress had been taken up (but not taken in). I also wore a hand-me-down-from-someone navy blue sparkly cardy, and so I was the picture of fashion in Malabar in the 1970s. It was an overcast day, but I had an added spring in my step because I had managed to scoop third place in the school cake raffle during assembly. It was a chocolate cake and I loved chocolate cake. I still do. And it was also the day before my birthday; I felt like the luckiest girl in the world. I smiled all day, but now my smile has a tinge of cringe as I realise Mum's wedding dress fitted me quite easily at the age of ten. Obviously, my mum was tiny when she married my dad in

1960. And clearly, the last thing I needed as a princess with a navy cardy was more chocolate cake.

Another school memory was the Easter bonnet parade in sixth class, where we could dress to match our headwear creation. My parents, as usual, had recycled someone else's bonnet from another school – the child of a friend in Matraville – because that's what neighbours did for each other in those days. So my 'bonnet' was a papier-mâché chicken's head (the Easter link being eggs, I guess) and it was probably the root of one of my nicknames – 'Chicken Legs' – later in life. I don't know who thought it was a good idea, or why my parents even let me wear it (perhaps they didn't even know), but to match my headwear I sported a yellow one-piece swimsuit I bought from Target in Rockdale on one of my little shopping trips while Dad was delivering desks. The unflattering suit was aimed to complete my chicken outfit, and I then clucked my way through the parade. Cringe factor: extreme! I'm scarred by that memory, and apologise to any other students who may be also.

It's an unfortunate reality, though, that the most vivid and easily recalled memories that come to mind of life at my little Catholic school in the 1970s are sad, painful ones. These memories take me back to a time in history where there were no racial vilification laws and where the television show *Kingswood Country* was an Australian favourite. A satire based on and targeting a certain Australian working-class demographic, its lead character, Ted Bullpitt, openly called his son-in-law, Bruno, a 'bloody wog' on national television, while Aboriginal characters were resigned to being garden statues named 'Neville'. While it's understood that the show was meant to be a send-up of what today are termed 'bogans', there is a danger that many viewers don't appreciate it's satire and may think the representations and language are acceptable.

It was around this time that I first learned that I was different to other kids at school, and that name-calling could often cause a five-year-old to go home in tears. By all accounts, my older sister was proud of my academic achievements in primary school. I remember sitting in the playground at the age of five and my sister bragging to her friends about my counting skills. So I counted to 100 for them, like a performing monkey. One of my sister's friends made a comment along the lines of, 'You're a good counter for an "abo".' I felt insulted at the time, knowing that 'abo' was one of those bad words you never used. I don't remember telling Mum about the incident, but I do remember standing alongside her in my sister's classroom the next day. Mum on one side, a teacher on the other; I was like an ant between giants as I was instructed to 'Point out the one who said it.' It was a pivotal moment, marking the beginning of my life reacting to racism, and the beginning of my primary school career of being a dibber-dobber, apparently.

I guess it's fair to say the coolest boy in school is never going to fancy the dibber-dobber, but we were friends, mostly. His name was Phillip Harcourt, and he was without doubt the spunkiest boy in my class. He lived close by, as did most of the kids who went to St Andrew's. Alas, by Year 3, racial taunts hadn't escaped the spunk's vocab either, and Hunky Harcourt felt the need to refer to me as an 'abo' one day in class. And it hurt. As the dibber-dobber mantle dictated, I told Mum that night. While I didn't know what racism really was at that age, I did know the words that Mum and Dad had told us never to repeat or use against *anyone*. Dad also said you should never call anyone stupid, a pig or an idiot. When I repeated the c-word I'd heard at the park around seven years of age, I was *very* firmly told *never, ever* to use it again.

So I told Mum that Hunky Harcourt had called me an 'abo', and she was on the phone in a flash that night calling his mother, who was embarrassed and apologetic like any good churchgoing mother would be. The next morning as I stood in the classroom near the windows overlooking Ireton Street, I remember Phillip coming up behind me and saying, 'I'm sorry for calling you an abo, and it will never happen again.' Although perfectly scripted and rehearsed, I continue to believe there was sincerity and remorse in his words and, indeed, it never happened again. By Year 4 when I got a mini-bike – a yellow Honda 50cc – Hunky Harcourt was the first kid in the class to arrive at my house to check it out and have a ride. My fleeting moment of tomboyishness had also found me some interest with other boys at school. But when the bike disappeared to the Hartley Valley holiday farm, so did the interest and the hunks.

By far my most dreaded moments in primary school were getting myself from Anzac Parade over the Lawson Street hill and into Cunningham Street. This was despite the fact that it was a time when it was safe for kids to walk to and from school without the fears that parents live with today. Sometimes I walked with my siblings, sometimes I walked with my best friend, Melinda, to the top of Lawson Street where she lived. Sometimes I walked alone. I had two great fears on the homeward journey. The first was walking past the laneway between Franklin Street and Lawson Street where the Matraville High students would have their regular punch-ups and 'initiation ceremonies'. Students would often come out the Lawson Street exit bloodied and battered. I walked particularly fast on those days, and minded my own business. I smile now recognising that the dibber-dobber was unusually silent at those times.

The second daunting aspect of my after-school walk was being confronted by Troy and his gang from Soldier Settlement Primary School. I wish I could say it was a public school versus Catholic school issue, but it wasn't. I was just a little brown girl minding my own business and skipping down the hill trying not to sprain my ankle (I hold a record number of sprains from the Lawson Street hill). Even though I wasn't disturbing anyone, I often got abused by Troy and his boys who were some years older and twice my size. Troy was obese, and his sheer mass next to me was scary enough without his added verbal abuse.

We nearly always met at the same spot: the corners of Wilkes Avenue, Blaxland Street and Lawson Street, less than 400 metres from the security of my home. I was always on the lookout for the boys and would cross to the other side of the road if I saw them. I can't say we had exchanges because I never actually said anything. I was five; *he* was huge, and he was a *he*! And everyone knew that boys were stronger than girls anyway. I'd become accustomed to having Troy and his crew sing out, 'Coco pop, chocolate drop, abo, boong and coon.' Often, if I was really scared, I'd turn left into Blaxland Street and walk home the long way. Sometimes I would cry with fear of the boys following me, of their words still taunting me and, more so, fear of the venom and ridicule in their tone. *Why were they so cruel? Why were they picking on me? Why was I brown anyway?*

'You've been kissed by the sun,' Mum once told me, as she wiped my eyes in the small blue-and-white bathroom at home. 'And they are just jealous.' Still not understanding the concept of Aboriginality at such a young age, I thought I now finally understood why in fact I was brown, unlike the other kids at my school or my siblings, who had much fairer skin than I. I remember when I was about eight years old going to Brownies – the younger version of Girl Guides – for all of two weeks (I think I lasted that long at jazz ballet as well), while my younger sister, Gisella, said to Mum she wanted to go to Whities.

Anyhow, now I knew that the sun had apparently puckered up and kissed me! With this new knowledge, I was prepared for the next time the nasty boys from the public school – otherwise known as 'pubos' – said something about my skin colour, or anyone in the playground for that matter. I would tell them, 'I've been kissed by the sun,' just like Mum said. But I never did use that phrase. It wasn't strong enough against the cannonballs of ignorance. I just walked the long way home again. I don't know how old I was when I finally realised the truth about my tan and what 'being Aboriginal' meant, but I always remember my mother trying to make me feel better that day.

I don't recall noticing the difference between my parents as a child. My father worked outside and so in summer his skin went very brown. We laughed as kids because he'd have milk-bottle-white legs from wearing long socks in the sun, and a natural white singlet when he took his navy blue Bonds one off. I know I boasted at school that my dad could yodel (which he was mortified by when they invited him up during Education Week to perform) and that my mum was beautiful, but the colour difference, or that Mum was Aboriginal and Dad was Austrian, was never a cause for discussion or angst.

However, the job of telling me who I was in the white world had been done. My sister's friend and Hunky Harcourt and Fat Boy Troy had essentially *made* me their kind of 'abo' by telling me who and what I was. Certainly my parents only ever made a baby. That's what people do. Even Blackfellas make babies – well, not me because I don't have the patience to be a mother, but that's beside the point. The point is that when I was born, the doctor didn't slap me on the arse and say, 'Congratulations, Mr and Mrs Heiss, you have a bouncing baby Aborigine.' No, he said, 'Congratulations, you have a bouncing baby girl.' My parents created that little girl, and in many respects whitefellas created the 'politicised Aborigine' I am today, because I realise now that everything I have become in terms of my writing and advocacy has been in reaction to what other people perceive me to be. I have long reacted to racist comments I have heard personally or that have been directed at me, and in my writing responded to racial stereotyping. I was formed as a political being in the 1970s, a time when racism was so heavily entrenched in the Australian vernacular and humour that it was considered 'normal' or acceptable.

My days in high school in the 1980s were different, though. I spent the first half of the decade at a Catholic convent school in the eastern suburbs of Sydney, wearing grey stockings and navy blazers and pale-blue aprons over my uniform on the playground. It was an experience that remains bizarre even as I write this. Like my primary school, I was pretty much flying solo as a Blackfella, aside from my sister and one other girl, neither of whom I hung out with. Even though St Clare's had large Greek, Italian and Asian student populations, there were very few 'brown' girls there. I'm glad to say, however, that I never experienced or saw blatant racism at that school. One would get a Saturday morning detention in full school uniform – including stockings and blazer – if one said any-thing 'un-Christian-like' at St Clare's. And quite frankly, I'm pleased about that: prevention of racism by threat of losing a weekend seemed to have worked, at least there. It didn't mean that racism didn't exist in the lives of those I went to school with, it just meant that, for me, high school was a racist-free safety zone. That meant that the most important thing about high school – meeting boys at the bus stop and on Bronte Beach – could be focused on.

My school was at Charing Cross, Waverley, down the road from Waverley College and just a few kilometres from Bondi, Tamarama and Bronte beaches. Because of its location, there were a lot of blond, Anglo, surfie types around, and girls from what I imagined were the more wealthy families of Rose Bay and Vaucluse. I often felt like the triangular peg in the square hole: not only was I Koori, but I came from west of Anzac Parade, regarded by some as equivalent to the western suburbs and almost another city away. Few in my class had heard of Matraville, let alone been there. And *no-one* would ever visit just for the day. It required a sleepover/slumber party to get anyone to travel *that* far to see me.

One exception was a day in 1983 when two friends appeared at my place to tell me a guilty secret. It was always going to be a profound moment when friends from Bondi and Clovelly had caught two buses to Malabar and then walked to my house in Matraville, uninvited and unexpected. I remember lying on my bed in a room with hideous purple floral wallpaper and seeing a hickey on the neck of one girl. I thought nothing of it; hickeys were popular when I was young. A confession flowed quickly that she had kissed my pseudo-boyfriend. I don't know what impressed me more at the time – the trek or the truth being spilled. Either way, the friendship didn't last, nor did the boyfriend. While honesty is always appreciated, so too is loyalty and fidelity.

When I was in high school, glamorous or 'normal' cars would wait for students in Church Street or Carrington Road, and until I had a boyfriend with a car who waited also, I'd wait at the bus stop outside Waverley College and stand curbside in the hope of flagging down my dad in his famous white kombi van. On the odd occasion we'd see each other, he'd pull over and I'd climb in the back and sit on a milk crate among his toolboxes and empty thermos or esky jug. Sometimes my mate Anne would climb in the back too. Anne lived in Chifley, and we were two of the few 'westies' at school. By Year 9, we'd traded the three busses from our place to Bronte Beach on the weekend to hang out at our own local beach, South Maroubra. It was an easy walk to the beach, over the Malabar rifle range or through the swamp, which is now covered in mansions bordering the St Spyridon College Greek Orthodox school.

But before the change, I remember my parents being very concerned about my long journeys from Matraville to Bronte in the summer of 1983. 'There's more than sand and surf at that beach,' Dad would say, suggesting that somehow boys were the real interest at Bronte. Parents, in fact, *do* know everything. I have specific memories that come to mind when I think of my days at Bronte. Days when it wasn't even sunny. Rainy days in the sheds where I wore a yellow corduroy skirt and carried a Pretender's album I'd bought at Bondi Junction. I'm not sure why that is a constant memory, perhaps because it was one of my first albums. These were the same years when we'd go to five-dollar concerts at the Hordern Pavilion and see bands like the Radiators, Dragon and the Allniters. These were days when I'd have 'Gimme Head' blaring from Mum's stereo and not even know what it meant (nor Mum for that matter!). I wonder what the neighbours must've thought!

While I may have felt the need to keep up with the groovy eastern suburbs girls at the beach, I never actually felt that I fitted in. Everyone else was thin, rode blue coolite surfboards and wore Speedos or bikinis. I never tried to ride a board, wasn't overly confident in the surf and, for one summer at least, wore a peach-coloured one-piece from Best and Less. Admittedly, I also came from one of the biggest families with five kids; most of my friends were either only children or one of two or three, so there was often more disposable income in their homes.

At school, I studied Modern History, which was mostly about wars (although not the invasion and colonial warfare in Australia). My greatest educational challenge as a secondary student in relation to Aboriginality was that I knew more about Aboriginal Australia than my teachers. The positive in this negative is that I always received top marks. It wasn't even that the content of my essays was always correct, but the teachers didn't know enough to challenge my commentary or knowledge. Mostly, my words were opinions I'd formed on fleeting pieces of conversations I'd hear about the place. My parents certainly didn't sit us all down and teach us Australian history or Aboriginal issues and politics. My parents, like most parents at the time, expected the school system to provide my education on history, society and so forth, but an education on the true invasion and consequences of colonisation were never on the syllabus when I was at school. Aborigines were pretty much talked about in the past tense, if at all, and there was never any discussion of Aboriginal warfare like Windradyne and the Wiradjuri Battle of Bathurst. Rather, we learned about the World Wars and the Cold War. I also studied Society and Culture, which at least dealt with some realities of life in the modern world, although the course and assignments were on Japanese culture rather than anything closer to home. In English we studied Jane Austen, Mark Twain and Shakespeare: all dead white writers.

However, life as an undergraduate at the University of New South Wales (UNSW) in the late 1980s and early 1990s was a whole different world. It was where I would meet and make my lifelong Aboriginal friends. After finishing Year 12, I qualified and enrolled through the mainstream channels of UNSW, although I made it clear in my admission papers that I was Aboriginal. I wanted to participate with other Blackfellas on campus, having not had any of these networks throughout my school years. I was excited about being a 'uni student', and what I thought uni life meant: seeing bands, joining clubs and meeting hot guys to hang out with on the library lawn. Actually thinking and analysing issues, politics and history never really appeared on my radar when first contemplating my new life.

I did my undergraduate degree alongside the Janke sisters, Terri and Toni, who were both studying Law along with Larissa Behrendt, Barry Williams and Nathan Tyson. Later

94

on I'd meet two staunch women friends in Rhonda Jacobsen (better known as Jake) and Robynne Quiggin, *also* studying to be lawyers. I would watch these people at various times and be in awe not only of their dedication but of their intellect in studying such a crucial field, and I felt constantly inadequate as a student next to them. Socially, though, we were on an equal playing field: hanging out at the uni bar, going to balls at the Roundhouse, having parties at Botany Street and building lifelong friendships. I wasn't sure what my career would be when I started my Bachelor of Arts, but I was absolutely certain that it would have to be in an area that did not require me to read something called torts. The enormity of the required reading for that subject alone was enough to put me off any remote thought of enrolling in a Law degree. I knew very early on that Australian history, politics and literature were enough to challenge my wannabe academic brain and my social calendar.

In my second year of uni I started pulling beers and cleaning ashtrays at Yarra Bay Sailing Club, just a few kilometres south of Matraville, near La Perouse. It was 1988, I was working the day of the Bicentennial March in Sydney, and the club was packed with Blackfellas later that afternoon. I worked at the club for three months before starting at Matraville RSL, and more than once I was surprised to find someone impressed with me for simply going to uni. I would say, 'I'm just doing an Arts degree, all the other Blackfellas are doing Law.' I really did feel dumb next to my peers, and even today tend to devalue my own work alongside the significant life-changing work they do in intellectual property, Native Title rights and consumer rights.

Enrolling in Australian History was eye-opening because it was the first time I sat with whitefellas and learned about the true history of Australia's invasion in an educational setting. More significantly, these students were sympathetic to the cause: left-wingers who by today's definition would have a 'Black Armband' view of history. These classes gave me hope, gave me strength, and gave me some sense of solidarity for the first time. I spent my days hanging out and writing my essays at the Aboriginal Students' Centre (now known as Nura Gili) on Botany Street, Randwick, where I'd see my close-knit group and others on a regular basis. People would flit in and out between classes, eat lunch together, book time on the computers to meet assignment deadlines and, if necessary and possible, sometimes one could catch a nap on a couch if it were quiet. While I would have done well as an undergraduate anyway, I know having a designated space to study each day and supportive peers at the centre – particularly during my honours year – largely assisted my emotional and social wellbeing while at uni.

We also had great social events at the centre, including NAIDOC activities. One of the most memorable was when Peter Garrett (then Midnight Oil hero, now my local member) and journalist Stan Grant Junior came to our NAIDOC flag-raising ceremony, and the party afterwards. I wonder, was ours the only flag flown upside down that day? No-one was game to point out the mistake at the time as we watched it raised on the main campus. Both men raised the flag together, so no-one was to blame. And we didn't have the guts to say something after the event either. We just huddled in the kitchen and said, 'Did you notice . . .'

For many of the years I was at the centre, a woman named Laurel Russ was the caretaker. Her son, Kristien, was an IT whiz who'd come to the rescue when computers were over-worked, when students lost documents or the printer just wouldn't print. I always thought Laurel was impressive; in fact, I wrote a comic story about some of her life when I was at Streetwize. Laurel was the first Aboriginal airhostess in 1966 and flew with East-West Airlines, the country link for Ansett Airlines. When I look at her life now, I've no doubt it was the energy and inspiration from the other Law students that compelled Laurel to enrol in a Law degree while I was still studying my undergraduate degree. And when she graduated in 1992, the rest of us were inspired by her incredible accomplishment. But she didn't stop there: she was admitted as a solicitor in 1994, worked with the Legal Aid Commission in a number of legal positions, and then headed to the Aboriginal Unit of the New South Wales Ombudsman's office. The office had been established in 1995 in response to a recommendation made by the 1994–97 Wood Royal Commission into Police Corruption in New South Wales, which exposed endemic and systematic corruption and the need for police to be accountable.

In need of a change of scene, Laurel says that, 'After four years, in early 2000, I took twelve months off and went back to work with my mob on Gibb River Station as the administrator, which was absolutely fantastic. But we know what working with family members is like *and*, more importantly, I missed the city life and the luxuries too much.' She started work back at the Ombo's (Ombudsman's) in 2001. However, with itchy feet again, she took up a senior position with the Legal Aid Commission as the Aboriginal employment officer in 2003. In that role, Laurel set up traineeship and cadetship positions and employed more Aboriginal people across the commission. In 2005 the Ombo's office called her back, though, and she has been there ever since.

Thinking of Laurel's extraordinary journey from being a caretaker to becoming a lawyer implementing major policy direction for our mob in New South Wales inspires me. It also confirms that determination, belief in self and drive, once married with opportunity, can result in great things for individuals and whole communities. When I think of Laurel's success, I'm reminded of all the women I studied with who have gone on to do important work in their fields: Terri Janke & Company is the longest-running Indigenous-owned law firm in Australia and Terri was NAIDOC Person of the Year in 2011; Robynne Quiggin is a senior manager of the Australian Securities and Investment Commission Indigenous Program; Rhonda Jacobsen is a senior legal officer for the North Queensland Land Council; Toni Janke is a musician and minister with Catholic Education in Queensland; and Larissa Behrendt is director of the Centre for Strengthening Indigenous Communities at Jumbunna (University of

Technology, Sydney) and was NAIDOC Person of the Year in 2009. And I haven't even covered their community involvement through boards, committees, commissions, tribunals, ambassadorships, mentoring and so forth. I also haven't showcased their long list of achievements professionally and personally, both as individuals and as members of their own mobs. I am in awe as I list where they are all at today, and where we have travelled from in our lives. The influence of these women on my own sense of self, my sense of commitment to the cause, and my capacity to continue is immense.

Remembering my days at UNSW through my time with the mob in Botany Street reminds me of how much I liked most of my university studies: Australian politics, history, English and some incredibly basic and barely passed economics and industrial relations courses. While studying English I failed Chaucer, and it was at that point I decided that examining the literature of dead white male writers was irrelevant to me as a young Aboriginal Australian woman. Having said that, aside from Chaucer, even in the subjects I found dry and uninspiring I managed to motivate myself. I went to lectures and tutorials and, from memory, only asked for an extension for an essay on one occasion. I found my days on campus mostly stimulating, especially being at the Aboriginal Students' Centre, but in hindsight I know that I didn't push or challenge myself anywhere near as much as I could (or should) have. That 'push' came later when doing my doctorate and carries on today. In fact, I feel 'pushed' writing this right now!

I am so grateful for my education. Even as an undergrad working nights at the Matraville RSL to pay my uni fees, buy books and save for my big backpacking trip, I had always been self-motivated and valued education. More to the point, I valued the effort my parents put in: they not only wanted all their children to have more opportunities than they had, but they were determined we would have an extraordinary education by comparison. And we did. When I was old enough to understand and appreciate their efforts, I knew I owed them a practical return on their hard work and sacrifices, and that's one of the reasons I went back to study later on.

I completed my Bachelor of Arts at the end of 1989, and the following year went to Canberra for twelve months as a cadet with the Australian International Development Assistance Bureau (now AusAID). Realising how much better uni life was to life in the public service, where I clearly did not belong, I went back to UNSW in 1991 and completed my honours degree in History, writing a thesis on the 1967 referendum and citizenship rights for Aborigines. I wrote it because, at the time of the referendum, my father was counted on the census even though he didn't become a citizen until 1968, the same year I was born; my sister, who was two years old at the time, was also counted on that census because she was the daughter of a white man. But my mother wasn't counted. When I was old enough to understand that dogs and cattle were 'important' enough to be numbered in the census (their owners had to register them) but that Aboriginal people weren't, it was easy to see that the government considered animals more valuable than my mum. I was duly pissed off. That's when I decided on my thesis topic.

As a cocky undergraduate, I remember being surprised that my father didn't know much about the referendum or the changes to the constitution requested through the 'Yes' vote in 1967. He put me in my place quickly when telling me why he was not politically active during the campaign: 'Your mother and I were working hard to keep a roof over our heads. We didn't have time to sit around and talk politics. I was exhausted every night.' I'm angry at myself at times for not realising the poverty my parents came from and the enormous leaps that we made in one generation to be educated and have a voice in a previously voiceless society. All the while my father was a foreigner with English as a second language.

I enjoyed my time at UNSW because I was free from racist taunts and ignorant educators, and my teachers finally knew more about Australian history than I did. When I say 'Australian history', I mean everything post-1788. I don't subscribe to the categories of 'pre-history', 'Aboriginal history' and 'Australian history'. Aboriginal people didn't massacre themselves, we didn't write the policies of protection and assimilation, we didn't remove children – so it should not be called 'Aboriginal history'. The reality is Australians and Australian governments are responsible for such acts – practical and political – hence why it is all *Australian history* and why it needs to be taught as part of the national Australian history curriculum.

I must admit that in the first semester of my honours degree I would literally cry every Tuesday afternoon, which was the day before I had my Industrial Revolution subject. I remember driving along Botany Street in my ugly blue Commodore, weeping with anxiety. The pickings for subjects in my honours year were slim, but I still don't know why I chose the Industrial Revolution, I just know that I hated it. And I hated the students who got excited about the subject matter that bored me to tears – literally. The saving grace of the class was a woman in her late sixties writing all her papers and her thesis on a typewriter. She was the greatest inspiration for me in that room.

I didn't want to attend my graduation ceremony because back then I thought the pomp and pageantry was essentially a wank (I definitely would not call it that now as I have been the invited speaker at graduation ceremonies at Macquarie University and UNSW and know the importance of them to students and their families). At the time, I agreed to go to my graduation ceremony essentially for my parents. Decked out in a red, black and yellow suit under my gown and mortar, I took to the stage and Mum told me later she and Dad were the proudest parents there.

In 1992, six months after completing my honours, I became coordinator of Aboriginal projects at Streetwize Comics, a publisher of free education media for young people. As part of the program, I spent time with Koori lads in Reiby Juvenile Justice Centre at Airds, near Campbelltown, and at the Yasmar Training Facility, where I ran poster workshops on safe sex and HIV/AIDS. In these settings I saw young men who'd been forced to grow up too fast, and had done some terrible crimes, but who showed me only respect when we worked together. These were young men that broke my heart, because I knew their lives were tainted in so many ways beyond their control, and for some there was no return. However, between them they were able to come up with slogans and artwork for posters that would be distributed to health and community organisations nationally. In the first instance the boys didn't want their names on the posters, but when they saw drafts of the work, *their* work, they were all proud. The posters were something they could show their families and friends on the outside.

After establishing a rapport with some lads at Yasmar in the classroom, I went back to visit the boys after the whole project was completed in 1993. There were five Koori lads involved, so it meant five blocks of chocolate, five bottles of soft drink and five packets of chips. There was not going to be any sharing, or so I was told. I felt compelled to visit these lads purely because I knew most didn't get visitors and they sometimes fronted court without family support. While I know some had done terrible physical harm to others, to me they were always courteous and hopeful for themselves. I understand why others had their misgivings, though. I remember Dad hosing the front garden one Saturday, asking where I was going as I climbed into my Commodore. I told him I was going to visit the lads. 'Why?' he asked. I replied, 'Because they have no-one, and I have you and Mum and I can spend twenty dollars and two hours and it will mean something to them.' He just nodded and kept hosing. We never spoke about it again.

I didn't know enough back then to know that after every visit the boys had to have full body searches. When I learned that, I said I wouldn't visit again because I didn't want to put them through it. But they argued with me because they appreciated the visits and said the search was worth it. We would sit in the yard and yarn. They offered to get me a video camera and to have my car pinched if I needed, much to my mortification. Underneath it all, I knew their offers were made because they were boys who were grateful for someone who took the time to visit them. It saddened me that I was often their only visitor. I brought them some sort of entertainment and caring when there was no other. They started calling me at home and at work and I was advised by others to cut the ties. I was in my early twenties and took the advice, but I was left feeling like I too had abandoned the boys.

In late 1993 I was at the Covent Garden Hotel in Sydney's Chinatown on a Thursday night, which was traditionally Koori-oke night. It was particularly popular with Block Release students who were in town for their intensive residential study programs at UTS and Tranby Aboriginal College. I was standing at the bar when a tall, lean, young Koori lad shyly said, 'Hello.' He was one of the Yasmar boys, now out and doing his artwork seriously. He offered to buy me a drink with money from a painting he had sold. And that was a moment I will never forget. Not all stories are as positive as that, and I don't know where he is now, but for that fleeting moment back then, I saw some hope for his future.

After I completed my honours I never imagined returning to study. I'd had my fill of academic life – weekends in libraries, stressful exam periods, not enough boys on the library lawn – and I wanted to be out amongst it in the real world: working, making change, making my mark. However, in 1995 I applied for and won an overseas study award through the then Department of Employment, Education, Training and Youth Affairs. The opportunity took me to two Native newspapers in Canada to research and complete work experience in publishing houses, with the aim of bringing knowledge and new skills back with me.

The first paper, *The Eastern Door*, was a privately owned weekly published on the Mohawk Reservation of Kahnawake in Quebec. It was a welcoming community on the banks of the St Lawrence River a few miles from downtown Montreal and I remember vividly arriving on a Saturday afternoon and being toured around the town by the publisher, Kenneth Deer, and his wife Glenda. It was an extraordinary experience for me, having had no real experience of Canada's First Nations peoples before, aside from meeting delegates at the World Indigenous People's Conference on Education in Wollongong in 1993. Kahnawake itself was like a small country town of 7000 people with food outlets, a fire station, radio station, sporting grounds, schools, cafés and numerous cigarette outlets, which were a main economic growth area for the locals. In my six weeks there I researched and wrote articles on everything from staffing issues at the local radio station K103 to an enormous wedding of two locals with nine bridesmaids and a magician. I reviewed CDs, went to protests and book launches and met many of the locals. I was glad to be part of a completely Native-owned-and-operated publishing house, and I was inspired.

From Kahnawake I went to *Windspeaker*, the national Native newspaper published in Edmonton (known to some as 'Deadmonton'), Alberta. It was a place where I had discussions about lower case 'aboriginal', and what was of interest to readers of the country's most widely read Native newspaper. Unlike *The Eastern Door* – where positions were staffed solely by local Native people – at the time there were only two Native staff members at *Windspeaker*: the publisher and the financial director.

It was while I was working on these papers that I decided to go back to study, hoping to do a doctorate on Aboriginal literature and publishing. I wasn't inspired by the prospect of another long degree, the work involved or the title it would bring. But I wanted and needed the structure that only a university approach would give me. I knew I required the structure in order to get the research done. However, when I approached someone working in the field at the time and asked them about applying to their university, our phone conversation left me feeling bewildered and frustrated. I felt that I was being blocked in my attempts to even apply.

It was six months later, when someone pointed it out to me, that I realised the person on the phone may have been hostile to the fact that I would be encroaching on their 'turf', an area *they* had been teaching and publishing in for over a decade. It's not something I talked about much at the time, or since, but the more I thought about that 'turf', the more I wanted to do a doctorate in Aboriginal literature, because I wanted to give a voice to Aboriginal writers themselves. I wanted students in the future to be able to quote *us*, and not just another white academic. I wanted students and researchers to be reading the voices of Blackfellas talking about our own writing, not the voices of white academics who'd written about Black authors after doing desktop analyses of what other white academics had written about Black authors.

I made another phone call, this time to the post-graduate office at the University of Western Sydney, whose whole approach was far more accommodating and welcoming than my previous experience. The school went into overdrive to assist me applying and, once I was accepted, the department strategised to find the appropriate supervisor for me, settling on Peter Kirkpatrick, a whitefella. There were no academically qualified Blackfellas working at UWS at the time and in 2001 I was the first Black doctoral graduate. While I had no relationship with the Indigenous unit at UWS when I was a student – my capacity to give back to the university now as an ambassador and advocate for the Badanami Centre for Indigenous Education, is great. I'm proud to be able to speak to students and staff there with the aim of inspiring others to use their education strategically. As western Sydney has the highest population of Indigenous people in the country, UWS should see large numbers of Blackfellas graduate in the future.

Chapter 5

Being Ridgy-Didge

I started my doctoral research in early 1996 while living in Matraville with Mum and Dad, before moving to Runaway Bay on the northern tip of the Gold Coast in Queensland in February 1997. Exhausted from a dysfunctional relationship, I jumped on a plane, got off at Coolangatta airport and drove up and down the coast for two days looking for an apartment that I could afford and could make a good escape from my chaotic life in Sydney. I liked the name 'Runaway Bay' – it summed up what I was doing – and I found a flat in a small complex that looked like a comforting and safe place to heal me while away from the family.

I was already twelve months into my PhD and had managed to move forwards in a productive way, and I remain grateful for the years that followed when Peter Kirkpatrick and I worked more closely. He never wanted to change my content or vision, but rather ensured I met all the academic requirements to graduate. I had done my literary desktop research, had a filing cabinet full of articles to read and a bookshelf of Aboriginal-authored books to keep me company. I took the opportunity to marry the hot weather and need to read by sitting by or standing in the pool of my complex, 'studying' in the sun. Finding the humidity of the Gold Coast debilitating on some days, I would head over to the local, poorly stocked library to read and write in the air conditioning and I aimed for a minimum of five quality hours per day. I loved my time at Runaway Bay, the morning walks along the Broadwater at Labrador, and the ability to park with ease almost anywhere. I smiled a lot, but I missed my family and friends terribly. There was no real soul on the coast like there is in Sydney; there was a Joh Bjelke-Petersen hangover and everywhere I turned were busty, bleached-blonde bikini babes. My attempts at engaging with some of the local mob didn't get me far, so I felt a bit of an outsider on all fronts.

I moved back to Sydney in March of 1998 because Mum had a stroke and Dad was out of action with major operations on both shoulders. I lived with them but rented a writer's studio at the New South Wales Writers' Centre in Rozelle, on the site of the old Callum Park Hospital (formerly known as the Callum Park Hospital for the Insane). Back at home, it wasn't that big a deal to anyone that I was doing a PhD, or at least we never really talked about it. My siblings are good at different things and not all are interested nor inclined to be academic. I don't even consider myself an academic, even though I've jumped through all the hoops. My sister, Gisella, has a degree in Early Childhood Education from Macquarie

University and is currently coordinator of Aboriginal and Torres Strait Islander programs for KU Children's Services of New South Wales. Mark has a degree in Education from the University of Sydney and teaches at his alma mater, Marist Brothers, Pagewood. Josef started a degree at the Catholic University, but is currently a parking patrol officer for Waverley Council. It's amazing how you gain more respect for a position when you have a family member in it. I want Joe to write a book one day: *100 Excuses for Getting Out of a Parking Fine*. He's heard them all.

While working on my PhD between 1996 and 2000, I was fortunate enough to do various projects, including running writers' workshops in regional New South Wales. Under a community writing program, funded by the Community Cultural Development Fund of the Australia Council and auspiced by the New South Wales Writers' Centre, I visited Moree (I ended up featuring the town in *Paris Dreaming*), Bathurst, Orange, Dubbo (which gave me the opportunity to work on Wiradjuri country), Armidale (I ended up going back and doing a lot of work with the Koori students at Duval High) and Walgett (where I was introduced to the Walgett races, the exceptionally good food at the Walgett RSL and local emu-egg carvers).

The workshops were essentially to impart what I had learned about writing and publishing through the release of two books and my time at Streetwize Comics. I also needed to earn an income while I was enrolled in my doctorate. One of the aims of the workshops was to offer regional Aboriginal writers an opportunity to receive group tuition and personal guidance. I also ran similar workshops around western Sydney through Gadigal Information Services. These workshops, although requested by the community, weren't generally well-attended, to my frustration. However, on 21 February 2011, I sat next to playwright and performer Lily Shearer at the state funeral of Wiradjuri elder Aunty Sylvia Scott, an important advocate for our people. While waiting for the mob to arrive, Lily reminisced about a workshop I'd run in Blacktown in the 1990s when she was the only Blackfella to turn up. While I recalled being disappointed and angry that those who had requested a workshop didn't actually come along, Lily told me she was grateful because she got to have me to herself for three hours. I've learned over the years that the quality of students is much more important than quantity, and that individual output is more important than bums on seats.

Lily now heads Gadigal Information Services – home of Koori Radio and the Gadigal Music Label – while also working on a multi-arts performance piece about William Dawes, an officer of the First Fleet whose journals document much about Aboriginal Sydney's language which he learned from a young Gadigal girl by the name of Paytegarang. I like to believe our three hours together back in the 1990s assisted Lily's professional growth in some small way.

In terms of my actual thesis, the research involved many literary searches on the *AustLit* Australian literature database and going through academic articles and reviews of Aboriginal works. But I wanted to be different: I wanted my research to be the voices of the writers themselves, and so I set about interviewing largely those writers I already knew professionally and personally, including Jackie Huggins, Lisa Bellear, Melissa Lucashenko, Bruce Pascoe, Kerry Reed-Gilbert, Kenny Laughton and Cathy Craigie. I wanted to know from writers themselves why they wrote, who they wrote for, and how they saw Aboriginality impacting on their own creative production. I wanted students of Australian literature to one day be reading these words. How better to understand what the writer means than hearing from the writer themself?

I was also interested in comparing Aboriginal literature here with that produced by Maori writers in Aotearoa/New Zealand and Native writers in Canada. With the assistance of an Association for Canadian Studies in Australia and New Zealand (ACSANZ) post-graduate award through the Canadian High Commission, I attended the second Aboriginal Publishers Conference in Vancouver in 1998, visited the En'owkin Centre for international Indigenous writers and home of Theytus Books in Penticton (British Columbia), and then went to the Aboriginal Media Conference in Toronto, where I heard speeches from long-admired Native American novelist and broadcaster Tom King, author and playwright Drew Hayden Taylor (*Funny, You Don't Look Like One: Observations from a Blue-Eyed Ojibway*) and poet, journo and children's author Jordan Wheeler. I also saw renowned performance poet Joy Harjo live on stage, and my inspiration to write soared.

In 1997 I travelled across the North Island of New Zealand, driving south from Auckland via Hamilton, Rotorua and on to Wellington. It was on this trip I met for the first time the poet Robert Sullivan, multi-award-winning novelists Patricia Grace and Witi Ihimaera, and Samoan writer Albert Wendt. The generosity of these authors and academics, as well as other authors across genres, all happy to talk to me about their writing production and publications, was extraordinary. It gave me an insight into why and what was being produced in Aotearoa and by whom. Time with publishers Robyn Bargh (Huia Press), Maarire Goodall (Aoraki Press) and Annais Allen and Janine McVeagh (Te Reo Publications) also helped me understand the process across the Tasman.

During my 'student phase' I gave many guest lectures, some required by my post-graduate degree and others by invitation. While I was studying I understood there were less than twenty Aboriginal people in the country who had graduated with doctorates – a very small number in the big scheme of things – so within the education sector I assumed it was easy to track down post-graduate students for lecturing. One day I got a call from UNSW asking me to give a lecture on Aboriginal women's feminism. I responded, 'That's not my area of expertise, my area is Aboriginal literature.' They replied, 'Oh yes, but you are Aboriginal and you're a woman, so you can do it.' I did the lecture and used Romaine Moreton's powerful and challenging poem 'Ode to Barbie' to demonstrate the different realities between Black and white women. But those were the pre-life-coach days, when I found it difficult to say no out of a sense of obligation and easily induced self-imposed guilt.

I've heard over the years from academic whitefellas who've claimed to have contacted Blackfellas to give speeches and heard nothing back or didn't receive the response they wanted. While I understand the overwhelming sense of annoyance these random emails and requests bring to people who are being asked to offer advice, opinions and work (often unpaid), I don't want to be the one who doesn't respond to communications. Having said that, my attitude has shifted somewhat in recent months after an increasing stream of requests. Often these are questions from writers concerned about Indigenous content in their books who want my advice on how to phrase things correctly. I figure now that if they can find me and my email address on the internet, then they can also find Terri Janke's protocol guides on the Australia Council and ASA websites.

~

In 2004 I was part-time writer in residence at Macquarie University and spent my writing time working on my novel *Not Meeting Mr Right* and the initial research for *Yirra and her Deadly Dog, Demon*. In 2005 I was appointed deputy director of the Warawara Department of Indigenous Studies at the uni. In a single semester I enjoyed the company and challenges of some 200 students in the Introduction to Indigenous Australia course I coordinated and co-taught with the director, Michael McDaniel. Michael is a Wiradjuri man with over two decades of experience in education, implementing major reform at Macquarie, the University of Western Sydney and the University of Technology in Sydney. He was also on the National Native Title Tribunal for five years and is involved with the Wiradjuri Council of Elders. I first met him at the World Indigenous People's Conference on Education in Wollongong in December 1993. We were introduced by our mutual friend, Sonia Nitchell, who I had met at the Aboriginal Students' Centre at UNSW in 1992. We'd both applied for the job of lecturer in the Aboriginal Education Program, which involved academic and personal support to students, coordinating the Aboriginal Tutorial Assistance Scheme and the admissions process, as well as recruiting students and monitoring the academic perfor-mance of enrolled students. Sonia got the job. For years she let me rave on about how I would've got the job had I been in the country (I was in Austria at the time and couldn't do an interview). Then one day years later, after another debrief on our working lives, I finally admitted, 'There's no way I could've done that job!' Sonia said, 'I know.'

Sonia (affectionately known as Sonny) is one of my closest non-Aboriginal friends. She is energetic, honest, extremely reliable and good for a girly gossip. We meet at my place a few times a year. We have sleepovers in order to catch up on what's been happening in between visits. We view each other's photos, and I attempt to cook something she will eat. Sonia is a fantastic cook so it's always a challenge. Sonia is like one of the family, and the last time she visited me we both went down to Mum's for my nephew Matty's first communion celebration. Mum loves Sonia too, and doesn't even flinch on the odd occasion she may drop the c-bomb.

Mum knows Sonia bore the brunt of some very unhelpful staff at UNSW's Aboriginal Education Program for years, even though whatever they were complaining about in terms of the institution was never her fault. I've seen a few good whitefellas damaged by working with the mob because it's easy to blame the whitefella when something goes wrong. In fact, when there is infighting or serious community politics involved in some of the organisations I have been involved in, it makes me want to ask the whitefellas why they choose to be stuck in the middle. At least it's not like *we* have a choice. But most of them do it because they sincerely and genuinely want to be part of making positive change. And so Sonia, who went to uni at UWS with Michael McDaniel in the eighties, was the link that brought Michael and I together as friends and colleagues. It's safe to say Michael is one of the wisest and most considerate people I have ever met, and so the opportunity to teach alongside him was also an opportunity to learn.

At the time, roughly only 10 per cent of our Indigenous Studies students were Australian, while the rest were international students mostly from the United States of America and a few from Europe. We also had a sole Japanese student who desperately wanted to do the course, but struggled with the language coupled with complex issues. I was often asked why the numbers of Australian students were so low. In short, it was generally believed that there was no relevance of Indigenous Studies to their future professional lives. 'How will it help me get a job?' is what most students needed to know. Generally, those Australian students electing the subject did so for one of two reasons. One reason was that they wanted to learn about Indigenous society and culture because many of them were going to be teachers; they sought ideas and resources they too could eventually use to tackle issues and concepts in the classroom. It was clear that those students chose the course because their own compulsory subjects did not provide adequate education on the subject.

The second reason, it seemed to me, that Australian students elected to do the subject was because they wanted to deal with their own racism. I had two male students in their early twenties admit they had enrolled because they wanted to change their racist attitudes towards Aboriginal people. These students tended to make my already challenging classroom life that much harder, throwing endless questions at me each week, often with a smirk. 'Why are there direct entry programs to university for Indigenous people?' or 'Why do people make a big deal about black people who excel in sport, like Tiger Woods?' and so on. I took them aside one day and asked why they appeared to be waiting for me to crumble. 'That's just what we do,' they responded.

In writing, both students admitted to me that they were racist and didn't want to be, and that they were doing the subject to learn about (and stop being racist towards) Aboriginal people. I gave them kudos for their honesty, and for paying to do a university subject in an effort to change their ways. I've never forgotten those two. On the odd occasion I would see them on the campus after our course, they would eagerly and proudly update me on their learning. They told me once that because of our thirteen-week journey together, they both decided they wanted to teach Australian history 'properly' when they became teachers, inclusive of the shared history with Indigenous Australia. That is what made the challenge of teaching them worthwhile. I recently learned that one of those students is a 'very good History teacher' in a high school in country New South Wales.

Just as an aside, I don't think *any* Australian student should be graduating from *any* Australian tertiary institution without having done at least one unit on Indigenous Australia, regardless of whether they are studying Education, Medicine, Law, Politics or Engineering. A basic understanding of Australia's history and current issues/demographics in relation to Australia's First Peoples should be considered, in my view, a basic expectation of students, teachers and employers. Such an introduction would ensure that misrepresentation and misinformation about Aboriginal people and identity would not appear in mainstream forums. When I left Macquarie in 2006, Indigenous Studies was not compulsory for any degree. I was trying to get it approved as a compulsory unit for first year students doing Media, but the proposal did not receive enough support from academics in that division. I felt like the academics were more worried about losing income and enrolments in their own subjects than they were about what kinds of media professionals we were producing.

As I mentioned, most of my Indigenous Studies students were from the United States and were in Australia for a semester or two on exchange. Many of the Americans – as expressed in their compulsory assessable journals – wanted to learn about the 'Aborigines', their minimal knowledge of whom was often based on *Crocodile Dundee*, the 1986 film about a fish-out-of-water Aussie cowboy in New York, and Marlo Morgan's book *Mutant Message Down Under*, a fabricated account (originally published as autobiography) of roaming the desert with a tribe of Aborigines, during which Morgan says she had access to sacred ceremonies, had her own epiphany and lived to tell the story. Sometimes my students were unaware of the controversy surrounding Morgan's book and the fact it was not real; this was unsurprising, given the students also knew little, if anything, about their own First Nations peoples back home. On most occasions, these students would arrive at their first lecture with preconceived notions of Aboriginal identity and what kind of person they expected to see up the front of the class. They certainly didn't expect to see someone who looked like me.

Like I said, nearly all had seen David Gulpilil's cameo in *Crocodile Dundee* (as had my audiences during my tours of the States for a peace and justice lecture series in 2003, 2004 and 2006), and so I came as a bit of a disappointment. Many expected me to know how to throw a boomerang, cook bush tucker and dance on cue, in part because of that film. (Bearing in mind, though, some of the students had also expected to see kangaroos when they landed at the Kingsford Smith international airport.) They didn't necessarily want to hear from a fair-skinned, blue-eyed, sometimes bleach-blonde professor. They wanted a ridgy-didge-hopefully-playing-the-didge Blackfella. I started by telling them:

> *I don't wear ochre, I wear Revlon or Avon, or Clinique or whatever is on special when I enter the department store. I don't go walkabout for work or social/cultural reasons, because I drive a sports car; it's faster. Why would you think that Blackfellas would want to get somewhere any slower than a whitefella? In fact, I am most annoyed when whitefellas use the term 'walkabout' loosely to describe almost any moment that a Blackfella is not where they are 'supposed' to be. Most think they are being funny, or worse, intelligent, when in fact they are only demonstrating they know nothing about the concept they are talking about.*

> *I don't speak creole or pidgin or my Wiradjuri language. I speak the coloniser's language, and I take some joy in talking and writing about colonisation and its consequences using the language that was once forced – often physically – onto*

my people. There is some irony in me being invited to the UK to tell my audiences about the harsh realities of the colonisation process and the impact of their own imperialistic policies of the past.

I don't tell time by using the sun; rather, I tell time by Dolce and Gabbana, a gift from my late father on the first Christmas after his passing. Of course, this breaks the stereotype that still exists because of that famous scene in Crocodile Dundee *where Gulpilil pretends to tell time by the sun. It is funny, if you get that it's a joke.*

I don't collect berries either, but I am collecting something from every Tiffany's store around the world. What? We like pretty things too? Why shouldn't we like things? As my wise friend Michael McDaniel pointed out one day, the reason we didn't have 'things' in the past is because we had to carry everything; now we have cars to put 'things' in that carry for us. I like Tiffany's, and there's still plenty of room in my fast, silver convertible to fit a few more 'collectibles'!

I like pointing out to my students that I participate in the *very* Aboriginal activity of hunting kangaroo, at which point they look grateful for some semblance of Aboriginality, only to be crushed when I tell them I hunt where other urban Blackfellas do – in the supermarket. Having dropped a few brand names like D&G and Tiffany's, I then ask my students to participate in an exercise I first saw Michael McDaniel set during my Macquarie days. I ask the students to think about who makes up the top 1 per cent of their society and to consider the following:

> *Who are they?*
> *Where do they live?*
> *What occupations are they in?*
> *How much power do they have?*
> *How much money do they earn?*

They usually cite media moguls, property developers, politicians and the like as being in the top 1 per cent. I explain that I am the top 1 per cent of the bottom 2.5 per cent of Australian society, and that's only because I have an education, a job and a car. In a non-Indigenous context, having these things would not rank me as anything out of the ordinary, but in an Aboriginal context I am completely privileged. When I was at Macquarie I knew my students already had their own idea of what Aboriginal identity meant, before they even entered the learning space. And that's why it is crucial for my students to consider who has been responsible for actually defining Aboriginality, and what kind of language has been used to define us.

In the early 1980s, the Commonwealth Department of Aboriginal Affairs proposed a new three-part definition of an Aboriginal or Torres Strait Islander person. It has since been adopted by government agencies and Indigenous community organisations as a working definition. It reads as follows:

> *An Aboriginal or Torres Strait Islander is a person of Aboriginal or Torres Strait Islander descent who identifies as an Aboriginal or Torres Strait Islander and is accepted as such by the community in which he [or she] lives.**

Throughout the western world there were and are government definitions of Aborigines based on a caste system defined by blood quantum (half-caste, quarter-caste, full-blood, quadroon). These definitions are used as a means of watering down and eliminating Aboriginal peoples in Australia. Furthermore, there is a whole language outside of government to define Aboriginal society, but while it is a language used by westerners about 'the other', it is not a language they use about themselves. Slang terms like 'abo', 'boong', 'coon' and the American term 'nigger' have also been introduced into the Australian vernacular.

Another example of words westerners would never use to define themselves, as flagged by Michael McDaniel are

---

* Department of Aboriginal Affairs (1981), 'Report on a Review of the Administration of the Working Definition of Aboriginal and Torres Strait Islanders', Commonwealth of Australia, Canberra, cited in J. Gardiner-Garden (2000), 'The Definition of Aboriginality: Research Note 18, 2000–01', Parliament of Australia.

'half-caste' or 'part'. Never, in any discussion about race, identity or patriotism, have I *ever* heard a white person say they are 'half-caste Australian' or 'part-Australian' because they have Irish, English, German or other ancestry. White Australians allow themselves to have one identity (Australian), albeit with mixed heritages, but Aboriginal people are relegated to a caste system defining us as 'part'. However, the way in which we choose to define ourselves is similar to these white Australians: that is, we have one identity (being Aboriginal) and many mixed heritages (mine is Austrian, of course). Australians are very good at one minute giving someone an identity and the next minute taking it away. 'You are an abo, but you're only half-caste because your father is white.' Ironically, my father himself dealt with the issue of being an Austrian migrant who would never be completely accepted as 'Australian' by the British-descended Australians because of his lifelong accent.

The power of language to create identities is extraordinary, and often debilitating. Consider the following points, raised by ProfessorMcDaniel during the very first class of the Indigenous Studies course we co-taught:

> *When western societies evolve they call it 'modernisation'.*

> *When we evolve we're told we have 'cultural loss'.*

> *Western societies have 'development' but when*

we develop we're told we're experiencing 'cultural disintegration'.

Western societies are allowed to 'progress' but when we do, we're told we're 'trapped between two worlds'.

Western societies become 'cosmopolitan', but we're told we're being 'urbanised and losing touch with our roots'.

Western societies become 'multicultural' but we're apparently becoming 'culturally contaminated'.

Western societies are allowed to 'adapt' a culture but when we do, we're told we're actually 'becoming the other culture'.

Western societies, as mentioned above, are allowed to have one identity with diverse heritages but we are told we are 'half-caste', 'part' and so on.

~

I relish the challenge of lecturing, but my greatest joy in teaching is working with Koori kids in schools. In 2010 I had the great privilege of running a literacy-based project with twelve Year 7 Aboriginal students in south-western Sydney as part of the Twugia project coordinated by the New South Wales Department of Employment, Education and Training. These students were the top achievers in the region and were involved in a filmmaking project in 2009. Such extracurricular projects are incentives for Koori students to do well in the NAPLAN testing, and each school supports their students participating during school hours. As a Sydney-based Koori and author it would be an understatement to say that facilitating the Twugia writing workshops was an exceptional journey for me. Every week I entered our space at East Hills Girls High School to find not only energy and enthusiasm among my students, but overwhelming talent, creativity and a positive attitude from each and every participant.

The Twugia project and the anthology the students produced – with poetry, book reviews, short stories, artwork and biographies – highlights the enormous artistic potential within our young population in south-western Sydney. As part of our workshops, the students wrote about places that were important to them, and about issues around their own Aboriginal identity.

My experience with the Twugia project reminds me of some of the most emotionally challenging and yet rewarding work I have ever done: working as a workshop facilitator with Koori kids in detention with South Sydney Youth Services (renamed Weave in 2010). In 1995 – before beginning my PhD – I visited Mount Penang Detention Centre (maximum security) and the Minda Juvenile Justice Centre as part of cultural awareness training workshops. In the workshops, students were given poems and song lyrics to read and discuss on issues such as domestic violence (we used Archie Roach's 'Walking into Doors'). To inspire the lads in terms of their identity, and to give them a place to write from and about, we used a poem of mine titled, 'The Koori Flag'. It seemed apt, given that many of the boys actually had the flag tattooed on their arms, wrists or ankles.

THE KOORI FLAG

There's Black for our skin
And what we feel within.
There's yellow for the sun
Giver of life since time begun.
Then there's red
To signify our bloodshed.
And there's the meaning of the Koori flag.
We fly it with pride
We ain't got nothin' to hide.
We look to it for inspiration
Guidance and motivation.
And as for the Union Jack
They can take that back.
That ain't Black Australia's flag.
The flag draped across her back
Cathy ran around the track.
With pride she did a victory lap

That somehow got Tunstall in a flap.
The power in our flag we now can see
It gets up the nose of our enemies.
Cos racists hate the Koori flag.
But in many places it now flies
And it signifies,
An acknowledgment for us Blacks
Something white-Australian history lacks.
That we have a place in this land
As owners since time began.
There's a good history behind our flag.
Our flag is a banner
Used in different manners.
Marching for Black deaths in George Street
Flying on a building belonging to DEET.
Wrapped around a child that's cold
Rekindling memories of the Tent Embassy for the old.
The Koori flag to me is everything.
SYDNEY 1994

After that session, Shane Brown, the director of the youth service, received a phone call from Minda asking us not to return because of the poem used in my workshop. I was allegedly giving the boys propaganda about the Aboriginal flag. Really? That was not the most distressing thing that happened because of those workshops, however. The worst part was sitting in a circle during the program and giving each boy the chance to say an affirmation like, 'I'm not coming back here. I won't be coming back here.' As we went around the circle, many boys would say the mantra or make up their own with a similar message, adding their reasons why: a child they wanted to see grow up, a girlfriend they wanted to love or a desire to have a car and their own place with mates. Every so often, someone would say, 'I'll be back because this is the only family I know. I get three meals a day here and a bed.' That was when I was at my saddest, and most grateful for the home life I was so fortunate to have.

Chapter 6

Epista-What?

In 2006, five years after completing my PhD, I was sitting in a lecture theatre in Fiji contemplating why I had agreed to be a keynote speaker at the Pacific Epistemologies Conference in Suva. By the third day of the event, when I was due to speak, my head was spinning from the previous discussions on the theory of knowledge, how we know what we know and so forth. As the rain came down I was mentally exhausted and less than inspired, and I realised I wasn't in that 'happy' working place where I could be most productive.

My presentation was after lunch, and I'd already thrown out my PowerPoint slideshow and any jargon I had thought to use; I just wanted to have a conversation with my audience, which included scholars, academics, artists and, most importantly to me, local community members. There were also non-academics who had English as a second language, like my friends Tahitian writer Chantal Spitz and Déwé Gorodé, a Kanak writer and then vice-president of New Caledonia.

I chose not to speak as an academic or an author that day, but simply as an Aboriginal woman from Australia. The reason being that when I mentioned to other Kooris that I was going to speak at an 'epistemologies conference', they all responded similarly: 'Epista-what?' It was a gentle but subtle reminder of the incredibly privileged space I found myself in that week, the same privilege as when I entered my workplace at Macquarie University, or was flown to the UK, Paris or the US to speak.

With that in mind, whenever I was forced in my role as an academic to engage with a language that includes terminology like epistemology, discourse, intersubjectivity, deconstruction, pedagogies, comparative approaches, dualities, and – my all-time favourite – post-colonial (let's face it, we're still being colonised!), I was always uncomfortable. This was because it was a language that, while trying to define and discuss Blackfellas, also served largely to alienate the very people it was talking about. It's a language that, on a day-to-day basis, is rarely used among ourselves, even among those with post-graduate degrees. And in reality, it's a language that cannot be read by a large proportion of *us*, due to appalling literacy levels in Aboriginal communities in Australia.

That day in Fiji I used lay speech also out of respect for those in the room who had English as a second language and who were not academics and so were struggling with the scholarly discussions that week. I never understood the point of academics talking purely to academics when those in the 'real' world needed and wanted to engage as well. This is probably why some may see me as a failed academic. I can live with that. The title of my conversation that day was 'Being a Walking, Talking Aboriginal Encyclopaedia', because for me, Aboriginal people, particularly those who have a platform to speak, are often expected to be all things knowledgeable when it comes to 'Aboriginal history' (can you tell us about the Myall Creek Massacre?), art (can you explain dot painting?), spirituality (what is Aboriginal spirituality?), law (what does it mean to go through the law?), land (what's the difference between land rights and Native Title, and can you explain your special relationship with the land?), language (what is the Aboriginal word for this, that and the other?), and current issues (how do we solve the Aboriginal health crisis?). These are all questions that have been posed to me in recent years.

I have also been asked – not even in the classroom or on writers' festival panels, but in such venues as the laundromat or by strangers at the bus stop – to talk about, for example, Aboriginal political systems of the past (of which I know nothing). But when I respond by asking if they can tell me about the Westminster political system we live under today, the difference between the House of Representatives and the Senate, the Legislative Assembly and the Legislative Council, how a bill is proposed and possibly legislated, what the Speaker of the House is responsible for and other details of our political system, very few Australians can. (Mind you, I majored in Political Science at uni – what now seems a lifetime ago – and would struggle to explain these today also!)

Generally, when I am asked to speak at a mainstream

event, I know it is not only because of my writing abilities, my teaching methods or my research area (which is specifically Aboriginal literature and publishing). My writing and research is not necessarily what impresses others or the reason for my invitation; rather, it is the Aboriginality that I bring with me, and the *assumed* knowledge that my Aboriginality brings with it. It is somehow believed, because of the great western wisdom imparted on white Australian society, that 'Aboriginal blood' equals Aboriginal knowledge. I go to great lengths to tell my inquirers that there is, in fact, no such thing as Aboriginal blood as such – I am in the B+ blood group – and knowledge doesn't come from genetics, but from learned experience.

I watched a documentary about reconciliation with my classes at Macquarie University when I was teaching. It's called *Whiteys Like Us*, by Rachel Landers and Tom Zubrycki. In it, an Aboriginal heritage officer, Dave Watts, speaks with a reconciliation circle – a group of whitefellas on the northern beaches of Sydney. Dave is specifically knowledgeable in the area of sites and heritage protection in the northern Sydney region. But the first question thrown at him is about why Aboriginal people die so young. I felt Dave's exhaustion when that question was asked, the struggle to be the font of all Aboriginal knowledge for white people – to be that walking, talking Aboriginal encyclopaedia who has to attempt to answer questions that your learning might not have provided you with answers for, and is expected to respond to complex questions on the spot without time to consider them fully.

Do you think that a white criminal lawyer invited to speak at an event would be expected to talk about Aboriginal literacy rates or nutrition? I don't think so. In my experience, whitefellas do not expect themselves to have the same level – or anywhere near the same level – of knowledge of their own 200-year history or their own current social issues that they expect Aboriginal people to have of over 50,000 years. Nor do I believe that many white people recognise that current issues of Aboriginal life-expectancy rates are *Australian* issues, not simply Aboriginal issues. *All* Australians need to understand these problems and work towards a solution.

It is inspiring to see an increase in the interest in learning, though, that in many ways is brought about by the reconciliation movement – a process designed to unite Indigenous and non-Indigenous Australians and work at the issues that cause division between the two communities. To be honest, I haven't always been an advocate for reconciliation. When the Council for Aboriginal Reconciliation (CAR) was set up in 1991, I was all of twenty-two years old and had a very simplistic view of it. I thought it was bizarre to have a government appointed body established to essentially tell whitefellas to respect and be nice to Blackfellas. I told you my view was simplistic. I was also annoyed that, as an Aboriginal person, I was expected to participate in the process, because it was 'Aboriginal reconciliation' (that is, for *us*), while non-Aboriginal people could choose whether they participated or not.

I kept my distance from anything reconciliation related until 1997, when I was living on the Gold Coast and received an invitation from my friend Jackie Huggins – a member of the CAR for six years – asking me to attend a women's reconciliation dinner in Brisbane. I went because Jackie was and remains one of my dearest sisters. It was at that dinner, where 400 women were squeezed into a hall that officially held 250, that I had my epiphany. I was confronted by the reality that there was a whole grassroots movement of Australians wanting to live respectfully and peacefully alongside Aboriginal people, who were happy to be part of a process that made that possible. At the dinner, I recall getting up on my chair to take a photo of all the non-Aboriginal women in the room standing and reading a pledge to bring others into the process. It was quite an extraordinary moment, although so too was the moment when one of the speakers suggested it was the perfect time to hug an Aboriginal woman if they hadn't had the opportunity to do so before. For the record, I don't want to be hugged just because I'm Aboriginal, okay?

Since then, I have spoken at many reconciliation meetings and have seen the success and sustainability of the Residents for Reconciliation movement. Indeed, I believe it is one of the most successful grassroots movements this country has seen. It has outlasted a Labor government, a Liberal government, and will no doubt outlive the current government. I know this because Reconciliation Week 2011 took me to both Deniliquin and Wollongong in New South Wales, where I saw the strength of conviction the supporters of reconciliation had, and I was blown away by the warmth and generosity of spirit of all those who participated in the events I went to.

The reconciliation movement is an example of the importance of symbolic gestures. One of the most significant of
these was Prime Minister Kevin Rudd's Apology to the Stolen
Generations on 13 February 2008, when he said 'Sorry'
on behalf of the Australian government 'for the laws and
policies of successive parliaments and governments that have
inflicted profound grief, suffering and loss on these our fellow
Australians . . . We apologise especially for the removal of
Aboriginal and Torres Strait Islander children from their
families, their communities and their country.'

But there are other acts that are also necessary to not
only recognise and respect Aboriginal Australians, but
also to build bridges between Black and white Australia.
This includes acknowledging country at events, meetings,
festivals and in Parliament. There are those who think
otherwise, like the Premier of Victoria, Ted Baillieu, who
was quoted in a statement from his office in May 2011 as
saying, 'Acknowledgement of country is not mandated, never
has been, and nor should it be. The Coalition government
believes that such acknowledgements may be diminished if
they become tokenistic.'

Contrary to his thoughts on the matter, I was pleased that
only days after this statement, on my visit to Melbourne to
be part of the Long Walk and the Emerging Writers' Festival,
everyone I met supported maintaining the status quo on that
front. It is not tokenistic to acknowledge country unless in
your heart you don't mean it – if the act means something to
the individual, then without question it is of value. And it will

always mean something to the traditional owners and care-takers of country where an event is happening. I was relieved at the 2011 New South Wales Premier's Literary Awards that both the premier and our new arts minister, George Souris, both sincerely and effortlessly paid respects to country.

Another important gesture is flying the Aboriginal flag at schools, council buildings and town halls. While I was disturbed that my visit to Deniliquin in 2011 revealed their local council had (with no logical explanation) voted against permanently flying the Aboriginal flag, I'm grateful that my own local council in Randwick and many other local councils do fly the flag full-time. This symbolic gesture is a basic rec-ognition that a government building stands on the traditional lands of a specific Aboriginal group. Quite simple, really. When I drive along the street in any town or suburb and I see the Aboriginal flag flying, I don't say to myself, 'Well done!' Rather, I say, 'About time.'

~

To return back to my feelings of being overwhelmed at the epistemology conference in Fiji, it's fair to say that, while I was employed as an academic, I felt my own brand of first-hand research in Indigenous Studies was not really valued. I felt that the learned knowledge of many whitefellas in the academy and in the area of consultancy – desktop analyses and the fly in, fly out, approach of researchers with their note-pads, tape recorders, video cameras and observer's gaze – was worth more than the learning of people like me from our entire lifetimes of *being* Aboriginal.

A colleague of mine says I shouldn't worry, since anthropology has always just been brown stuff that passes through white people anyway. And to some degree it is. It is our intellectual property passed through them as a medium to be accessible to a white audience. Many of these anthropological textbooks are never read by Aboriginal people, and often only read by other white academics and white lay people. But before any anthropologists jump up to defend their own work in the field and the contribution they make to Indigenous people, I absolutely and gratefully recognise the essential role they play in Native Title claims and so forth. But one of my concerns in this area is about who owns the copyright (the legal and economic rights to publish, distribute and perform creative material) on the information that has been extracted from Aboriginal communities and individuals through anthropological processes.

Who owns the oral testimony or the photos? Who now owns the rights to reproduce that cultural knowledge? The name that stands beside the copyright symbol in the publication is the quick answer, and often that name belongs to a white academic, historian or anthropologist. And who gets the royalties? According to the Australian *Copyright Act 1968*, it's whoever records the story or takes the photo or films the dance: that, to me, is where the problem lies. This is one reason why I didn't record my lectures when teaching at Macquarie University: it would've meant that my material in the oral form would have been legally owned by the university. What many authors, researchers and those being researched don't know is that you can share copyright. For example, I share copyright and royalties (fifty-fifty) with the La Perouse Public School for our Yirra novels. And there are others – like Gillian Cowlishaw and Tex and Nelly Camfoo and their book *Love Against the Law* – who share copyright between the storyteller and the story recorder. In mid-2001 I was in north-west Western Australia at the Wangka Maya Aboriginal Language Centre, South Hedland, speaking to staff about publishing and their rights as authors and knowledge holders. At the centre I heard the story of a white linguist working in a community in the region where there were only a handful of language speakers left and all were old and sick. Everyone knew the urgency of getting the language recorded and, while the linguist was keen to do the job, she wouldn't agree to do it without full copyright of the text resting with her. You see, she needed the publication for her academic promotion, but the community was smart enough to know not to sign away their intellectual property. They knew that their language belonged to the community and the stalemate stood for some time.

According to Nadine Hicks, the current manager of Wangka Maya, today the organisation has a Copyright, Traditional Knowledge (TK) and Intellectual Property (IP) policy developed with the help of Terri Janke. This allows researchers to use the results of their work for academic publications while ensuring that copyright, TK and IP remain with the language speakers. She says, 'That way, we can get the benefit of the work done by students and researchers, while ensuring that local people retain control of their cultural heritage. Under this policy it would be agreed in advance that the researcher can use the work for specific purposes in stated publications (such as a thesis) and for any additional uses they must come back to the community and seek new permission.'

Academics working in Aboriginal communities need to understand that they function in a privileged space, and that they should consider themselves the facilitators of knowledge transmission rather than self-appointed gatekeepers or modern-day owners of cultural material that has belonged communally to specific Aboriginal clans, language groups and nations for tens of thousands of years. When I first arrived at Macquarie University, I heard of at least one non-Aboriginal academic defining themselves as an 'Aboriginalist': someone who is an 'expert' in the area of Aboriginal studies. Only a white person would give themselves a title like this. I've been Aboriginal for forty-three years and am still learning. I would *never* consider myself an *expert* in anything, least of all 'everything Aboriginal'. So there we have it: non-Aboriginal career-makers who are 'Aboriginalists', and those of us who are just 'Aboriginal'.

Turning again to the topic of copyright and creative ownership, in my opinion this western idea of 'artistic licence' – in which you can write anything and do anything in the name of creativity – has led to decades of appropriation and exploitation of Aboriginal cultural material in the arts. Because of this, official bodies like the Australia Council for the Arts work to help safeguard Indigenous knowledge and keep it in the control of Indigenous people. As an Aboriginal writer, I'm intrigued by others in my field who complain about protocols related to creative production. They argue that they have the right as artists to imagine and create what they want in their literature, and that it's the role of the artist to imagine the life of their characters. However, a counter-argument to that is that true art should never hurt or exploit the disadvantaged. And surely, a true artist should be able to create their own art and not need to appropriate someone else's. Either way, I for one am grateful for the guidelines developed by the Indigenous intellectual property lawyers Terri Janke and Robynne Quiggin to assist both Indigenous and non-Indigenous people working in the areas of literature, performance, new media, song and visual arts. My bible in this area is *Writing Cultures: Protocols for Producing Indigenous Australian Literature.*

The guidelines are not bound by Australian law, but they at least provide suggested boundaries to ensure codes of ethics are followed when working in Indigenous communities and with Indigenous knowledge. The Australian Society of Authors, of which I was chair (2008–09), also has a basic code of ethics checklist and a free publication, *More Than Words – Writing, Indigenous Culture and Copyright in Australia,* for Australian authors wanting to include Indigenous cultural material in their works. For example, you may want to appropriately include and acknowledge the Aboriginal language used in a creation story from a particular region. As an artist, I appreciate that I am not restricted by these protocols, but rather am empowered to do the best work I can without needlessly destroying or dishonouring another's culture.

Back in Fiji, it was important for me to talk about the incredible clash of value systems when it comes to acquiring knowledge in western societies as opposed to Aboriginal Australian communities. I focused on how education and knowledge had become a consumer product of sorts. For example, in the US there are 4000 universities and junior colleges *competing for students* who happily pay for their 'right' to gain knowledge. In Australia, there are forty-two universities, two self-accrediting higher education institutions and over 150 accredited higher education providers for which students 'compete' for a place in order to gain knowledge for a fee. In both instances, anyone can *buy* knowledge.

However, in traditional Aboriginal societies knowledge was not a right but a privilege. It could not be traded or bought, and with earned knowledge came responsibility to use the information appropriately. That sense of responsibility remains part of our lives, so there is a clash between the western values of competition, individual gain and rights versus the Aboriginal values of cooperation, community benefit and accountability. Nevertheless, Aboriginal students today are now part of this western system where they need to buy knowledge in order to participate in education, employment and industry. We need to do this if we are ever to have any sense of self-determination and control over our futures.

At the end of my 'yarn' in Fiji, I was honoured to be sung to by the Maori delegation, including academic Jo Diamond, a senior lecturer at the University of Canterbury in Aotearoa/ New Zealand.

I have to admit that the word 'epistemology' had not passed my lips too often before that conference – nor since. I understood what it meant in lay terms: it's what we know and how we know it. What I didn't understand was why, as Indigenous people, we needed to have a conference to share our knowledge with whitefellas who, I felt, had already exploited and appropriated what knowledge we had shared already in Australia. I wondered what I was doing in that forum, knowing I had accepted the invitation because it had been extended by deadly playwright Larry Thomas, whose work I admired.

I decided in Fiji that I would leave academia, and soon afterwards I resigned. I don't miss it at all, although I enjoy the appearances I make at the University of Western Sydney in my unpaid role of adjunct associate professor attached to the Badanami Centre for Indigenous Education, with the function of raising the profile of the centre, particularly in potential school-leaving communities. On the odd occasion I attend conferences and seminars, I am reminded of my own capacity to think a certain way. Most recently, as part of the Alex Miller Symposium at the University of Sydney in May 2011, I was honoured to speak alongside Frank Budby and Liz Hatte on whom Alex's novel *Journey to the Stone Country* was based. Our panel, while the least academic or analytical, was, in my subjective view, one of the most important in terms of expressing and sharing knowledge.

However, sitting in the John Woolley Building I realised how inept I was at analysing the literature that was going on around me. *Is it enough to create literature?* I asked myself while driving home. *Do I need to be able to academically analyse it as well?* I recognised and appreciated that with my ability to write my own works came a waning of my interest and capacity to be critical of other works. And while I was okay with that, I wasn't sure if those in academia, for instance, were okay with it. Was Dr Anita Heiss, former chair of the ASA and PhD graduate with a thesis on publishing Aboriginal literature, expected to always be involved in literary discussions?

CHAPTER 7

ON BEING INVISIBLE

I n the Aboriginal community I'd be regarded as privileged because I've long had access to education, quality health services, housing and the right to manage my own affairs and income (unlike those living under the NT Intervention). Essentially, I am afforded the basic human rights that any child anywhere should have, and that sometimes makes me stand out as 'lucky'. However, in a non-Aboriginal context I'm seen as fairly 'normal' and I am very much like my neighbours in many ways: we are all living comfortably in the suburbs. We mostly all have cars, mortgages, local GPs, gym and library memberships, access to social services and jobs.

Always conscious of the social advantage I have over others in the Aboriginal community, I try to use my speaking and writing opportunities to bring about change for those who have been denied a comfortable, wholesome, dignified life. I use every opportunity to provoke thought in my audiences and hopefully instil some sense of action.

Although my methods may be different – they are fiction and poetry – I have the same motives as and pay tribute to the work of organisations of the past like the Federal Council for the Advancement of Aborigines and Torres Strait Islanders (FCAATSI), which was originally set up as the Federal Council for Aboriginal Advancement following a meeting in 1958. As an undergrad, I learned from reading about FCAATSI and those involved, including Joe McGuinness, Kath Walker, Pastor Doug Nicholls, and long-time Aboriginal supporter, South Sea Islander, Faith Bandler, that if you had the opportunity to help your people and make positive change for the community, then that's what you did. That's what it means to be Aboriginal to me: to be active, to be political.

Although my type of work is different to most, I am happy to be the workaholic I've previously described myself as, spending countless hours writing every week. Everyone knows that if you do something you love, it doesn't feel like work. And seeing as I don't get paid for a lot of my daily activity, I do have to remind myself that it *is* still work. I also appreciate that hard work, determination and perseverance has given me a job where I get to travel. In 2011 alone I visited Armidale, Gunnedah, Deniliquin, Bathurst, Tumut, Hobart, Melbourne, Brisbane, Adelaide, Thursday Island, Perth and Ubud, Honston and New york – all through my work as an author, Indigenous Literacy Day Ambassador and valued member of the Aboriginal (and specifically Wiradjuri) community. Many of these trips are 'love jobs' (that is, unpaid), and on these trips I am always reminded of my grandmother's working life. I have whitefellas carrying my bags and cooking for me now. How times have changed.

Although as an individual I have a public profile, I often feel my community generally is invisible. This is why I feel compelled to use my profile to highlight issues such as Indigenous literacy, and why I end up with overwhelming requests to do public speaking. In some regards, my public profile is also a burden in that I am constantly and consciously aware of my behaviour and anxious not to reflect badly on my community. Don't get me wrong, it's not like I want to run amok in the middle of the night when I'm on the road, but I rarely, for example, ever drink alcohol before I speak at an event. Even at my own book launches. I'm paranoid about being perceived as the nasty stereotype of the 'Black drunk', even though in my head I know that I shouldn't be held as a representative of all Aboriginal people. Still, I know how often our community is judged by the actions of one person.

On a Qantas flight from Sydney to Los Angeles in 2003, I overheard a conversation between an American tourist and a guy from Melbourne. Let me preface this firstly by saying that I wasn't intentionally eavesdropping; the American was some number of rows behind me, he was just speaking loudly. The tourist said, 'I've just been in Australia and I met a fourth-generation Australian. That's pretty good, isn't it?' The guy from Melbourne responded, 'Well, you just don't get any more Australian than that!' My Wiradjuri colleague Michael

McDaniel and I turned to each other, almost laughing, and said, 'Try four-thousandth-generation Australian!' It was painfully clear as we took off in the flying kangaroo that our long history – tens of thousands of years of existence – didn't count as being part of the Australian identity. It was a shame, too, that our American guest hadn't had any interaction with Aboriginal Australians on his visit.

Although the 1967 referendum was about making Aboriginal people count as Australians, I believe that we still generally remain invisible on the Australian identity radar. In society today we still categorise levels of being Australian: 'New Australian' has been replaced with Greek-Australian, Italian-Australian, Chinese-Australian, Lebanese-Australian, for example. Our language still separates those who are 'un-Australian' from those 'real' Anglo-Australians who can trace their family heritage back to the convicts who made up the First Fleet: the original boat people, reluctant refugees to the great southern land from 1788 onwards.

From what I can see, this country's national identity has struggled for clarity ever since 1770 when Captain Cook planted the Union Jack at Possession Point off the coast of far northern Queensland and claimed the east coast of Australia under the doctrine of *Terra Nullius* (a Latin term meaning 'land belonging to no-one'), even though there were people here. Since then, the notion of Australian identity has somehow accommodated convicts and settlers who became 'landowners', those who built the economic backbone of the country by raising cattle and sheep and doing it tough in droughts and floods. But because Aboriginal people did not use western agriculture or 'farm the land' like Europeans, they were deemed invisible, hence in part the assumption that they had no rights to the land under *Terra Nullius*.

In later years, Australians fought and continue to fight wars that aren't theirs, and from those wars identities were created. Each year Anzac Day commemorates our diggers, those Australian and New Zealand troops who died at a beach on the Gallipoli Peninsula in 1915. Aboriginal Australians are generally not considered part of this tradition and do not feature in much of the written history of Australia's participation in world wars, although they also fought. According to an Australian War Memorial article on 'Aborigines and Torres Strait Islanders in the Australian Defence Force':

> *Aborigines and Torres Strait Islanders have contributed to Australia's military forces for many years. Exact numbers are not known, however Aboriginal trackers served in the Boer War and approximately 400 to 500 served in the First World War. In the Second World War as many as 6000 Aborigines and Torres Strait Islanders served as enlisted servicemen, members of irregular units, or in support units. The Second World War Torres Strait Light Infantry Battalion had around 745 Indigenous Australians in August 1943. The Northern Territory Special*

*Reconnaissance Unit was one of several irregular forces raised.**

The Department of Veterans Affairs has also estimated that, 'Dozens of other Indigenous Australians served in the Malayan Emergency against Communist guerrillas, in Borneo against Indonesian forces, and the Vietnam War.' The Department of Defence's website states generally that 'Indigenous Australians have made a significant contribution to protecting Australia and its national interests for over 100 years, serving in every military conflict Australia has been involved in since the Boer War in 1899.'** According to Lieutenant Colonel Deborah Warren-Smith, the Australian Army has had several Indigenous persons serve recently on overseas operations, including in Iraq, Afghanistan as well as East Timor. She said, 'Our young as well as our more experienced Indigenous soldiers serve across a range of different corps and trades and they serve with distinction and pride.'

The lack of adequate acknowledgement of our contribution to defending the country in war is a reflection of the wider failure to record in history books the role Aboriginal people have played in the development of the country. The need for a shared recorded history is obvious, and so I was pleased to launch the Deniliquin Shared History

---

* 'Aborigines and Torres Strait Islanders in the Australian Defence Force', Australian War Memorial, Canberra: www.awm.gov.au/encyclopedia/aborigines.

** 'Indigenous Overview: A Proud History', Defence Jobs, Commonwealth of Australia, Canberra: www.defencejobs.gov.au/indigenous/aProudHistory.aspx.

Project in 2011. Designed by the local Nyerna Deniliquin Reconciliation Group, it focuses on the positive roles pastoralists, land-owners and traditional owners have shared in Deniliquin and the surrounding regions. The project is designed to highlight the role Indigenous people have played in the farming industry and the development of the region. I was grateful to be part of the launch of the project at the Deniliquin Library, where locals brought contributions of their own to add to the photos, letters, oral histories and other documents already being exhibited. I think it's a fantastic template for communities around the country.

From the nation-building history of the trenches we hit the suburban backyard, where throughout the 1980s and 1990s our Crocodile Dundee, Paul Hogan, told us he would 'throw another shrimp on the barbie' as part of the Australian Tourism Commission's campaign designed to tempt Americans to our shores. But Aboriginal Australians were not a part of this campaign, although the middens (traditional food waste dumps) made up of shellfish remains up and down the coast are testament to our taste for crustaceans and our life on the coast (i.e., at the beach!). I understand that the Paul Hogan campaign was concerned with marketing Australia as a place of summertime barbecue bliss, but I believe it would have served more than one outcome to acknowledge that the country has been practising cooking seafood outdoors for thousands of years!

I feel that being invisible in terms of the Australian identity radar is a form of racism. Being invisible and ignored is also painful. While there was a lack of conversation about identity and Aboriginal heritage between my dad and his family, this was because we were part of their lives. We were already engaging with each other, so we didn't need to talk about it. But when you are invisible in society engagement is unlikely, and therefore learning about each other is near impossible. It is that lack of education about the other that leads to racism and intolerance, which can in turn lead to violence, like the riots at Cronulla Beach in Sydney's south on 11 December 2005. Following the assault of local lifeguards by 'Lebanese-Australian' men, locals retaliated. According to images in the media at the time, Anglo-Aussies were proudly wearing the Australian flag as a political statement, standing their ground against the Lebanese-Australians who had apparently ganged up. I don't think it was a 'skips versus Lebs' situation, rather it was idiots versus idiots, and even racists versus racists.

Regardless, it was an opportunity for the self-appointed identity police in the general public and the media to decide who was and who wasn't Australian. The angry mob of violent, flag-wearing (yet shirtless) drunks chanted, 'F— off, Lebs,' and bellowed *Waltzing Matilda* in an attack on those who appeared to be 'un-Australian' – 'of Middle Eastern appearance'. (I've always wondered why media commentators don't use the phrase 'of Australian appearance'. Maybe no-one wants to admit that looking 'Australian' means, if the Cronulla riots are any guide, being white, drunk, violent and possessing a mob mentality.)

The same proud Aussies sent inflammatory text messages

to each other to 'bash Wogs and Lebs'. This reinforced their slogans on self-made posters and placards that read 'Ethnic Cleansing' and 'Aussies Fighting Back'. Active, blatant racism became the 'Australian way of life' in Cronulla that day. There was even one poster for a local sausage sizzle that proclaimed 'Free snags – no tabouli'. Even culinary fusion was out.

Personally, I remember the day of the Cronulla riots clearly. I was meant to be having an early Christmas dinner with my close friend Michelle Wong at a seafood restaurant at Brighton-Le-Sands. Michelle and I speak every other day. I met her standing by the photocopier at the Australia Council in 2001. The machine was shared by my employers, the Aboriginal and Torres Strait Islander Arts Board (ATSIAB), and the then Community Cultural Development Board (CCDB). I was trying to print labels for a mailout of ATSIAB's glossy magazine *Arts Yarn Up* which I edited. I was having no luck: my technological abilities are up there with my cooking skills. Out of nowhere appeared super-admin assistant Michelle Wong. She was working for CCDB and was more than happy to help me. And that's how we became friends.

Since then we have set ourselves the tiresome task of finding the best salt 'n' pepper squid in Sydney. We have eaten in many, many, *many* Chinese and Thai restaurants in Maroubra, Randwick, Coogee, Kensington and the city. We've also eaten Spanish, Greek, Italian, Vietnamese, Korean and French. Michelle and I do food. That's our thing. And sometimes we do the movies – just for the choc tops. Food.

Movies. Family. That's what we talk about too. And work and travel. That's enough of a foundation for any friendship about to celebrate its tenth anniversary (you already know I like to celebrate milestones). Michelle is a Leo Princess also, and she doesn't mind the idea of a party: food, wine, laughter and the odd pressie.

After organising serious birthday and Christmas dinners for the first seven years, where we would inevitably give each other very similar gifts (chocolates, beauty products and jamies), we decided we'd just give each other handmade cards or gifts. This is fine for Michelle because she is very crafty – in the practical arty sense – and I am not. The non-cooker is also a non-crafter. What friendships like mine and Michelle's highlight is that all relationships are richer for their cultural differences, and that sameness is also possible. Neither of us is confined or censored in our friendship by our different heritages, and our identities aren't challenged by the other's identity either.

With that celebration of just being friends who like to eat (a lot!), we love eating out together, but we have also been there for each other during times of family crisis. My father's funeral was the first that Michelle had ever been to. She was lucky that no-one close to her had died. Unlike in my world, where funerals are almost common community events and we attend those of people who may not be biologically related to us but are still considered part of our extended family. Michelle was one of my crutches during Dad's illness, always there, calling, offering help and food and coordinating things on the day of the funeral. In fact, when Dad was in hospital for his final operation and I needed a break from the sterile space one Saturday, Michelle ate hamburgers with me in Centennial Park. It was just an hour, but it was an hour I will never forget. I'm not even sure what we spoke about at the time. I just know it was a moment I will always appreciate because I needed a friend and to just sit.

Michelle is probably one of the least judgmental people I know. And she is calm. I've never seen her get angry, she rarely swears and she is polite, *always*. I know when I send people via email or phone to her in her job – she now works for ATSIAB – that even if she can't help them herself, she will generously do what she can to point them in the right direction. I could learn a lot from her.

On the day of the Cronulla riots we were both concerned though, and although we'd planned our night out weeks ahead, in the end neither of us was keen to head that way – although it was only a ten to fifteen minute drive from my place – for fear the ugliness was heading north. I called the restaurant to explain and the owner was supportive: she was also fearful about what was happening, and worried about the impact it would have on local business. It turns out we were right to be cautious, as the violence did in fact find a place at Brighton and Maroubra on the following nights.

Amidst the boozing, brawling and bellowing in the name of protecting the 'values' and authenticity of being Australian, no-one asked for a response from the local Aboriginal community about the chaos at Cronulla, which ironically sits adjacent to Kurnell Peninsula, the first landing place of Captain James Cook in 1770. Placards by the local surfer crowd that read 'We were here first', made many Aboriginal people and our supporters laugh. They should have carried placards reading 'We were here second'.

Well-known local spokesperson for Aboriginal affairs Merv Ryan has long been active in ensuring that the Sutherland Shire's Aboriginal culture is preserved and the 1700 local Kooris' spiritual connection to the land – and beaches – is acknowledged. He's been an active participant in establishing a reconciliation statement with the council, and regularly performs the 'Welcome to Country' ceremonies on behalf of the Dharawal nation. Interestingly, though, Merv remained unusually quiet during the riots. This was a self-imposed invisibility, however, for his own safety, because being Black and visible that day would have been dangerous, not only physically, but also in terms of how the media portrayed Aboriginal involvement. In our world, any more than two Blacks congregating with a flag can be termed a protest or riot! Merv also encouraged young Kooris to stay away, out of sight of the mob.

There is a difference between someone choosing to fly under the radar at a specific moment in time, and a society making you invisible all the time. Merv was strategic when choosing not to speak out on the Cronulla issue. At a local community forum after the riots, all he said about the 'Take Our Beaches Back' slogan was: 'These people are claiming this beach because they've been here for 230 years. We've been here for 60,000!' A relevant point, delivered with dignity. I am inspired by Ryan's style in educating everyday Australians on such significant social issues.

On the topic of the flag-wearers and of national emblems being attached to identities and communities, I wonder what kind of response there would have been if thousands of Aboriginal flags had been waved that day in Cronulla – if the focus had been on claiming inherent rights to land as First Peoples and values of societal inclusiveness and sharing, as opposed to focusing on excluding those who were different (non-Anglo Australia) and coupling that with physical attacks.

What I learned from the surfside identity wars is that our national identity needs grounding more than ever. We need to understand what makes up this country so we no longer remain a society of intolerant, violent and directionless idiots waving a flag with the Union Jack on it despite the fact that many of us have no genetic or cultural affiliation with Britain at all. We need a flag that captures our diversity – that shows we are a nation made up of more than Anglos.

The prevailing attitude in Australia towards migrants, which resulted in the Cronulla riots, strikes me as being scarily close to the notions of Aboriginal assimilation as laid out in government policy in 1951 and amended in 1965 at the Native Welfare Conference. As stated, 'The policy of assimilation seeks that all persons of Aboriginal descent will choose to attain a similar manner of living to that of other Australians and live as members of a single community

– enjoying the same rights and privileges, accepting the same responsibilities and influenced by the same hopes and loyalties as other Australians.'*

~

I travel the world teaching and performing, and it concerns me how Aboriginal Australia generally is perceived by the international community. Blackfellas are *still* seen as boomerang-throwing *Crocodile Dundee* extras, because that remains the identity portrayed to most of the international market, twenty years later. This stereotype was supported by the government-backed film *Australia* (2008), which not only has a limited portrayal of Aboriginal people on the land but seems to also have little respect for cultural values and protocols. In November 2008, *The Age* newspaper reported that Aboriginal elders from northern Australia were upset at the forty-million-dollar Tourism Australia campaign, based around the Baz Luhrmann movie, which suggested it was 'okay to trample all over our culture'. Doc Reynolds, chairman of the WA Aboriginal Lands Trust said he was concerned the ads showed images of people in 'culturally sensitive areas' without seeking permission from traditional owners. 'It seems to be hypocritical to promote Indigenous tourism but not uphold the values and traditions and sensitivities of these areas,' he said.

* Cited in Lorna Lippman (1991), *Generations of Resistance: Aborigines Demand Justice*, 2nd edition, Longman Cheshire, Melbourne, p. 29.

Who would be surprised, though? The official trailer for the film focuses on the two main white characters (Nicole Kidman and Hugh Jackman) apparently defying destiny, falling in love and making the most of life on the land. A glimpse or two of a young Aboriginal boy does nothing to tell of the story of the Stolen Generations, the lack of ceremony around the death of his mother, or the reality for Aboriginal people living on the land at the time the film is set.

In public forums I try to contain my frustration over the reality that urban Blackfellas – one-fifth of the Indigenous Australian population in Australia lives in Greater Sydney – remain invisible. In the classroom I can at least attempt to redefine what Australian students understand Aboriginal identity to be and teach my students how it evolves. In a classroom full of antsy hormonal teenagers, I do my best in one hour to help the student community understand more about who we are. But getting an entire nation to understand that we need to be included within the main national identity is another story.

The Canadian and the US governments appear to hold their Indigenous populations in higher esteem, defining them in official documentation as 'First Peoples' as opposed to Aboriginal and Torres Strait Islander or Indigenous in Australian documentation. In Aotearoa/New Zealand, Maori is spoken widely and the government recognises the role their First Peoples have to play in policy-making by having designated seats for them in Parliament. They have the Treaty of Waitangi – an agreement between the British Crown and representatives of Maori Iwi and Hapu – and there has been much debate on the interpretation of the nation's founding document, which is written in both Maori and English. In short, according to the official government website NZ History Online:

> *In the English version, Maori cede the sovereignty of New Zealand to Britain; Maori give the Crown an exclusive right to buy lands they wish to sell, and, in return, are guaranteed full rights of ownership of their lands, forests, fisheries and other possessions; and Maori are given the rights and privileges of British subjects.*

No such documents or guiding principles exist here in Australia. We don't appear on the national identity radar as anything other than a problem to be solved or an exotic fantasy, and we have no defined role in the Australian political infrastructure. If local councils can still refuse to fly the Aboriginal flag, we need to ask: what can we do to become visible? What avenues are open to us to have a say in the society where we exist and participate every day, but are almost unrecognisable? What forums allow us to represent ourselves and our identities and communities? How can we tell our stories and our shared histories? How can we make political statements that will affect social change?

In an attempt to answer some of these questions, the National Congress of Australia's First Peoples was created in April 2010, after a round of national consultations to help develop a model for a new national representative body. The congress's aim is to give our peoples a say on issues important to us, and to create a national voice for those opinions to be heard by all Australians. Since their first elected board took office in July 2011 they have issued statements to the government on the Northern Territory Intervention, Native Title reform, constitutional recognition and other issues such as health, cultural policy and anti-racism strategy. At this point there are just over 3300 individual congress members and 130 organisational members. It is still early days for the congress, and so the only real platform for a voice in the mainstream as I see it is our arts sector, which has a longstanding strong foundation. Our writers, storytellers, filmmakers, playwrights, new media artists, musicians and visual artists are using their skills, creativity and knowledge to make us more visible, not only to the rest of Australia but to the entire world.

When we were finally recognised in the census in 1967, Kath Walker was the only published Aboriginal poet with her collection *We Are Going*. Today we have many award-winning poets, like Samuel Wagan Watson, Yvette Holt, John Muk Muk Burke, Elizabeth Hodgson and Ali Cobby Eckermann. We have prolific poets like Lionel Fogarty and performance poets like Romaine Moreton. In total, we have almost 5000 published Aboriginal and Torres Strait Islander authors in Australia today and a number of Indigenous publishing houses: Aboriginal Studies Press (Australian Capital

Territory), Magabala Books (Western Australia), Institute of Aboriginal Development Press (Northern Territory), Black Ink Press and the Kardarair Press (both Queensland).

Fiction and non-fiction writing is also being used by Aboriginal writers to highlight historical and political issues such as the Stolen Generations, facts denied and ignored by the commonwealth government. This includes award-winning books like Doris Pilkington's *Follow the Rabbit-Proof Fence* (the true story of three girls removed from their family in Jigalong and placed in the Moore River Native Settlement in WA, only to escape and walk 1600 kilometres home along the rabbit-proof fence), Larissa Behrendt's *Home* (about three generations of stolen children), Albert Holt's *Forcibly Removed* (about life under the act on the Cherbourg Mission) and Glenyse Ward's *Wandering Girl* (about life on the Catholic-run Wandering Mission in Western Australia). Along with my own *Who Am I? The Diary of Mary Talence, Sydney 1937* (about the emotional, psychological and physical journey of a young girl removed to Bomaderry Aboriginal Children's Home before being fostered by a white family on Sydney's North Shore), these are just a few examples of our authors writing us into Australian history and, one hopes, the national psyche at the same time.

As an indication of the wide reach our writing has, our works are translated into many languages. Alexis Wright's and Philip McLaren's novels have been translated into French, while Doris Pilkington's *Follow the Rabbit-Proof Fence* has been translated into Chinese, Turkish, German,

Dutch, French, Japanese, Italian and Swedish. We are writing ourselves into the international literary world, asserting our identities on a global platform. Then there are the major literary awards being awarded to our fiction writers: both Kim Scott and Alexis Wright have been awarded the prestigious Miles Franklin Award, and in 2011 Scott became the first Aboriginal author to win the Commonwealth Writers' Prize for *That Deadman Dance*, a story of the early contact experience between the Noongars in Albany and Europeans. That novel also snagged him his second Miles Franklin Award.

Our playwrights, too, are making their mark. In 1968 we had the groundbreaking play by Kevin Gilbert, *The Cherry Pickers*, based on the experiences of itinerant rural workers, which explores issues of family, spirituality and dispossession. Now we celebrate having playwrights in every state and territory, three Indigenous theatre companies, and plays like Jane Harrison's *Stolen* (revolving around the lives of five Aboriginal children removed under government policy), being performed nationally as well as internationally, in London in 2001.

We also have Aboriginal theatre actors taking on mainstream roles, like Wayne Blair playing Othello in the Bell Shakespeare production that toured nationally in 2007. Deb Mailman, a television veteran, played the role of Kate in a La Boite Theatre production of Shakespeare's *The Taming of the Shrew* in 1994, and a whole cast of Blackfellas performed *A Midsummer Night's Dream* for Sydney's Festival of the Dreaming in 1997.

Our filmmakers as well are making us more visible, shaping the way history is remembered, politics is lived and the nation's conscience is guided. Our own filmmakers in recent years have given recognition to Blackfellas who went to war, like in Richard Frankland's award-winning film *Harry's War*, which tells the story of Richard's uncle Harry Saunders who fought for Australia in the South Pacific campaign during the Second World War. Films like *Rabbit-Proof Fence*, based on Doris Pilkington's *Follow the Rabbit-Proof Fence* (1996) and directed by non-Indigenous man Phillip Noyce, for the first time brought to mainstream screens an accessible story about the Stolen Generations. It was distributed internationally and revitalised sales of the original book. Another film on the international radar is Rachel Perkins's *Bran Nue Dae*, first produced for the stage in 1990, which reached even greater success when transformed for the screen in 2010, becoming one of the highest-grossing Australian films that year.

I have only scratched the surface here: there are many other Aboriginal creators out there, including visual artists, songwriters and dancers. The arts are a fantastic tool not only for expressing identity and politics but also for learning about them, and I often use films, novels, poetry, etc. as resources for teaching in the classroom. While we continue to remain invisible in the main Australian identity, we will focus on making ourselves seen via the arts, especially in Indigenous-focused programs such as the Message Sticks Festival at the Sydney Opera House each May. With a program mainly of films, it's an opportunity for both Black and white audiences to converge at Bennelong Point to view the latest cinematic offerings of Indigenous movies not only nationally but internationally.

~

At this point I need to acknowledge that there are some within the Aboriginal community who exclude others from their definition of a true Aboriginal. No-one has ever called me a 'coconut' – well, not to my face – but I've no doubt it's been said behind my back, because there is a feeling in my community that when you do well in a material sense, you are becoming white. For those of you who haven't heard the term 'coconut' before, it means someone who is brown on the outside and white on the inside. 'Coconuts' are considered to be sell-outs working for the white man, or working mostly for themselves instead of the community. To suggest someone is a 'coconut' is the ultimate insult. I don't recall ever using the term myself, but I've heard it used in the past about others. It's not a sentiment unique to Australia: in the US, Native Americans use the term 'apple' within their own communities for the same reasons (red on the outside and white on the inside).

For many Blackfellas who have been 'socialised' as a Blackfella – growing up in their own or another Aboriginal community and knowing their mob and family history – it is easy to criticise others who find their Aboriginality accidentally, discovering it while doing family trees and the like.

Sometimes these discoveries are intentional, when individuals are desperately seeking to learn more about the dark-looking relative in old family photos. For many of those who were removed under the Act of Protection, there is much angst and heartache surrounding the ability (or inability) to connect with their biological families.

There are also those who were lied to about their true identities, as explored by Lorraine McGee-Sippel in her memoir *Hey Mum, What's a Half-Caste?* It is not uncommon to hear stories of families denying for generations their Aboriginal ancestry. They attempt to shield family members from the retribution that can come when mainstream society knows such a deep dark secret. In light of this, it's a bit unfair when Blackfellas are brutal when talking about those who immediately declare their own sense of Aboriginality once they have confirmed a 'touch of the tarbrush' in their family. It's weird to consider myself fortunate for knowing my family never hid such truths from each other, and that I have grown up knowing exactly who I am and who my family are.

What age and experience moving around the country has given me is a better understanding of the complexities around individual and collective Aboriginal identity. One shouldn't be too quick to judge others, especially when some of us have been fortunate to know who we are all our lives and others haven't.

THE TRIAL: WHY GO TO COURT?

had a number of conversations with friends about whether to be part of the class action against the Herald and Weekly Times or not. There were originally seventeen Aboriginal people named in the article, and only nine took up the action. One significant conversation, which convinced me to be one of the nine, was talking to friend and lawyer Robynne Quiggin on the phone during our usual morning chats. I needed to be sure that I had the stamina to go through what could be a long, exhausting process, and I had a strong desire to win. It was more than just raising the issue in the public court, it was about the history of negative stereotyping of Aboriginal people in the media, the lack of fair response for us against such appalling journalism, and our rights particularly under the law, to self-identification. Robynne convinced me when she said, 'You've got some of the country's best legal counsel. Ron Merkel is not going into this case to lose, you can believe that.' I knew then that I had to have faith in the team I was still yet to meet, and that victory was always about what I believed was morally right, not simply about winning a fight.

The nine of us who would eventually put our heads on the chopping block had the option of pursuing our cases individually under the long-established Australian defamation laws. We chose instead to pursue the case under Section 18C of the *Racial Discrimination Act* (RDA), which states that, 'It is unlawful for a person to do an act, otherwise than in private, if the act is likely to offend and insult another person and the act is done because of race, colour or ethnic origin.' An act is viewed not to be done in private if it 'causes words or writing to be communicated to the public'.

The RDA was enacted to give effect to Australia's international treaty obligations under the International Convention on the Elimination of All Forms of Racial Discrimination. Its major objectives are to promote equality before the law for all persons, regardless of their race, colour or national or ethnic origin, and make discrimination against people on the basis of their race, colour, descent or national or ethnic origin unlawful.

There have been a number of cases brought under the RDA, mostly by Aboriginal and Jewish people. However, none of those cases involved conduct like Bolt's article, as they were more direct forms of racism. Our case was contentious because the form of racial discrimination involved was more subtle: it was an attack on the right and ability to identify as Aboriginal. Our case was also contentious because it was brought under a part of the RDA dealing with 'Racial Hatred', and according to the case led by Bolt and the Herald and Weekly Times, Bolt's conduct was not serious enough to be 'racial hatred'. We disagreed.

I saw the RDA as being the best forum to deal with an issue such as ours that affected a broader group of people. The defamation laws are largely based on the 'harm' done to the reputation of individuals, and this was not just about my reputation. While I needed to clear my professional name, I was more concerned about the greater ramifications for my own community at large and the damage and confusion Bolt's article had caused when it came to other so-called 'fair-skinned Aboriginal people' and their roles in our community. The RDA had the power to challenge these aspects of Bolt's article.

I was conscious that while we were a group of nine plaintiffs, we were also representing all those Aboriginal people likely to have been offended by the article. I was never interested in monetary compensation, which a defamation case would have sought to achieve. I wanted the publication of under-researched, race-based misinformation to end. The RDA was the only way to ensure that this might happen. As noted in my statement issued on the day of judgment, I was pleased (although not surprised) with the finding handed down by Justice Bromberg. I believed the result meant that Australia would have a higher quality, more responsible media, and that to some degree the persecution of Aboriginal people in the press would be lessened. That was why I chose to be part of this case: Australian readers deserve better.

In preparation for court, I had to read all the comments attached to the online publication of the article. It was one of the most emotional and traumatic experiences of the whole case. I sat at my desk in Rosebery and sobbed. Comments published behind pseudonyms like Captain Cabbage, Boy on a Bike and Eskimo (who got a legal snip by the moderator) suggested that DNA analysis would weed out the real Blacks and that the government should 'take away the gravy train and squillions of dollars and see how many want to stay black'. I shook my head at that, having received a letter from the Australian Tax Office in 2010 asking how I could possibly live on the $30,000–$40,000 dollars I had earned in the previous year. Where's my squillion? I ask.

Others commented that, 'Aboriginality is the get out of jail or get ahead free card.' Where did they get that idea? According to the Australian Bureau of Statistics, as of June 2008, 'Indigenous peoples in Western Australia were twenty times more likely to be imprisoned than non-Indigenous people.' According to other comments, I was part of the 'white Aboriginal scam' who had 'privileges', 'handouts' and a 'tenuous use of race to open doors'. None of those commenting provided statistics or sources, yet none of the absurdities were challenged or addressed by Bolt. The only time he appeared was to question comments made on his blog by Aboriginals (Westy of Footscray and Jenni of Adelaide). Bolt suggested that they too, given their appearance, would leave his readers: 'Cynical as to your motives . . . Curious as to your precise links to Aboriginal ancestry and culture.' To Westy, Bolt also went on to say that he was 'sceptical about your claim that you have found "no easy option coming my way" as an Aboriginal'.

Just before a teleconference with Ron Merkel and Natalie Dalpethado from Holding Redlich to discuss my witness statement to the court in early December 2010 – a week before we were originally scheduled to go to court – I sat in the sunny kitchen of my family home. Propped up on a stool at the breakfast bar, I sat waiting for the phone to ring. I re-read the blogs, yelling at the printed-out pages when I read phrases like 'free education' and 'it's all about the money!' I paid HECS just like other students, and I *know* that Andrew Bolt has made more money from writing about Blacks than I am *ever* likely to.

Eskimo had commented: 'The people in this article are not presenting themselves to be judged on their merits but are seeking advantage based on their ethnicity.' 'NO WE WEREN'T!' I scribbled in the margin next to that comment. We were all educated and hardworking; it was the writer of the article who was presenting us as using our ethnicity. The damage had been done: the readers now had a completely warped view of my professional reputation and of the reasons I do what I do. And this was the discussion I needed to have once I met up with Ron.

The hatred and misinformation continued to be spouted by commenters on the blog, and it just got nastier and more venomous as time went on. This was racial discrimination in action, and my name was being used to help generate it. I felt sick and unsafe. If this is what Australians thought was socially acceptable attitudes towards Aboriginals, what else might they do outside of an internet forum?

By the time we went to court, I was angry for so many reasons. I knew that no other group in Australia lived under the microscope like Aboriginal people do. That no other group would have to 'prove' their identity in a court of law. Imagine: 'You say you're a lesbian, but you don't *look* like a lesbian. Why and how do you define yourself as a lesbian? Can you prove your lesbianism to us?' Nobody should have to resort to a court battle to clear their unfairly maligned reputation but I had no choice. I needed to defend my integrity, my family name and all those who may not have been mentioned in the article but who fitted the definition of 'professional Aborigines' Bolt was espousing.

Chapter 8

WRITING US ONTO THE IDENTITY RADAR

'I WRITE
TO VOICE
THE WORDS
THE STORIES
THE HEARTBEAT
OF MY PEOPLE
I WRITE
AS A ROLE
AS A RESPONSIBILITY
AS AN ACCOUNTABILITY
TO MY PEOPLE
I WRITE
WITH A SOUL
WITH A PASSION
WITH THE EXPERIENCE
AS ONE OF MY PEOPLE
I WRITE BECAUSE IT IS THE ONLY WAY I HAVE A VOICE IN YOUR WORLD.'

AUSTRIA 2003

realised over twenty years ago that what was a great hobby of mine – epic letter writing – could be something much more powerful than making someone smile when they went to their mailbox. Apart from getting joy out of storytelling on paper and feeling a need to write, I soon learned the important ability I had to communicate through the written word.

In my later primary school years, I considered myself to be a rather fabulous and attentive pen-pal, writing letters to never-met-friends abroad via an international pen-pal organisation. I can't recall the names of those I wrote to now, I just know that I liked writing letters (and receiving them), and considered myself rather good at it. Letter writing is one of those gifts that has been lost since the introduction of emails, text messages, Facebook status updates and Twitter tweets. From my letter-writing exchanges grew my need to write letters later in life, when I travelled overseas in my twenties. As a backpacker on the move and during extended periods visiting family in Austria, I wrote lengthy letters to friends and family back home, when I should've been skiing, doing the Zorba, dining in trattorias, getting lost in museums and galleries and engaging more with locals in small villages.

I still have the letters I wrote to my mum when I backpacked across Europe over the summer of 1991 and 1992. I spent over $1000 on stamps and phone cards during that time because I was so homesick, but also because I felt the need to tell everyone about everything that was going on, in every minute detail. I'm not sure why I thought that my mother would be remotely interested in the sleazy behaviour of local men in Delphi and Athens, but I told her anyway. I also kept travel journals detailing where I went, what I saw, ate and purchased. No great work of literature but it's clear it's how I started penning stories in the commercial women's fiction genre, since I seemed to have kept a commentary on the increasing number of annoying couples being romantic (read: fornicating) in many of the significant historical and tourist sites I visited. This included but was not limited to: Pompeii, the Colosseum, the Acropolis, the Leaning Tower of Pisa (okay, so I was half of that couple), the Uffizi Gallery and other international landmarks.

The benefit of such basic and often critical observations penned in my journals was that almost two decades later I used some of those scribbles in my novel *Avoiding Mr Right*, where my narrator Peta Tully has amazing dreams in which she travels around the world. Disclaimer: I made up the sex scenes in that novel, and maintain that one of the joys of writing fiction is that you can write the sex you wished you were having, with whom and where!

When I got back to Sydney in February 1992, in those years between finishing my honours and starting my PhD, I struggled to get a job immediately. This was largely because I didn't just want a 'job', rather I wanted to embark on a career. I wasn't quite sure what that meant, and the search for it took a back seat, given it took me six weeks just to land a position pulling beers in a local RSL. I was grateful for that job, though, because I had credit-card debts to pay, board to cover, and a well-kept diary of IOUs to my father who sent me money while backpacking. 'You have to stop drinking champagne and start drinking beer,' he'd growled down the line at me when I asked for a few schillings more. Little did he know that beer was just as expensive as bubbly in Austria.

While I searched the newspapers for something that inspired me, I always recalled Dad and I having a conversation in the lounge room as I stood under the carved triangular wooden lights he'd made. He said, 'Anita, if you want to sweep the streets and that's what makes you happy, then that's what you do.' I was stunned at the time that he was being so generous in allowing me to find my own career path. I've often thought that being on the local council road gang wouldn't be a bad gig: working outdoors to set hours, exercising on the job, getting a uniform, holidays and superannuation. It would be a coup compared to the instability of the writer's life. I also calculated what I'd save on makeup.

Of course, my dad wasn't being literal when he suggested his tertiary educated daughter should sweep the streets. He clarified his point by adding, 'So many people around the world go to work every day and they hate what they do, but they have responsibilities like paying school fees, rent, raising families. But if you can do a job that you love and that makes you happy, then your life will be better.' That being said, he was less than impressed when I started pulling beers; luckily that stint didn't last long. If I hadn't landed another job within weeks of starting at the club, I'm sure I would've been sacked for challenging racism anyway.

As I stood at the bar on my second shift, a rather unattractive moustachioed man approached and asked a co-worker for a 'schooner of nigger'. I was gobsmacked, not only at the request, but that no-one standing either side of the bar said anything: not the barmaid, or any of the patrons. I looked around for some kind of physical reaction at least – a roll of the eyes, a tut-tut – but nothing came. I composed myself following the shock, and contemplated what I should do. I waited for him to come to the bar for another drink, and made sure I was there for his next order. Before he spoke, I said, 'If you want a beer from me you ask for a schooner of black or a schooner of Old.' He responded, 'No-one else has a problem with how I order.' 'I don't give a fuck what the other barmaids think or do or let pass,' I said venomously, heat rising in my face. 'You want a beer from me? Then that's the way you'll order it.'

I poured the beer; he paid and left the bar. I was hot and angry, my heart was racing and I was shaking my head. I'd have to quit, and so this would be the shortest employment contract I'd ever had. When the man walked off, about three other men at the bar said, independently of each other, 'Good on you!' However, none of them would confront him themselves, or even comment to each other about it. I then learned that the man with the moustache was a board member. I'd worked in an RSL before, and the chauvinism and racism had always bothered me, but the work was mindless, the pay good, and I had learned to pick my arguments. This time, however, I was worried. I advised my supervisor of the exchange and was told that my job was safe. At the next shift, the man with the moustache came to the bar and apologised, in a fashion. 'We're still friends, aren't we?' he asked. I looked at him coldly. 'I didn't come here to make friends. I pour beers; you drink them. That's it.'

Needless to say, I was grateful a few weeks later to land my first 'real' writing job at Streetwize Comics. Admittedly, when I was younger, I had imagined a career in the 'high end of town', wearing suits and court shoes. My vision back then was quite limited, and resembles nothing on my Vision Board now. I was never quite sure what I'd be doing, but I was convinced I'd be having lunch in Martin Place and getting the 394 bus from Malabar to and from work every day. So I was a tad surprised to find myself sitting in a warehouse full of boxes in Glebe, waiting for my first 'real job' interview. I was quickly woken from my glamorous career dreams.

I was interviewed by three women, including the writer I would be replacing as coordinator of Aboriginal projects. Kathy Kum Sing (who later took her traditional name of Kathy Malera Bandjalan) was leaving fairly big shoes to fill. I told her as much, and she replied, 'There's no way you could ever fill my shoes – I'm a size six and you would be at least an eight! We can't fill someone else's shoes, but we can fill our own.' She'd been a star in the job for some years (and would later employ my mum and one of my sisters in their first positions working with Aboriginal people at the Aboriginal Homecare Service), and I was a novice at everything – except telling off racist beer drinkers. I got the job and recall with a smile the excitement and enthusiasm I felt when racing home in my ugly blue Commodore to tell Mum and Dad about the interview and offer. I was turning twenty-four and was about to begin my career in writing, even if I didn't know it then.

I loved working at Streetwize Comics. My job involved coordinating and researching the Aboriginal projects – comics, workshops and posters – as well as writing scripts and editing the final product. I conducted brainstorming meetings with key stakeholders and the Aboriginal Support Committee. I also ran focus groups and workshops and liaised with the Aboriginal community, as well as funders on the projects I worked on. Futhermore, I attended board meetings as a director of the organisation.

The job gave me an insight into the issues relevant to our young people: from life in detention centres, to street kids, to those in urban centres, to remote communities. These experiences definitely went towards shaping me as an Aboriginal woman. In hindsight, I can say that scriptwriting was not my strong point – being naturally verbose is not conducive to writing short dialogue with one key message per page. But I gave it all I had because I believed in the concept, and I had the desire to get information out to our youth, specifically those with low literacy skills. My job also enabled me to do what I have ended up enjoying most in my career: visiting communities, working with school students, running workshops and encouraging young people to be whatever they want to be.

My first trip with Streetwize was in 1992. I visited Yarrabah Community for the first time to research a comic on education and training. In 1993 I attended the second World Indigenous Youth Conference in Darwin, coordinated by a committee of co-chairs: talented radio producer Lorena Allam and Kim Hill, with Alf Lacey and Peter Scotney. I attended as part of my research into a comic on the International Year of the World's Indigenous People.

In 1994 I travelled across Tasmania with Streetwize, running focus groups for a comic on land rights at a time when the state didn't even have land rights legislation for its Aboriginal population because they claimed there were no Aborigines left there. This was despite the fact the state government received federal funding for the non-existent population. The *Aboriginal Lands Act 1995* was not yet legislated. When it did come into practice, its purpose was 'to promote reconciliation with the Tasmanian Aboriginal community by granting to Aboriginal people certain parcels of land of historic or cultural significance'.* At last.

In the early 1990s many in positions of power and in the general community believed that Truganini – daughter of leader Mangerner, partner of Woorraddy and a guide to colonial appointee George Augustus Robinson – was long heralded as the last 'full-blood' Aboriginal Tasmanian. This thinking on the Aboriginal population in Tasmania has impacted on the way local Aboriginal people are treated on a day-to-day basis. At one meeting in Penguin or Burnie (I'm not exactly sure which because we drove to both in a day), I was distressed to talk to parents who said their children had to deal with locals telling them in one breath there were no

* '*Aboriginal Lands Act 1995* (Tas)', Agreements, Treaties and Negotiated Settlements Project, Melbourne: www.atns.net.au/agreement.asp?EntityID=896.

Blacks in Tasmania, and in the next breath calling them 'lazy Black bastards'. The identity issue for those across Bass Strait was more painfully severe than anything I had experienced in my urban environment on the mainland. They were even more invisible – at least back home I was acknowledged to exist, albeit in various imposed categories.

During that trip I recall walking through the city of Hobart wearing a long-sleeved black top with the word 'SURVIVAL' and the Aboriginal flag branded across the front of it. It was promoting the annual Survival concerts, now known as Yabun, held in Sydney every year on 26 January. It took me a while to realise that's what people were looking at when they were staring at me. The flag across my chest was a symbol that was challenging, and rarely seen in the little city I likened to a colonial town, right down to the cobblestones. It seemed uncomfortably homogenous in its population, and I was an unwanted visitor. I was also, compared to the locals, quite dark in complexion.

Some years later, in 2002, I was giving guest lectures on writing at the University of Tasmania, and staying at a boutique hotel in Hobart. One evening while waiting for my ride, I sat in the bar and chatted with the staff about the devastating Martin Bryant massacre at Port Arthur in 1996, which claimed the lives of thirty-five people and injured eighteen others. It was 'the worst massacre in Tasmanian history!' the staffer claimed, as he wiped the tables down. I was compelled to remind him of the Cape Grim Massacre of 1828, at the north-western point of the state, where four shepherds with musket guns ambushed over thirty local Blackfellas, killing thirty and throwing their bodies over a sixty-metre cliff into the sea. Offensively, the hill where the massacre occurred was later called Victory Hill by the shepherds.

The barman didn't know what to say, it was all news to him, and in his opinion Port Arthur was still worse than anything that had occurred in the history he knew nothing about. Not that there is a competition or a monopoly on who has suffered the most, or how to measure the tragedy of a massacre. Rather, the issue was the lack of knowledge that existed and still exists nationally in terms of the massacres, wars and carnage involved in the invading and colonising of this country. The Cape Grim Massacre is just an example of the history that few Tasmanians know or dare to acknowledge, it seems, at least on my visits there. These conversations remind me of the need for locals in Tasmania to write their stories, in order to demonstrate the different ways in which the colonised and the colonisers remember, recall and regard history. And what is 'our truth' in history? It's the reason books by the late Aunty Ida West (*Pride Against Prejudice: Reminiscences of a Tasmanian Aborigine*) and Molly Mallett (*My Past – Their Future: Stories From Cape Barren Island*) and the recent work by Patsy Cameron (*Grease and Ochre: The Blending of Two Cultures at the Colonial Sea Frontier*) are so important in documenting the history of the state.

Back to Streetwize Comics (and now you can see why I'm not good at writing short dialogue), it was in this position that I started writing more broadly: articles and columns for youth magazines, press releases and promo pieces for the organisation, as well as the variety of projects we were engaged in, including the first comic for deaf people on the topic of HIV/AIDS. I was part of a team where one could be creative with important information, and it was something I loved to do.

Unfortunately, it was in this job that I first experienced Black-on-Black prejudice. It was during a comic-writing workshop I was running with Kooris from around Sydney. One male participant in his twenties essentially claimed, 'You're not even Black. You wear lipstick and your mum drives a Pajero!' I still recall his words as he walked down the stairwell from the warehouse space to the front door leading onto Queen Street. I had to ask myself: *Am I really hearing another Blackfella tell me my identity is being defined by makeup and a car?* His notion that identity is linked to disadvantage is debilitating and damaging to the community. The sadder the story, the less you have, the blacker you are. The poorer you are, the more black you are. The less education you have, the blacker you are. Where did these ideas come from? I acknowledge that as Aboriginal people we can all have our own personal views on how we define ourselves, but I do feel that Aboriginality should be less restrictive and certainly not be determined by what one wears on the body or face.

I've never forgotten how damaged I thought that Blackfella must have been to think identity was so easily removed from an individual and, at the same time, negated by material items that most other human beings on the planet also used. Who knew that driving a car and wearing makeup would somehow magically make you a different person and change your identity? Maybe if I were a bloke wearing the lipstick . . .

I remember being confused by his comments and angry at the same time. I've always been a girly-girl, and my parents worked hard to afford the second-hand Pajero my mother drove. The truth was my father told me he bought that car because he wanted my mother to be safe when on the roads. She once rolled her little green VW beetle coming home from work in the 1970s.

~

I was at Streetwize for two years. I knew it was time to move on during an outreach event down on the south coast one day in 1994. I remember saying to the young Koori kids there something along the lines of: 'If you want to be in the red chair and you're sitting in the blue chair, then you need to get up and move, or at least work out how to get to the red chair.' It was a metaphor to help them with goal-setting and strategising, but I realised at that moment that I was, in fact, in the blue chair myself and needed to move. My motivation had waned. I wasn't in that 'happy place' my father had talked about.

I had a lot of leave saved up and took a trip in April 1994, travelling to Europe via Las Vegas and Washington, DC. I went to Scotland for three weeks to visit a friend I'd met in Austria in 1992 and had been writing epic letters to since.

We drove through the countryside in the rain listening to Rod Stewart. I loved conversations with locals there about Aboriginal Australia, and talking about the consequences of colonisation and particularly the 'real' history as I knew it. Talking about Aboriginal issues in Scotland was not like giving a lecture back home. The Scots I spoke to were keen for their own independence from England, and so were empathetic to the position of Aboriginal people in Australia.

I went back to Austria after Scotland. It was summer, and after three weeks of Scottish rain I needed to dry out. I had a lot of time to walk and think while my cousin Sabine worked long days at the hotel Pesentheiner Hof, and I lay by Lake Millstätter See contemplating life. It was by that lake that I had one of many epiphanies that would follow over the course of my adult life. Like being hit in the head with a ball because I wasn't watching the game, I realised that I needed to get out of my blue chair and fulfil my dream to write a book: just one solitary book about the issues that I came across in 1992 when trying to explain Aboriginality in that beer hall back in the Muhr. My mind was made up.

I returned to Australia, resigned from Streetwize Comics, set up my consultancy (Curringa Communications), and started doing some freelance writing, social research with Keys Young (now Urbis), workshops in juvenile justice centres with South Sydney Youth Services and the odd media/PR job. I considered the experiences I'd had in Austria and the stereotypes around Aboriginal Australia and how they were perpetuated by published documents written by whitefellas about Blackfellas. I knew I had to address the imbalance in these stories and I started to develop ideas in an exercise book.

I wasn't sure what or how I would write my book or what genre it would be. I considered my life at uni studying Australian history. My many days, nights and weekends had been spent scanning library shelves looking for the book that actually had us right, without the imperialistic or condescending view that accompanied most. I found few. This made me realise that Aboriginal culture and society in this country had been written about by experienced historians, anthropologists, authors and critics who were nearly always non-Indigenous. Much of what I had read was disturbing to me and I was annoyed.

With this in mind, I felt quite justified when writing on aspects of Australian culture that I had very little knowledge or experience with, such as Australian football. I am not a footballer, and I am not married to a footballer. (However, I have often heard whitefellas claiming to be experts in Aboriginal issues because he or she is married to an Aborigine. Newsflash: Aboriginality is not sexually transmitted; you do not get an access-all-areas pass and authority to speak because you are in a relationship with an Aboriginal person!)

To be honest, I'm not overly interested in football – other than to say my cousin Jim Williams is currently assistant coach of the Wallabies and Joe Williams once played league for the Bulldogs, the Panthers and the Rabbitohs. But even with my limited exposure, I had a vague idea of what a footballer was (I had dated someone who worked at Easts

Leagues Club – I was an expert, just like whitefellas who date Blackfellas), I'd been to the odd game and cheered my younger brother Mark from the stands of Redfern Oval when he played for the Coogee Wombats. I almost understood how men chasing an oval-shaped piece of leather filled with air could be an appropriate form of Australian male bonding. But the difference between what I would write about football and what those other authors wrote about Aboriginal Australia was that no-one would *ever* take me seriously in the football world. I wouldn't be asked to speak at conferences or give lectures or write policies or be quoted in the press on the topic of football. Nor did I want to. That was the point I was making. I would just be a Koori woman having a joke, and I was happy with that, but I was also trying to turn the tables by commenting on the white Australian lifestyle. My book turned out to be *Sacred Cows*, eventually published by Magabala Books in 1996, and was a satirical social commentary on my view of that lifestyle.

Inspiration hit me in the face when I contemplated the Paul Hogan 'throw another shrimp on the barbie' campaign. The target was the US market, and we were going to lure Americans to our shores with the promise of crustaceans on barbecues. I was a tad confused: I'd been to the US – Atlanta, Los Angeles, Las Vegas and Washington, DC – so I knew Americans had barbecues and seafood of their own. Why would they come here to do what they could do on their own soil? Perhaps they thought Australian men in stubbies drinking VB around the barbecue was an attractive sight, or that women grating cabbage and carrots for coleslaw was unique enough an experience to travel for.

What struck me most about the slogan was that Aussies had never eaten 'shrimp' before: Aussies ate 'prawns', either fresh or covered in honey and sesame seeds at the local Chinese restaurant. After 200 years of occupation of this land and fishing the waters off Australia, white Australians were now throwing 'shrimp' on the barbie, apparently. All of a sudden a whole new cultural tradition had supposedly begun because of a tourism campaign, and I wrote about it in the first chapter of *Sacred Cows*, 'Throw Another Shrimp on the Barbie'.

The second chapter I drafted was titled 'The Great Aussie Ale-Ment'. In it I aimed to give an insight into the only nation on the planet where you can bring-your-own alcohol to almost any activity: a barbecue, party, restaurant or picnic. I had to wonder if the Australian drinking mentality was born out of the history of beer-making as one of the oldest industries in the country. I was compelled to write a chapter on drinking because I was frustrated by the stereotypes and media representations of Aboriginal people and alcohol, and I wanted to reverse the roles in terms of writing about 'the other'. It was easy for me to unpack all the slang for beer and for getting drunk, and the rituals around consuming alcohol in Australia – drinking was as much a pastime as a way of life for many Aussies. I'd worked in clubs, was surrounded by whitefellas who drank a lot and, admittedly, had 'researched' with many of them as well.

In 1996 *Sacred Cows* was published by Magabala Books in

Broome after being rejected by every major publishing house in the country. Feedback from rejecters included: 'it read very much like work that would be terrific in performance', and 'your medium for the work is more likely the daily, weekly or monthly press . . . you would probably also do better financially taking that approach'. The ouch factor came with this one, though: 'Humour is a difficult area and needs to be absolutely top-notch side-splitting to succeed, especially without a strong "name" in the marketplace to push it along.' I recall having numerous conversations with others as I tried to understand what it would take to get published. Many suggested that *Sacred Cows* wasn't really 'Aboriginal literature' because it wasn't about land rights, Aboriginal health, politics and so on. These comments in part pushed me towards my doctoral research, which included considering what defines 'Aboriginal literature' and how Aboriginality impacts on our writing.

Author, historian, academic and my friend Jackie Huggins from the Bidjira nation tells me that *Sacred Cows* was for a long time her son John Henry's favourite book, and that's the feedback that is important to me. When I spoke about my books and writing on Thursday Island in June 2011, one of the aunties who had come over from Hammond Island to hear me shook my hand when I was finished, and told me how much she loved *Sacred Cows* when she first read it. She told me she looked forward to reading my new book and then passing onto her friends the signed copy I promised to send her following my trip.

In 1997, in the second year of my PhD research, I was writing for myself what I like to term 'social observations': short, punchy pieces that did not constitute prose, and weren't by my definition regarded as poetry. At the same time, I was keen to learn more about the publishing industry, having worked on Native newspapers in Canada. Aware that poetry did not sell well in Australia, the simple answer was for me to self-publish a collection of writing to learn the process of publishing while also assuming complete control over the work. In 1998 I released a slim volume of works titled *Token Koori*: short pieces largely born out of exchanges I'd had with whitefellas over time.

I had the original idea when I was at the Byron Bay Writers' Festival in 1997. I was the only Blackfella on the program, and there were a series of events which left me feeling like a completely tokenistic addition to the festival. However, it was during the screening of the Aussie romantic comedy *Thank God He Met Lizzie*, in the scene about having a Koori on the guest list so the wedding of Guy and Lizzie would be politically correct, that I had an epiphany. What if you opened an agency to rent out Kooris for weddings, parties, homecomings, housewarmings, conferences, corroborees and so on? I went on to develop this idea into a short radio play and three episodes of a dramedy for television with Geoffrey Atherden, of *Mother and Son* fame. In the first stages of writing these pieces, I produced a collection of social observations covering topics such as how entrenched racism was in the Australian vernacular, the reconciliation movement, and pride in identity. I also wrote about white perceptions of Aboriginality that were often based on what people read in the papers and saw on mainstream television – by and large negative stereotypes. I got tired of hearing the line, 'But you're not *really* an Aborigine,' and so I wrote a piece with the same title.

Within the collection I considered the concept of biculturalism: I was socialised, employed and educated through non-Aboriginal systems, but I have always been an Aboriginal person. Indeed, as mentioned previously, just like other Australians we can have many heritages and one identity. I still cringe recalling the times in my late teens and early twenties when the tone of my voice sounded almost apologetic as I talked about my family to other Blackfellas. 'Mum's Wiradjuri,' I would say proudly and then almost whisper, 'Oh, my dad's a whitefella,' as if it was something to be embarrassed about. I hate myself for that now. My father was my hero. But I knew the way some Blacks talked: those who would never date a whitefella, would never have a child with a whitefella, could never imagine falling in love with a whitefella. They could not, or would not allow themselves to understand that I was the proud daughter of a whitefella who only ever let me be me. So I wrote a poem called 'Bicultural Blackfella' which concludes:

> *I am who I am –*
> *I am a bicultural Blackfella*
> *And I apologise to no-one.*

Writing my first two books was a way of saying something I felt needed to be said. I didn't at the time think it would lead to a career. But considering that, for me, being Aboriginal is part of my everyday life and therefore part of every job I have had (either intentionally or not), it makes sense that I could easily have combined my thoughts and beliefs on issues, culture, the arts, and politics with storytelling. *Sacred Cows* and *Token Koori* acted as perfect springboards, and I have only looked forward since.

Chapter 9

Writing Us Into Australian History

I n 2001 I published *Who Am I? The Diary of Mary Talence, Sydney 1937*, a historical novel on the Stolen Generations. The novel deals with the emotional, psychological and physical journey of one girl who is removed under the Act of Protection in New South Wales and taken to Bomaderry Aboriginal Children's Home, before being fostered by an Irish-Catholic family on Sydney's North Shore. Within that journey we see the destructive forces of the assimilation policy and how government policies attempted – and often achieved – the disconnection of Aboriginal people from their true identities.

Mary's character also serves to demonstrate the confusion around identity for young children removed and raised with white families under the act:

I said I wasn't an Aborigine cos I felt ashamed. She said I must be a part-Aborigine cos I looked like one. That made me feel better cos she made out it was all right to be Aboriginal. I'm not goin' to start saying 'I'm a part-Aborigine' though, cos most people seem to think it's a bad thing here in the Hives . . .

Well I asked Ma B about talkin' to Dot and she got really angry with me again and got Pa B. He said the same thing. I was not allowed to talk to any Aborigines, and I was supposed to try and be more white, like Sophie and Sam, cos good people were white and bad people were the others. They didn't tell me what they meant by the good and bad people though. I don't want to be a bad person, but I look in the mirror and I don't really look white. All my real brothers and sisters are brown too, and so are my real parents, so how can I be white? And what about Dot? Is she trying to be white too? She can't though, cos she's real dark.

Who Am I? is a book I wrote to give a voice to those who are without one: those who don't have access to publishing or have the ability to tell their stories, whose lives previously hadn't been taught about in the classroom. Although I knew the need for and importance of writing a novel for young people on the Stolen Generations, I feared getting it wrong for those who needed their story told, so I sent drafts to Link-Up New South Wales (an Aboriginal and Torres Strait Islander support service), Eileen Stevens (who had spent nine years in Bomaderry and whom I'd met through Link-Up and interviewed for the novel) and Barbara Nicholson (a senior Aboriginal woman removed from her father at the age of four). Barbara is also the poet who penned the powerful poem of removal titled 'The Bastards'.

I am not motivated by royalties or glowing reviews, although they are appreciated when and if they arrive because they mean book sales, and more sales means more people reading and learning. I'm motivated by voicing our truths as we know them, and I am relieved when I have community members young and old tell me they are grateful for the story of Mary Talence. Although Mary is fictional, her experiences represent the experiences of thousands of Aboriginal children (now adults) as documented in numerous publications, particularly the report on a government inquiry entitled *Bringing Them Home: The 'Stolen Children' Report* (1997), which included submissions from 777 people or organisations, and detailed painful evidence of the removal of thousands of Aboriginal and Torres Strait Islander children from their families. The original inquiry that lead to the report included Recommendation No. 7 (a): that a National Sorry Day be held each year on 26 May 'to commemorate the history of forcible removals and its effects'. As a result, each year events are held nationally as a mark of respect and remembrance.

~

I do a lot of work in classrooms nationally as a guest writer. Many primary schools and some secondary schools invite me to talk about my books, especially *Who Am I?*. The challenge in many classrooms I go into is that many Australian students at the age of fifteen still don't know the basics about Aboriginal society or culture. They don't know the meaning of the Aboriginal or Torres Strait Islander flags. They don't know what the 1967 referendum was. They don't know who the traditional owners of country are in their local area. They don't know the demographics of where Aboriginal people live today. They don't know or consider that Aboriginal people live not just in rural and remote areas but also in Sydney and other cities, and even possibly next door to them. They don't know because they still consider that skin colour, education and economics is a measure of Aboriginality, and if you are fair, educated and financially well-off you can't possibly be Black. More concerning is that many of their teachers are ignorant on these basic facts also.

To me this is general knowledge that all Australian students should have in their grasp. When they don't it's a difficult task for me to go straight into talking about the policy of protection and the impacts of child removal if the class has no context of Australian history generally. While some students in some states can do elective Indigenous-related subjects, basic information – like demographics, roles in society throughout history, artistic output and so on – should be further integrated into the curriculum in subjects such as History, Geography, Science, English, Art and Drama, to name a few. Teaching an Aboriginal perspective on history is integral to ensure Australian students have a wholistic understanding and appreciation of their country. Those who develop and approve the curriculum could have their 'cultural antennae' up always, ensuring that there is a balance in what Australian students are reading and learning. Teachers and teacher-librarians could also avail themselves of the wealth of Aboriginal-authored literature across genres – easily accessible through resources like *AustLit*'s Black Words – as a means of engaging and entertaining students on topics like identity, connection to place and history, among others.

Because the curriculum does not always cover much of what I have mentioned above, and what I have covered varies in degrees in different states and territories (which is why I am an advocate also for a national curriculum), what should be a standard author visit where I talk about a book – the research, the storyline, the process of writing, the characters and settings – ends up becoming a crash-course in cultural awareness workshop where I discuss basic historical and demographic information.

My frustration with the curriculum in part led to my involvement with *The Macquarie PEN Anthology of Aboriginal Literature*, a collection of Aboriginal writings presented in an accessible way for teachers, researchers and students to use as a springboard for greater exposure to our voices. I had the privilege of starting work on the anthology with poet Peter Minter in 2005. As teachers and published writers, both Peter and I were aware of the need for a comprehensive resource that clearly demonstrated the volume of published work by Aboriginal writers and spoke of the historical, political, social and cultural evolution of Aboriginal society as demonstrated through the written word.

This anthology stands out from anything that has been published in the past, because it is the first ever anthology of Aboriginal literature from the beginning of our written word until the present time. The material published includes letters, political manifestos, song lyrics, poetry, play excerpts and fiction, but it is not just a book of literature. It tells the story of our nation from eighty-one different Aboriginal perspectives, rich with experience.

The selection process for the anthology was possibly the most challenging professional thing I've faced. Peter and I were looking for works that would demonstrate the way in which Aboriginal writing and storytelling has evolved over time and the way in which different genres of writing have been used by Aboriginal writers to often tell similar stories about the impacts of colonisation on our people. We also wanted to pay tribute to those who not only pioneered Aboriginal literature in this country, but have taken us to new levels in recent times, making us competitive in the international market. Orders for the *Anthology* by both colleges and school suppliers suggest the book has been set as recommended reading and is used in both universities and schools around the country, with an increase in educational use in 2011.

~

With all my books I receive feedback, written and in person, from mobs around the country who tell me that they have had the same experience of discrimination or racism, or that they were moved by a story or poem. I also have a lot of non-Indigenous people (the largest part of my audience because of population size), who tell me they have been challenged by what I have written and have learned from the experience of reading my work. This gives me more reason to write. I want people to be challenged, to think about their role in the world and how their behaviour impacts on other people, particularly Aboriginal people. I want readers to learn and appreciate and at times laugh and cringe at my stories. I want readers to hear an authentic voice when they read about us. By authentic voice, I mean an Aboriginal voice. And it doesn't matter where the author is located or what he or she looks like, rather that they *are* Aboriginal.

In recent years, I have written a number of novels with the intention of placing Aboriginal people on the overall Australian national identity radar, and I'm specifically committed to writing about those like me who live in urban settings. Between 2004 and 2011, I wrote two children's novels featuring the main characters of Yirra, a young girl, and Demon, her dog. They were a chance for me to do something for, and with, the local community near where I have spent most of my life: the coastal suburb of La Perouse. La Perouse has an important place in my personal history. I spent many,

many summers as a young person at the beach at La Pa. It is a beach I still prefer to swim at because there are no waves. I've sat under trees, in cars and on restaurant balconies there, eating fish 'n' chips. I first kissed a man I loved for years in that suburb, late one night in his red Ford Escort, after dancing at the Maroubra Seals, Kenny Rogers serenading us in the background. It is a moment I have never forgotten.

As a young person, I walked the wooden bridge to Bare Island. I watched the famed Snake Man charm his pets. As an adult I have taken my international guests to La Perouse to buy boomerangs and clap sticks from Uncle Laddie Timbery and Uncle Vic Simms. During the late 1980s and early 1990s I would take Sunday afternoon drives as a form of relaxation before a nap. I'd drive from Matraville along the east coast from Maroubra, to Coogee, Clovelly, Bronte, Tamarama, Bondi, over to Watsons Bay and back. Out to La Perouse and home. Not good in terms of the carbon footprint but it was a tradition of sorts. And I did it by myself mostly. In the ugly blue Commodore.

I wanted to show my appreciation and love of La Pa through writing. More importantly, I wanted to show the similarities that young local Koori kids have with other young Australians, and to de-marginalise them. I wanted also to show that these kids were strong in their own Aboriginal identities. The plan with these books was to consider the issue of sameness with the aim of my stories being shared in the school environment nationally. While it's important to make the point that we come from diverse nations within the one nation, there is much to be said for pointing out that we are also human and share the same human emotions, and that our children are like other children. Our kids, Aboriginal kids, also need to see themselves in Australian literature in picture books and novels, and I want them to be considered on the national identity radar, and to have their stories read by other Australian students.

With that in mind, I began work with the students from Years 3 to 6 at La Perouse Public School in Sydney in 2004 with the assistance of the New South Wales Premier's Indigenous Arts Fellowship that I won that year. The project plan was initially to write five picture books set in La Perouse and around New South Wales. But after a few introductory writing workshops, it was clear we were going to have far more content than the one slim picture book we aimed to begin with. Our first book became a short novel titled *Yirra and Her Deadly Dog, Demon*, published by ABC Books in 2007.

The students came up with the content: the characters, the settings, the voices, Yirra's lifestyle and personality. I wove it into a story that resembled something similar to their own lives but perhaps with a little more dog-related drama. The story is about ten-year-old Yirra – named after the Wiradjuri word meaning 'sun' – who lives on the mission, goes to La Perouse Public School, likes the beach, yoghurt, her iPod, Kasey Chambers, a boy at school called Matt and her Siberian husky, Demon. But Yirra's mum's sick of vacuuming up fur balls, the neighbours are fed up with having their undies nicked from the clothesline, and her stepdad just wants his slippers back. If Yirra doesn't find a dog trainer soon, she'll have to give her beloved Demon to a new family – one who likes dogs who run and dig a lot!

Working with the students and watching them get excited about creating characters and storylines and voting on character names filled me with joy. But nothing matched the thrill of watching all the students receive their own copy of the work at a community launch held at the school in May 2007 as part of the Sydney Writers' Festival. Her Excellency Professor Marie Bashir did the honour of launching the novel, heaping praise on the new Australian authors. The school hall was filled by the school community – parents, friends, locals – as well as media and staff from the New South Wales Ministry for the Arts. These kinds of moments bring communities together as a demonstration of what's possible for our young people when financial and moral support is strategically channelled. In the years following, another Australian author was working with students at Matraville Sports High School, where some of the students of La Pa had graduated in to. The author emailed me to say that when he had started there, my kids proudly announced, 'We've already written a book.' I firmly believe producing the work as a collaboration had a huge impact on the self-esteem of the students, especially since they can claim to be the first group of Australian students to have co-written a novel that is now held in local, school and university libraries nationally.

The sequel, *Demon Guards the School Yard*, was produced

with a different set of students at La Perouse and was released through Oxford University Press in March 2011. It allowed us as authors to talk about local native plants and history around the Bondi Beach area. Within the text, the characters also discuss identity based on skin colour. In one scene at the beach the following unfolds:

'So how many Kooris live in Bondi then? You don't see many round here,' John says innocently.

'What's that supposed to mean?' Judy attacks him.

'What?' John's a bit confused.

'You don't see many Kooris, but what're you looking for? Some Kooris aren't that dark you know,' Judy says. Mary puts her arm over Judy's shoulder. In the past, Judy's been given a hard time about being a fair-skinned Koori.

'I just meant that I know there's an Aboriginal mission at La Pa so there's lots of Kooris around all the time, but I didn't know if there's one here. Am I saying the wrong thing?' John's from England – and he's still learning about Australia.

'Did you know there are more Blackfellas living

in Sydney than in the whole of the Northern Territory and that one third of Aboriginal people live in big cities?' Judy is really worked up.

'How do you even know this stuff?' Matt, like everyone else, is surprised at what Judy knows.

'Cos that's what you do when you're a Blackfella in the city. You learn about where your mob have come from and why they are here and I want people to know that we didn't die out just cos there's cement and houses and other stuff in the city. My mob's from down south, but this is my home too,' Judy continues. Mary rubs her shoulders, trying to calm her down.

'I didn't mean to upset you Judy, really,' John says, embarrassed.

I believe Yirra's story gives young Australian readers a contemporary view of an urban Aboriginal world in coastal Sydney. The work also puts La Perouse on the map for something other than the fact the French landed there and Tom Cruise shot some scenes for *Mission: Impossible II* at Bare Island Fort.

～

Many people think the writerly life is all one glamorous junket. It's not. The writerly life, or mine specifically, is both rewarding and challenging but also hard work! I find joy in working with Koori kids to teach them the importance of books, writing and reading, and I love seeing them engage with the process when I'm in a classroom or even a tent, as I was in August 2010 when I worked with students at the Children's Literature in the Centre (CLIC) festival in Alice Springs.

The rewards are balanced out with the challenges, though, and the greatest one I face as an Aboriginal writer every day is knowing that I have the basic skill of reading while many other Aboriginal people are illiterate. I can read street signs, medicine bottles and warning labels. I can read books that take me to other parts of the country, to other cultures and even to other galaxies. I am incredibly lucky in the literacy skills I have, and this reality is another reason why I write books for and about young Aboriginal kids – to give them something they want to read.

I am an Indigenous Literacy Day Ambassador for the Indigenous Literacy Foundation (ILF), funded solely by donations, volunteers and in-kind support from the Australian book industry – publishers, booksellers, authors, and illustrators. The groundswell of support for ensuring that Indigenous kids have the same opportunities as other Australian kids inspires me, not only as an ambassador and an Australian author, but also as a Wiradjuri woman.

Above all, the development of English literacy skills is

important for the life opportunities of Indigenous children and youth. Being literate means they can participate in social activities, in the education system and the employment market. It means they have more chance of enjoying equity and improvements in health and lifestyle. But the reality remains that there exists an enormous gap in the English literacy rates of Indigenous and non-Indigenous people in Australia. That gap is even wider for Indigenous people living in remote and isolated communities.

According to the report 'Department of Education and Training, Western Australia (DET WA) Conductive Hearing Loss and Aboriginal Students, 2006', the gap between Indigenous and non-Indigenous students emerges early. Non-Indigenous students dramatically outperform Indigenous students in benchmark tests for reading, writing and numeracy in Year 3 and Year 5. By Year 7 the gap has widened, particularly for numeracy. What these statistics mean, in short, is that without some drastic improvement in the literacy rates of our young people, we will have another generation of Indigenous people reliant on non-Indigenous people to make decisions for them in key areas of their lives. There can be nothing more disempowering than having someone else decide how you live your life.

As an author, I am among many – my friends who are academics, booksellers, publishers, researchers, students – who depend on books every day for their own study and research, for their teaching and, of course, for their enjoyment. But I also know that there are others who still don't know how to read the books I rely on and enjoy every day. There are a shamefully high number of Indigenous people who cannot read. For example, the Council of Australian Governments (COAG) Reform Council stated in their 'National Indigenous Reform Agreement: Supplement on Literacy and Numeracy Achievement 2010' that in Year 9 only 40 per cent of Northern Territory Indigenous students could read or write at the national standard. This figure was both below the levels of Indigenous literacy in 2008 and significantly below the results of non-Indigenous students, with 85 per cent of non-Indigenous students tested performing at the national standard. Such huge gaps in literacy rates mean that only 22.7 per cent of Indigenous persons in remote communities are likely to gain a non-school qualification compared to 48.6 percent of non-Indigenous persons in remote areas.*

It is because of these appalling statistics and realities that face some of our Indigenous communities that Indigenous Literacy Day was first established by Suzy Wilson of Riverbend Books in 2004. She realised that Indigenous illiteracy is a national crisis. I have no doubt whatsoever that if the same statistics were attached to non-Indigenous Australian children then it would be front-page news and ministers' jobs would be on the line until real change had been made.

Through my various roles as a freelance writer and workshop facilitator, I work with a huge spectrum of Indigenous kids in classrooms: some are speaking English as a second

---

* Australian Bureau of Statistics (2006), 'Indigenous Statistics for Students: Education', Commonwealth of Australia, Canberra.

or third language in remote communities, others are in the gifted and talented programs in urban New South Wales. The differences between these groups in the classroom are extraordinary. The 'G&T' kids know how to dream: they have plans for their futures, they have read about Australia and the world in books, they engage with their friends in chat rooms and on Facebook because they can, because they know how to spell and read. Their self-esteem is heart-warming. At the other end is the heartbreak of knowing many children have not necessarily had the joy of reading books or websites, and aren't able to realise what's possible for them as grown-ups, as teenagers even.

One disturbing moment I have experienced while working in a school environment as part of my writing journey was related to a schoolteacher. I was visiting a remote school with a group of other people from different fields for specific week-long activities. The students were very excited and a little rest-less at the prospect of some fun activities after lunch. When they took longer than they should have to settle down, the teacher in charge threatened, 'Those who don't behave will have to go back into the classroom and write.' Writing was therefore their punishment – something that was not seen to be fun like sport when in fact literacy while a core to life's journey, can also be entertaining. I was mortified, not only as an author, but as someone who has worked for many years to encourage young Aboriginal kids to read and indeed write their own stories, and the ability to read is at the core of the efforts of the ILF.

I think my first official event for Indigenous Literacy Day was in 2007. I was part of a schools day at Abbotsleigh School for Girls in Sydney's northern suburbs, along with another author, Tara June Winch, my footballer cousin Joe Williams and actor Deborah Mailman. We all addressed the school about our favourite books and what we loved about reading.

I am thrilled to be a part of the ILF, but even before I was an official ambassador for the project I had always been an advocate for Aboriginal writers and writing through my role as the chair, deputy chair and management committee member of the Australian Society of Authors (1998–2008), and as national coordinator of the *AustLit* research community of Aboriginal and Torres Strait Islander writers and storytellers known as Black Words (2007–10). In all of those roles my aim was to showcase literature and to encourage more readers generally, but specifically to inspire more Aboriginal people – of all ages – to pick up books and read. And my advocacy on behalf of Indigenous writers is one of the reasons I was presented with the ASA Medal in 2003.

My nieces and nephews often receive books from me as gifts, instead of eggs for Easter and other consumables. I sometimes ask them what they are reading. Not all are into books like their authorly aunty, but all I'm sure are impressed that their aunty writes books. Ben, who is thirteen years old, reads for entertainment and Liesl, aged ten, is a voracious reader. She read eleven books in a few short months as part of the 2011 MS Readathon and will read in the back of the car when being dropped home from school. She also writes short stories, and is very funny, I might add. My brother Mark and I took Liesl out for pizza for her ninth birthday. I asked her what she wanted to do when she left school. 'Be an author!' she said, quite seriously. Needless to say, I support her career choice, but also suggested she takes up a second job for an adequate stream of income.

I am delighted that my niece loves books so much, but it makes me angry and sad that in the twenty-first century we still have illiterate Australian children. I'm part of the Indigenous Literacy Foundation because it's about making change for my community. Everything I am and everything I do is entrenched in my identity, which influences my writing and my desire to get Aboriginal kids to read and be proud of who they are.

Chapter 10

ON BEING KOORI BRADSHAW

'THE SUB-GENRE OF AUSTRALIAN INDIGENOUS
CHICK-LIT WAS VIRTUALLY INVENTED BY
HEISS AND, IN PROVIDING A MORE NUANCED,
ACCESSIBLE VISION OF ABORIGINAL IDENTITY,
SHE HAS ADDRESSED A GLARING ABSENCE FROM
THE LITERARY LANDSCAPE . . . IT PROBABLY
WON'T PLEASE FANS OF HER ACCLAIMED
HISTORICAL FICTION, POETRY OR SOCIAL
COMMENTARY – BUT THAT WAS NEVER THE
POINT. IT . . . BRINGS A FRESH PERSPECTIVE TO
AN OFTEN HOMOGENOUS GENRE.'

ANNE FULLERTON, THE HERALD SUN

n media related to the 2008 release of *Avoiding Mr Right*, my second adult novel, I was likened to Carrie Bradshaw from *Sex and the City* fame. Indeed, I coined and was happy to be considered as 'Koori Bradshaw', since at the time I wanted to have an apartment in Manhattan, a fabulous fashion wardrobe and a newspaper column. I still do. Let's face it: there are no Aboriginal columnists in mainstream print media in Australia, so maybe I'd have better luck in the Big Apple.

I never watched *Sex and the City* because I was without Channel 9 for eight years – you learn to adjust – but I watched the first movie in the franchise at least a dozen times, mostly on long-haul flights and in motel rooms when on the road for work. I loved it for its demonstration of friendship, for its ability to remind me of the pain of lost love and the joy of regained love. It made me want to go on a retreat with my besties to an island paradise, although I didn't want Carrie's humiliating reason for doing so. But even with my appreciation of the film, it's fair to say that I didn't necessarily connect with any of the characters, except Carrie – and only because she was a writer. While finding my own Mr Big is on the radar, it wasn't what interested me about Carrie's story. I do, however, know Aboriginal women who watched the series in its prime. Some had a favourite character, some dreamt about a trip to New York, others liked watching the fashions. (I finally watched the first two seasons in December 2011 while in NYC and realised I had very little in common with the women in that show – all they did was talk about men and sex – and to be honest the women in my life make far better conversation than the men!) I was probably the last one to start watching *Friends* as well, another New-York-City-based dramedy about the personal relationships of a core group of upper-class white friends.

In 2001 I was in a community school in the Pilbara, in north-western Western Australia, and saw a copy of *Harry Potter* sitting on the desk of a demountable classroom where I was running a writers' workshop. I was immediately happy – if not a tad surprised – and smiled because I didn't and don't care what our people are reading as long as they are reading. I realised then that if our people read commercial fiction then why shouldn't we write it? With that in mind, my commercial novels are, among other things, about us having a place in the commercial market. I think at this point I am still the only Aboriginal author of commercial fiction in Australia. We have several successful literary novelists like Alexis Wright, Melissa Lucashenko, Bruce Pascoe, Kim Scott and Tara June Winch, whereas as far as I know, Nicole Watson with *The Boundary* and Philip McLaren, with his crime novels *Scream Black Murder* and *Lightning Mine*, are the only genre fiction writers. With a commercial novel in mind, I was driven to write a book that other Australian women like me would read in the bath, on the beach or the train or bus and so forth. I read for escapism in these places, saving my more 'serious' non-fiction works, and particularly my precious hardcovers, for home and bed.

After being knocked back by three major publishing houses

for my draft of *Not Meeting Mr Right*, my agent, Tara Wynne, and I were thrilled when it was finally picked up by Random House Australia. My dream of being published (at least once) by a multinational was about to come true. My publisher, Larissa Edwards, knew my previous writings through her past work as a bookseller, and she believed the market would be open to the voice of my character Alice Aigner. It's fair to say that at the time I was a risk, given I was an unknown quantity in the commercial market. But the deal paid off and, within weeks of its release, the book was in reprints and we were offered an option by Essential Viewing for a potential TV series. I had, with one title, apparently managed to create a new genre known as 'Koori chick-lit', and had created a whole new audience of readers nationally.

I am aware that there are some who question the ability of commercial literature to tap into the national conscience, and there are those who question my portrayal of some women in my books. Obviously I want to increase my audience by writing a range of different stories with difference themes and concepts, but not just for the sake of book sales – although clearly the more books sold, the more people reached. My strategy in choosing to write commercial women's fiction is to reach audiences that weren't previously engaging with Aboriginal Australia in any format, either personally, professionally or subconsciously. And it is that non-Indigenous female market that is my key audience: let's face it, there are not enough Blackfellas to sustain *any* publishing venture, least of all an entire genre. With this in mind, I made a conscious decision to move into the area of commercial women's fiction, releasing four books in the genre of 'chick-lit' or, as my friends at Koori Radio 93.7FM categorised it, 'choc-lit'.

I have made no secret of my intentions in penning *Not Meeting Mr Right*, *Avoiding Mr Right*, *Manhattan Dreaming* and *Paris Dreaming*. I have heard whispers that I am 'dumbing down' my writing and betraying readers of my serious work, but those who criticise the genre miss the point of the efforts I've made as a Black writer in Australia to broker new publishing ground and enter the incredibly difficult space as a minority in mainstream publishing. I'd hazard a guess that there are more Aboriginal women now reading my novels than reading any Indigenous-authored academic books, unless the women are working in academia themselves.

I am defined as a 'choc-lit' author because I use the genre to write about the women I know, the women in my world, women who inspire me, motivate me and are role models to me. My characters reflect their strength, resilience and intelligence. These women are urban, educated, articulate, career-minded women, some with or wanting kids, some not. These are Aboriginal women who did not appear in contemporary Australian women's fiction until I put them there.

I wanted to write these Aboriginal women into Australian literature because they did not exist in *any* genre. I wanted to reach an audience of non-Aboriginal Australian women – largely aged between eighteen and forty-five years of age – who may not have ever heard of Anita Heiss or cared about Aboriginal women in Australia before. They may never have shared a coffee or dined with or worked alongside an Aboriginal woman. I wanted these readers to have an insight into just *some* of the realities of just *some* of the Aboriginal women like me. I knew that the way to reach them was to look at the things we had in common in life – such as the issues around personal relationships – and then to ease them into my world as an urban Koori woman and all that entails.

When I write my novels, I want to use my storylines to challenge the notions of what it means to be Aboriginal in the twenty-first century, with a focus on urban experiences because they are what I know best, having lived in Sydney, Canberra and on the Gold Coast. I like my stories to be saturated with capable, savvy and sexy Aboriginal women but of course, like other human beings my characters are flawed, often in terms of their personal relationships. Therein lies the universal connection between character and reader: this is what ensures pages are turned, empathy is encouraged and understanding of the shared human experience is acknowledged.

I feel that within mainstream media generally there's too much emphasis placed on the differences between human beings, and the fear of difference is what leads to intolerance. Difference, while important in many ways, is too often used as a tool to alienate and often denigrate individuals or even whole communities. I wanted to be positive with my writing. I wanted to demonstrate through the *Mr Right* and *Dreaming* novels that Aboriginal women, like most women, prize their friendships and desire companionship. We fall in love, we fall out of love, we make love, we have dates from hell, we are disappointed when romance fails, we fear rejection and some of us dream about Mr Right (or Ms Right depending on persuasion). Like our non-Aboriginal counterparts, many of us also live by the beach and drink cocktails, we go to the gym and do Zumba. We work in private and public schools and talk politics over coffee and green tea. We get waxed, and have periods – all because we are women! There is much that we share with women of many different backgrounds, but we are *all* Black, regardless of the path we follow or how we follow it.

It's important to note here that I have never tried to define any one kind of Aboriginal woman in my books, although I try to ensure that my characters have good values and are capable and strong human beings, even though they make mistakes and poor choices at various times in their lives. I admit, though, that all my female protagonists are very politicised, because most of the Aboriginal women I know are on boards and committees of community organisations. It's important to note as well that all my protagonists evolve throughout their stories. I know that a lot of Aboriginal women in their twenties read my books, and I am conscious of creating characters that they can also see themselves in – in both the good and bad.

The point I'm making in my novels is about identity: we are modern women and enjoying being a woman does not make us any more or less Black or white than the next person. While my characters are conscious of their Blackness, they are never debilitated by it, because I'm not debilitated by my own identity. For me, I've never wished to be anyone other than who I am, although I've often thought about what I'd do with my life if I'd been born to different parents. What would I do if I were born white? What purpose would I find in my day? Would I choose to be part of the reconciliation movement, part of social change instead of being expected to be part of it?

With this in mind, one complex topic in relation to identity that I tackle is interracial relationships. My characters, like me, don't want every first date to turn into a cultural awareness training workshop, and they don't want to be the 'exotic other' girlfriend. My characters date people from various cultural and social backgrounds. Being the product of an interracial relationship myself, I am sensitive to and interested in writing about such dynamics in my books. There will always be differences between, say, an Aboriginal woman and a non-Aboriginal man, but I believe in love, the love I witnessed between my parents.

To show you how I put all these ideas into practice, I'll describe the first adult Aboriginal protagonist I wrote about, Alice Aigner in *Not Meeting Mr Right*, who has an Aboriginal mother and Austrian father. Alice works in a history department at a private girls school in Sydney's eastern suburbs, and her discussions at the local history association allow her to unpack the terminology around invasion versus colonisation. In scenes of her in the classroom, I wove in dialogue about Aboriginal women and voting. Then, like lots of Kooris in Sydney, Alice heads to the Yabun Festival to celebrate Invasion

Day on 26 January, and does Koori-oke down at the Covent Garden with the Block Release students from the University of Technology. I think you can see the parallels with my life there!

We meet Alice's tidda Peta Tully in *Not Meeting Mr Right*. Peta lives at Coogee as well, but is Bundjalung, from Coolangatta. She works in developing policy and curriculum related to Aboriginal education. With Peta, who also appears in *Avoiding Mr Right*, I pushed the boundaries further in terms of women's fiction. Peta tackles not only interracial relationships, but the relationship between the Aboriginal community and the police force, giving commentary on Black deaths in custody. She marches against the Northern Territory Intervention, has conversations about methodologies of 'studying' Indigenous people in communities and Indigenous intellectual property, and attends numerous NAIDOC events around the state of Victoria. I've always felt that being an urban Black means being part of public life. Standing up and being counted. Showing solidarity. As I've aged and experienced different forms of political activism, I've saved my feet somewhat and used my hands to write more. My own identity and my expression of identity is therefore translated onto the page as the story unfolds.

I created a new set of characters for *Manhattan Dreaming*. Lauren Lucas, a Wiradjuri curator of visual art who goes from the fictional National Aboriginal Gallery (located in Old Parliament House in Canberra) to the National Museum of the American Indian (NMAI) at the Smithsonian in New

York, ditching her footballer boyfriend along the way. I did quite a bit of research for this book in our nation's capital. I stood in the ex-Country Party rooms of Old Parliament House and looked down onto the Tent Embassy, imagining moving the mob there into the space that in the novel is home to the National Aboriginal Gallery. I had worked as communications advisor for the Aboriginal and Torres Strait Islander Arts Board of the Australia Council from 2001–03, under the direction of Cathy Craigie, and through that role gained a foundation and further interest in visual arts and artists. Back in the 1990s I was a regular Boomalli Aboriginal Artists Cooperative visitor, launching my first book – *Sacred Cows* – at their then Abercrombie Street site in 1996. In 2001 Aden Ridgeway launched *Who Am I? The Diary of Mary Talence, Sydney 1937* at their site on Parramatta Road, Annandale, and in 2002 I was thrilled to launch Kerry Reed-Gilbert's collection of poetry, *Talkin' about Country*, at the current Leichhardt site.

I wanted the New York material in *Manhattan Dreaming* to be authentic, and although having been there many times before, I was prepared to suffer further for my craft and made the journey over there again. As you can imagine, research in New York was tedious at times – shopping on Fifth, Sixth and Seventh avenues and Macy's, around the streets of SoHo, Broadway and the designer department store Century 21. Naturally, I also researched more serious material. I was in Harlem – predominantly and historically an African-American hub and a centre for the civil rights movement – the day Obama was inaugurated, because I wanted to be there and knew my character Lauren Lucas would've too. That day inspired me as a Black woman from the suburbs of Sydney and they inspired my character.

At the time I was researching, in January 2009, there was an exhibition on at the NMAI called 'Fritz Scholder: Indian/ Not Indian', which tackled some identity issues in Native art. It reminded me of the role of Aboriginal artists here and the debate around what is and isn't defined as 'Aboriginal art'. More importantly, it reminded me of who does the defining in terms of Aboriginality today. I included Scholder's work briefly in the novel, because I knew these kinds of discussions weren't part of the regular conversations that the women buying my books would have, but it was a key issue for my character and one that my readers should be aware of. It's important to understand that when writing in the genre of commercial women's fiction, there's only so much politics you can include before it turns into a different kind of book for a different kind of audience.

I know I am right in sticking to my genre when I have long-time residents of New York admit they knew nothing about the NMAI until they read *Manhattan Dreaming*. I am reaching a new audience who knows little about Indigenous cultures, and therein lies another feeling of obligation – to incorporate as many diverse Indigenous cultures into my work – an obligation I feel not only as a writer but as an Aboriginal person who is a member of an international First Nations community. I therefore took the opportunity to weave into the novel a discussion on 'Welcome to Country' protocols. While we sometimes follow them here in Australia, they weren't apparent at all when I attended public events in New York. And these public events were 'Australian-organised', like the opening of a Torres Strait Islander exhibition I attended as part of Australia Week. *No-one* acknowledged the Haudenosaunee nations – the original landowners located in what is now New York State, with boundaries to the east by Lake Champlain, Lake George and the Hudson River. Although the practice is not common in the USA, it is a protocol that we follow at home, and one we know to do when on the land of other Indigenous people, so I was embarrassed as an Aboriginal woman and as a visitor in that city to see the protocols weren't being followed.

Because I want to use my novels to showcase as many diverse Aboriginal creators as possible, I'm not embarrassed to say that I have unashamedly plugged some of my favourites in *Manhattan Dreaming*. Included are visual artists Jenny Fraser, r e a, Karen Mills, Judy Watson and Gordon Hookey. I try to contact any artist I include in my books for the approval of the text and, if I can't get in touch, I only use material that is already in the public domain, such as their biographical information and commentary on their artwork. I send drafts of text where I can to ensure artists (or their representatives) are happy with how I have portrayed them but, from my perspective, in all cases the inclusion is about recognition and praise, and the artists generally understand this too.

In *Paris Dreaming*, the sequel to *Manhattan Dreaming*, artist Merrill Bray called me from Adelaide the minute she received my email requesting permission to write on her to tell me how pleased she was. She then emailed me to say, 'Good luck with your *Paris Dreaming* novel, and I am chuffed and grateful that you mentioned my work.' I wrote to artist Nyapanyapa Yunupingu via the Buku-Larrngay Mulka Centre in Yirrkala, and received an email back from Will Stubbs, coordinator of the centre. He wrote: 'Thanks Anita . . . It seems like a wholly positive reference. As a veteran of the Musée du Quai Branly opening with Nyapanyapa's sister Gulumbu, I can't wait to read the book.'

It's not only visual arts that I showcase: Lauren Lucas also curates a film festival while at the NMAI, and that side to her professional life gave me the opportunity to promote the work of Wayne Blair, Pauline Clague, Romaine Moreton and Warwick Thornton. I also showcase the diversity in our musical genres, writing about Sharnee Fenwick (country), Charlie Trindall (country/folk/rock), Emma Donovan (gospel/soul/reggae), Munkimuk (known as the grandfather of Aboriginal hip-hop) and the beautiful Shauntaii (gospel/R&B/jazz/classical), among others.

I've received many emails from women who read my novels. They come from everywhere: from Melbourne to Maningrida, Perth to Parramatta. Some are non-Indigenous, but increasingly more and more Aboriginal women are contacting me as well. Some of these women are in their sixties, some are in their twenties. This validates my hope that the stories I am writing are universal and serve as the hook to get women to read and engage more fully with more Indigenous literature after finishing my book. I feel that, for many, these small steps I help them take to learn about a range of Aboriginal experiences are big steps in terms of understanding Aboriginal identity in the twenty-first century.

I am also validated by the assessment of my work made by reviewers. In the March 2010 *Bookseller and Publisher*, one reviewer writes, 'Like the author, Lauren is a member of the Wiradjuri nation. Her deep connection to her people and culture is a vital part of the story – and what sets *Manhattan Dreaming* apart from other chick-lit.' Interestingly, the reviewer was a bloke – Lachlan Jobbins – and so I feel even happier that my intended audience of women is being extended to the other gender. I've certainly noticed an increasing number of men not only attending events related to my books, but buying and reading them. One-fifth of my audience at Concord Library in March 2011 was men over fifty years of age. At the Noosa Longweekend Festival in 2011, there were also a handful of men all over the age of fifty who had read *Paris Dreaming*. One asked during question time, 'I'm interested to know why a male didn't appear in the novel until page ninety-eight?' Why indeed? I was forced to ask myself.

I've also been incredibly validated by the Deadly Awards I've won for Outstanding Achievement in Literature. The Deadlys were established in 1995 and recognise and show-case Aboriginal and Torres Strait Islander achievement in the arts, sport, health and education. The community endorsement the awards represent is a huge boost to the self-esteem of any artist. I've been fortunate enough to win four Deadlys: for *Not Meeting Mr Right*, *Manhattan Dreaming* and, with Peter Minter, *The Macquarie PEN Anthology of Aboriginal Literature* and in 2011, for *Paris Dreaming*.

Of course, the reading experience is subjective; some won't like my books at all, and that's fine, they're not for them. What's important is that I know I am making a difference to the literary landscape. In an article written by Margaret Merrilees in *dotlit*, the University of Queensland's creative writing journal, the author asks, 'Can an Aboriginal literary character ever just go shopping, do the dishes, laugh, vote: be "ordinary" rather than "different"?' The reason Merrilees asks this question is because often white writers only include us as something that appears alien to their normal everyday lives, since most of them don't have us as part of their everyday lives. And these are the people who *shouldn't* write about us at all – when they imagine us to be some kind of unknown species, without feelings or ordinary human experiences, they deny the common bonds that we all share, and this can only be damaging. Merrilees's question highlights *exactly* why I write the books I do.

THE TRIAL: IN THE COURT

On Sunday, 27 March 2011, I flew to Melbourne to meet the legal team. Three of those bringing the case gathered in Ron Merkel's chambers, and it was the first time I'd seen co-plaintiff Pat Eatock and her daughter Cathy since the 1990s, when they were both working in Aboriginal media. I met Bindi Cole for the first time. Together we listened to barristers Ron Merkel QC, Herman Borenstein SC and Phoebe Knowles on how they would present our case and what they imagined the defence might ask each of us.

I felt calm when I left, and I slept easy that night. I had lots of messages of support by the time I walked towards the federal court the next morning. At 9 am I was sitting at the offices of Holding Redlich in William Street, waiting to be ushered to court. Right up until we left the building I was hoping Andrew Bolt's lawyers would convince him that it was best to just make the apology and move forward, and the whole case could be settled. That never happened.

Court was already in session when we walked in, and I sat

in one of the first seats I could find. Our QC Ron Merkel was already opening the day. In front of me was Kirstie Parker, the only Indigenous media representative there, and a number of other reporters from the mainstream media. A few rows ahead of me was journalist and friend Martin Flanagan and Koori academic friend Michelle Evans, and across the room I saw non-Aboriginal Twitter friends Michelle Nicol and Toula Karayannis. Michelle was wearing red, black and yellow in support, and threw me a smile as if to say, 'She'll be right.'

I was ready to have my say, speak my truth, challenge the lies that had been written about me, but I very quickly learned that I was not going to be called by the defence, despite what I had previously been told. I was disappointed, annoyed, confused. But I realised that to put me on the stand would have been dangerous for the defence team; perhaps I was darker than they had thought I was, which would have thrown off their argument. And then there was the error in the witness statement about the photo of my mother and her alleged mixed heritage.

As I sat in court, I thought about my ancestors. I thought about Windradyne, the Wiradjuri warrior who had led the Battle of Bathurst and lived his life fighting to protect his people and land. I thought about my grandmother Amy Williams, who had been removed under the Act of Protection, one of the Stolen Generations. I thought about all those who had attended the 1938 Day of Mourning Protest and Conference calling for equal rights for Aboriginal people. And I thought about myself sitting in a courtroom, now fighting for my right to self-identification without persecution by the press.

I gained strength from those thoughts of my old people, and they also reminded me of my responsibility in this struggle. At the very least I needed to honour those who had gone before me and step up and fight. It was my job to fight this latest form of cultural genocide now being implemented by someone who had more power than me.

I also remembered Barangaroo, second wife of the well-known Wangal conciliator Bennelong, whom Bennelong Point in Sydney was named after. Barangaroo is known to have been an incredibly strong, capable woman with a powerful presence among the Cammeraygal around Sydney. Barangaroo was against any form of negotiation and, although encouraged to eat and dress like a European as her husband so easily did, she refused to assimilate. She chastised her husband publicly and also made known her absolute disgust at a public flogging of a convict. When the city of Sydney announced a precinct around the Sydney foreshore was going to be named after her in 2006, I was in Canberra as a writer in residence at the ANU. My phone rang early in the morning, and on the line was the now late Aunty Beryl Beller Timbery from La Perouse. She had just read the news and had called to say that when she thought about Barangaroo, she thought of women like herself and me. It was one of the highest compliments I had ever been paid. I thought of Aunty Beryl that day in the courtroom, and how she would've urged me to fight.

I was in awe of our barrister Ron Merkel in action. In opening our case under Section 18C of the *Racial Discrimination Act*, Ron said:

> *And what this* Racial Discrimination Act *has done is, in 18C, it has defined . . . 'Conduct likely to offend'.*
>
> *And the conduct likely to offend is on the grounds and by reason of the race, colour, ethnic origin or nationality of a persons or a group of persons is in contravention of 18C. That was as has been discussed in a number of the cases . . . And it's often thought . . . by those that take a narrow view of this, and say this is somehow an impediment of freedom of speech, that this is all about racial vilification and racial hatred as such . . . The Holocaust in the 1940s started with words and finished with violence. This Act tries to stop those words, stop the shouting of 'fire' in this arena, in a crowded theatre.*

I got goosebumps when Ron said those words, which were as positively powerful as Bolt's had been negatively powerful. I knew at that moment that we would win. This case was fighting for the society in which we should all want to live; a society that allows racial hatred, discrimination and vilification was not one I wanted to be in. During our lunchbreak, I sat with a group of women – some Black, some white – all there to support those of us in the case. Belinda Duarte and Michelle Evans, both Aboriginal women living in Melbourne, understood the importance the case held for our mobs. The mood was positive: Ron had set the tone for the trial, and we believed we were on the right track. After lunch, I re-entered the courtroom and sat in the front row, only metres from the man who, to date, appeared to have no remorse for what he had written.

Following a debrief session that day, I flew home to Sydney. I wasn't able to sit through the entire trial although I wanted to be there. It was only a few days before *Paris Dreaming* was due for release, and I was about to embark on a book tour. I received the daily transcripts of the hearing, as well as calls from those who were attending. And of course, the press reports were endless.

Chapter 11

SLEEPING UNDER THE STARS

Everyone knows I hate camping. My idea of *Survivor* is a night in a caravan: the last one I slept in was when I was seventeen and up on the Central Coast, just ninety minutes north of Sydney. I am still haunted by having to cross the holiday park barefoot to use the loo in the middle of the night. This is not how a 'Koori Princess' – as I was once defined by a whitefella I was dating – wishes to spend her weekends away. I was with my more adventurous boyfriend at the time, but even then I took flannelette sheets and an esky full of chocolates and other treats to comfort me.

When I was young, no-one in our circle had major trips overseas to places like Disneyland or resorts in the Pacific, not like today. Back then families went camping and fishing and visited other family. I was born before my time; I should've been born now, when air travel and international holidays are normal for many children, because I was *never* one for sleeping rough. However, as kids, we did pitch tents in the backyard occasionally, and would stay there as long as we could before the dew set in and we got scared.

When I was seventeen I also went camping (I swore it was for the last time) on the Hawkesbury with my immediate Heiss family and extended Austrian family. I say Austrian family, but we're not blood-related. They are the closest thing to family my father had in Australia, so we say we're cousins. I was so bad at being 'at one with nature' during my time on the Hawkesbury that after one night of sleeping in Dad's kombi, and another sleeping in my boyfriend's VW station wagon, my parents sent me back to my blissfully comfortable home in Matraville. I think they were completely over my whining, but it wasn't my fault that anything that was capable of biting or stinging found its way onto and into my very sensitive, brown skin.

Mum tells me that Uncle Willi Knorr could be heard to ask after me by inquiring, 'Where's the Whinger?' because of my efforts that weekend. I hate to say this because I love my family, but I have no real fond memories of that time other than seeing the men with their kombies and their folding chairs all strategically positioned for the best yarn and rest. I just wanted to get home – it was the same weekend Westfield Eastgardens was opening, and it was the biggest thing to happen locally since the drive-in closed, so Matraville was going to become prime real estate very soon.

I went back to the Hawkesbury when I was eighteen or nineteen with the same boyfriend. He hired us a houseboat and it may as well have been a tent in terms of luxury, but at least I didn't have to sleep in a sleeping-bag. The door to the boat didn't lock and I was frightened of pirates – not that well known on the Hawkesbury but, since the mozzies would always find me, I was convinced the pirates would as well. Yes, I have always been paranoid and big on creating stories in my mind; perhaps I should write *Pirates of the Hawkesbury* and have Johnny Depp play the lead in the film adaptation.

Refusing to even attempt sleeping in a tent, car or houseboat ever again, I stayed in a cabin down at Ulladulla in my twenties with my tidda, Murri musician Toni Janke. We were on a girls weekend down the coast, arriving late on a Friday night with rest and relaxation on our minds. Toni had not long before released her debut EP *Hearts Speak Out*, with the powerful and enduring anthem 'Black Woman'. I remember our time away fondly: we talked non-stop, laughed and pretended we were private investigators ready to expose cheating husbands at a bowling club nearby. At dusk we sat eating oysters and prawns by the water before roughing it by 'camping' in the cabin, with no stars to be seen past the brown panelled walls and curtained windows.

This story reminds me of another trip to Ulladulla with Toni's sister Terri and a group of friends from Sydney. We drove in a convoy on a Friday night, stopping for pizza on the Princes Highway. I was in my ugly blue, six-cylinder Commodore. It was heavy enough to always feel safe, but something was always wrong with it. When we reached our final destination I turned the engine off and heard a whole lot of racket in what should have been the still of the night.

I said to my travelling companion, 'Fuck, there's something wrong with my car.' She responded with a laugh of disbelief. 'They're just crickets, you idiot!' So out of touch with nature was I that I had confused the sounds of nature with the sounds of engines.

More proof of my being out of touch was my first visit to Bermagui for the Shorelines Literary Festival in 1998, where I stayed at a bed and breakfast courtesy of some very generous locals. I couldn't sleep for the noise coming from 'nature'. Earplugs, alcohol, pillows over my head – I tried everything. I even suggested leaving baits out for the possums crawling all over the roof and veranda of a night. I must confess here that I called them 'squirrels' at the time, but as you'd be aware, we don't have squirrels, I mean possums, in Matraville either.

In 1993 I attended an Indigenous sport and recreation conference on Melville Island off the tip of Australia, home of the Tiwi Islanders. I was there as part of my role at Streetwize Comics, hoping to drum up support for a health comic for young Aboriginal and Torres Strait Islander people. Completely focused on my project idea, I gave little prior thought to the actual geography and logistics of getting to the conference occurring in the island community of Pularumpi.

I was daunted before even leaving the mainland when, as well as my bag, I personally had to be weighed at the airport prior to boarding the light plane from Darwin to the island. Having been obsessed with my weight since primary school, the obligation to get on the scales in front of strangers who weren't at a weight-loss meeting was mortifying. Not that anybody there cared how much I weighed – they would have been more shocked by the fact I embarked for my flight wearing a fitted navy-and-orange linen frock and court shoes. Thank God I'd packed my clothes in a sports bag and not a suitcase (given that we were staying in tents), because I'm sure even the most generous-spirited delegates there would have found it hard not to comment. As I've always joked to people, I'm a conference 'delicate' rather than a delegate.

The flight over to Melville Island was thrilling, if not too thrilling, since the pilot advised that light planes such as ours did not appear on airport radars. I'm not sure if he was kidding or not, but I wondered how we'd ever be seen by another plane as we flew through the clouds. Being back on the ground near Matto seemed very attractive at that stage. Weigh-in and flight successfully completed, the next step for this already-challenged Sydney-based writer was setting up 'camp' in the army tents erected for us in the local football field. I remain grateful to this day for the staff in camouflage gear who also set up the camping cot beds for us, knowing there was no way I could've managed it myself. I'm a thousand-threadcount-sheets-four-feather-pillows-and-doona kind of girl.

To my surprise, I soon learned that some conference attendees were staying in air-conditioned demountables with amenities that those of us in tents were without. *How did I not know I could have booked this instead?* I would've paid the extra costs with no second thoughts. But no, I was accommodated in a dorm-like tent with about eight other women, sharing the newly built toilet block with few showers and no mirror. As it was, I was glad there were no mirrors because roughing it meant no blowdryers, no makeup and certainly no irons. Court shoes and linen frocks were back in the bag, and shorts, T-shirts and hiking boots were donned for the rest of the week.

While not overly comfortable in my tent, it wasn't long before whispers across the conference site changed my mind about wanting the alternative. The young women from Victoria who had booked and moved into the demountables were being quietly criticised for not being able to 'rough it', for separating themselves from the rest of the mob. How grateful I felt for the accident that I was in a tent. And how sorry I felt for them being criticised for wanting to be comfortable and have privacy. To me it seemed their 'Blackness' was being questioned because of their choice of sleeping arrangements, choosing the assumed 'whitefella way' of sleeping indoors over the 'Blackfella way' of camping outdoors. I may be wrong, but it was what I felt and thought at the time.

The after-hours activities at the conference included going to a local swimming hole. I'll never forget the looks I got from other Blackfellas as we piled into the back of a people mover and I asked if anyone wanted 30+ sunscreen. The glares they gave me made me feel as though I were offering a vegetarian a rare steak to eat. *Why would a Blackfella want sunscreen?* Someone laughed; others shook their heads. I put the tube back in my bag. I didn't say it then, but the truth is that I am terrified of developing melanomas given the amount of time I spend in the sun, usually at the beach.

There's this myth that because Aborigines have dark skin we are immune to sun cancer but, according to research published on Australian Indigenous Health *Info*Net run by the Kurongkurl Katitjin Centre for Indigenous Australian Education and Research at Edith Cowan University, there are alarming statistics related to Indigenous Australians and skin cancer. For example, In 2005–06, three of the five most common malignant cancers for which Indigenous males were hospitalised were lung cancer (140 hospitalisations), skin cancer (106 hospitalisations), prostate cancer (fifty-nine hospitalisations).' So while some make fun of me as a Blackfella wearing 30+, I know I'm a healthy Blackfella wearing sun protection. My character Libby Cutmore in *Paris Dreaming* says at one point that she almost wishes a Koori got sun cancer, just to prove the point that Blackfellas aren't immune to sun exposure.

The camping dilemma arose again in the summer of 1994 when Kerry Reed-Gilbert and I were invited to the Woodford Folk Festival (previously known as the Maleny Festival) to perform as writers on the Murri stage. If you've been to Woodford, you know it's one big campsite, which translates into my idea of hell on earth! The thought of showering with hundreds of hippies – Black, white or brindle – didn't inspire me at all, no matter if I was showering with people I knew or strangers (even though I have been to a Korean bathhouse in Sydney). Don't get me wrong, I love performing to audiences, just not naked. I don't even own a pair of thongs, which I'm told I'd need to wear when showering in public places so you're not standing in someone else's bodily fluids. Enough said.

I'd agreed to go to Woodford and do the camping gig because I was doing it with Kerry. We'd become instantly tight when meeting through Streetwize Comics, where she was on the external Aboriginal Support Committee for the organisation, along with Denis Maher from the New South Wales Aboriginal Land Council and Marjorie Anderson from ABC television. Back then, Kerry, Marj and I were good friends, playing pool regularly at the Britannia Hotel on Cleveland Street, Chippendale, and having 'meetings' there with other Blackfellas after work. There was nothing we sisters in arms couldn't do together. And we *always* had fun; laughter was found even on the days when we were banging our heads against the wall regarding various political issues.

Kerry was writing poetry at the time and, being the daughter of the late, great Kevin Gilbert, had expectations placed on her by both the Black and white communities. However, the festival was not about expectations: it was going to be inspiring and food for the soul – a place for creativity to be born and grown. Despite these positives, in the back of my mind was a repetitive mantra unlike the affirming mantras my character Alice Aigner appreciated in *Not Meeting Mr Right*. The Anita Heiss mantra just kept nagging, *I really don't want to camp, I really don't want to camp. I really, really hate to camp!*

As our plane descended into Brisbane, I wondered how I would broach the issue of staying in a hotel in the city rather than camping at Woodford. I needn't have worried at all.

Kerry suffers from chest infections, and not sleeping in a bed didn't inspire her either. She was happy to 'camp' at the Travelodge and drive the seventy-five kilometres north every day. We made a pact not to tell anyone for fear of retribution for not being 'one of the mob', not being 'Black enough' and being 'too uptown'. In hindsight, we should've done what we do today: *be comfortable* in the choice *to be comfortable*. Newsflash: you can camp in a hotel and still be Black!

In 1995 I visited British Columbia, Canada, while doing work experience as part of an Aboriginal and Torres Strait Islander Overseas Study Award given by the then DEETYA (now known as the Department of Education, Employment and Workplace Relations). Some say that if you are going to camp, then it should be in a place like the Canadian Rocky Mountains with stunning mountain views, glistening lakes, horse-riding trails, hiking and fresh air. At first it wasn't that hard to momentarily push into the back of my mind the *I really don't want to camp* mantra.

It was knowing I was in the Canadian Rockies that excited me as my colleague from the Aboriginal Multi-Media Society (AMMS) and I drove towards the ranges. I thought back to my childhood and how I enjoyed the Rocky and Bullwinkle cartoons with Bullwinkle, the Canadian moose, and Dudley Do-Right, the Canadian Mountie. I had lost track of how many girlfriends had urged me to find a Mountie of my own while there, but I wasn't sure as I didn't know enough about the status of the relationship between the Royal Canadian Mounted Police – founded to establish and maintain amicable relations with the Native peoples of the Northwest Territories – and the First Nations peoples of Canada. I needed to do research and, until I knew more, I would be dodging all handsome Mounties in uniform.

My AMMS colleague was one of the very few First Nations peoples in the publishing house where I was doing my work experience. She was Metis: in some states of Canada those First Nations peoples with mixed European heritage, usually French, are classified as Metis. I was impressed that she knew how to pitch a tent, how to make a fire and how to cook over it. Unlike me, she found joy in the experience of camping.

We spent our first day climbing down Sulphur Mountain – smartly taking the famous gondola up – and on reaching the bottom enjoyed the hot sulphur pools with mountain views. The experience was at once exhausting and relaxing, and by nightfall I was pleased to be able to lie down *anywhere*. As a bonus, there was a brick toilet block nearby with power points for us city dwellers to plug in blow dryers and irons – not that I did, but it was comforting to know I could. To my surprise, someone had plugged in a rice cooker! Hygiene issues aside, I thought it was ingenious.

Weeks later, when I was back in the comfort and safety of my family home in Matraville, I relived stories from my four months abroad. As I sat at the dinner table with Mum, Dad and my brothers, I was gobsmacked to see a news report of a bear attack near the camping ground where I had stayed. Not that there are bear fears here, but it further cemented my argument against sleeping outdoors when much safer options were on offer, such as the world-famous Fairmont Chateau Lake Louise with day spas, canapés and suites with king-sized beds and furnishings with burnished brass and wood accents. Now *that's* my idea of camping!

In the late 1990s I was in Fitzroy Crossing in the Kimberley region, working on a research project related to Indigenous education. I was staying at one of the few hotels in town. It was comfortable, clean and conveniently close to the local communities I would visit by car in the day. But there were geckos and spiders and other bugs, and I recall walking along the veranda to my room and wincing at some bug that flew towards me. My non-Indigenous colleague said some-thing along the lines of, 'What's wrong with you? You're Aboriginal; surely you're used to the bush.' How could I be used to the bush if I was born and raised in the suburbs and only went back to country for funerals or to give talks in schools? And even if I *was* used to the bush, I would still never get used to creepy-crawly things. I had matured by this point – I didn't feel challenged at all as a Blackfella on that day. Rather, I felt dismayed that even among my 'politically correct' peers there was a level of ignorance that I thought would've been dispelled by that stage in our work-ing relationship.

It would be some years before I would sleep in a swag or sleeping-bag again, mainly because life hadn't called for it. I'd stayed in a few dodgy hotels in towns I won't mention here for the sake of not wanting to offend anyone, and even in some nicer establishments I could sometimes feel my city roots challenged. Choosing not to 'go bush' still came with its critics, however. In 2007 I was excited about heading to Woodford for the Dreaming Festival at the invitation of Rhoda Roberts, where we were launching the BlackWords: Aboriginal and Torres Strait Islander Writers and Storytellers research community, an online resource of bios, publications and histories of Indigenous literary producers. I would also read from some of my work. The annual festival is the perfect opportunity for reunions and catch-ups. My excitement levels were also raised because I knew I was staying in a hotel in Caboolture rather than the campsite during what was extraordinarily cold weather. It was so cold that one friend from Darwin had virtually cried herself to sleep with the chill, and even those who had brought coats and gloves were buying earmuffs and scarves. The thought of queuing for a hot shower after a frozen, sleepless night of drumming and other campsite activities made me even more grateful for my urban ways.

Sure enough, it wasn't long before I was accused – some might say jokingly – of not being a Blackfella because I didn't want to 'sleep under the stars'. '*Five stars* are the only stars I want to sleep under,' I joked. 'My mum was raised in a humpy on a mission. You fellas are going backwards. I'm going back to my hotel with the heater and the electric blanket and I'm going to be warm tonight. Oh,' I added, as I walked away, 'don't be asking if you can come use my *hot* shower. You can be as Black and cold as you like tonight.' The reality is when I'm at events like that I'm also working and I need to have slept in order to do my job. I can't sleep when I'm on the ground freezing my tits off and fearing spiders, snakes, grizzly bears or, God forbid, intruders (like pirates on the Hawkesbury River).

In 2008 I went on my first ARMtour with the National Aboriginal Sporting Chance Academy (NASCA). ARMtour stands for Athletes as Role Models tour (clearly I'm not an athlete, but I did don a tracksuit *and* I can skip) and the trip involves teams of athletes and others heading into five communities in the Northern Territory. The ARMtour program uses sporting and high-profile role models to encourage Aboriginal youth in remote communities to stay in school, lead healthy lifestyles and make positive choices in life. Our aim is to promote the importance of education and improving literacy and numeracy. The overall goal of NASCA is to inspire young Indigenous people to greatness – whatever that may mean to them as individuals and community members. I got involved at the time because my cousin Joe Williams was working with the organisation and had put my name up for inclusion.

My first tour took me to Mutitjulu with three male and one female footballers. With my Melville Island memories in mind, I packed lightly for the Northern Territory: uniform-black NASCA shorts, leggings, orange ARMtour T-shirts, NASCA tracksuit and runners that I'd throw out after a week in the red dirt. I allowed myself one lip gloss, some foundation, one mascara and that was it in terms of beauty regime. I had a sleeping-bag and cushion. I packed, but then unpacked, the jewellery, cleanser, toner, eye cream and hairspray. I took one book, the David Unaipon Award-winning *Me, Antman and Fleabag* by Gayle Kennedy. At the last minute I squished in three more black tees, a pair of cargo pants, two pairs of sexy knickers – just in case Mr Right was in the Red Centre – and my cozzie.

I was excited about going back to Mutitjulu; I hadn't been there since 1998, when I was invited by the Ngaanyatjarra Pitjantjatjara Yankunytjatjara Women's Council to speak at the Kungka Career's Conference at Yulara. At that conference we had the choice of camping or hotel accommodation. I assumed all the other women would camp, because I was sure I was the only pathetic 30+- wearing city-slicker. I didn't want to segregate myself so asked to hotel it for the first and last nights and camp the rest. However, I arrived to find that nearly every other presenter had chosen the hotel option. I'm grateful that musician Kerrianne Cox allowed me to share her room for a couple of nights. Phew!

I imagined Mutitjulu would be different since the introduction of the invasive Northern Territory 'Intervention' in 2007, which included the suspension of the *Racial Discrimination Act* – the very act that Andrew Bolt was found to be in breach of – in order to deny basic human rights to services without agreeing to sign over land-leases and imposed a system of income management on only Aboriginal people. I had heard about the changes the Intervention had brought when I had chaired a public forum organised by Women for Wik at Australia Hall in Sydney on 14 September 2007. There, hundreds of Sydneysiders in attendance had the opportunity to hear firsthand from Northern Territory Aboriginal women about what was happening in their affected communities. Olga Havnen, Eileen Cummings, Raelene Rosas and Rachel Willika shared stories to a packed hall of concerned Australians wanting to know how they could help get the power back into the hands of those who had lost control over their own lives.

With memories of their heart-wrenching stories in mind, I headed to the community at the base of Uluru, which happened to be the original target of the Intervention policy. I was keen to get to the community to work with the kids in the school, and hopefully catch up with Uncle Bobby Randall. I'd not seen him since we both spoke at the Children's Book Council of Australia Conference in Sydney in 2006 and shared some laughs together. At that conference he had been a hit as the opening speaker, and as cheeky as ever. 'There's a list going around the conference about you meeting Mr Right,' he said to me with a chuckle. 'I put my name on it.'

Before leaving Alice Springs for Muti, our group learned of some hiccups with our accommodation arrangements and we left town knowing we had two options ahead: camping outside or sleeping in a Winnebago motorhome. Neither inspired me. As we've already established, the ground and I are not good sleeping partners, but the thought of being a Blackfella pulling into a remote community in a Winnebago – which happens to be another name for the Ho-Chunk tribe from land now known as Wisconsin and Illinois – not only didn't sound right, but sounded very, very wrong.

I opted to arrive in the four-wheel drive, waving as we passed our fellow teammates in the Winnebago. When we all reached the Erlunda Truck Stop Desert Oasis Resort – 200 kilometres away from our destination – for 'supplies', I almost keeled over with laughter. It was taking the fellas – Black and white – a notable amount of time to find where to actually put diesel into the vehicle. While I had been very conscious of being a concrete Koori, I hadn't been quite sure what they were. It was a funny moment.

It was a surreal experience driving from Alice to Mutitjulu, crossing the deep red landscape while talking to driver and team-leader Simon about everything from the Intervention to how cattle is raised on the land in the Northern Territory, volunteer work, the Stolen Generations, the David Peachey Foundation (set up by Wiradjuri man and rugby league legend David Peachey to support young people through educational scholarships, sporting grants and programs and overseas exchange opportunities), youth issues and the impact of careers on family life and vice versa. It was a trip where hours passed quickly as we both fought for air time, yarning constantly, only getting a chance to speak while the other took a breath.

I have always loved waking up in Matraville, it is my home. I feel safe and secure there and it is a place where I feel at peace because it's somewhere I know intimately, a place full of childhood memories and familiar faces. I am on the road so much that I am never happier than when I wake to the sun streaming through the gum tree outside my window (even though the birds might annoy the hell out of me) and I'm in my southward-facing bed, which is the correct feng shui for me, apparently. But waking up in Anangu country, Mutitjulu, watching the sunrise over Uluru and then later sunset over Kata Tjuta, was a memory that no camera could ever really capture, and a gift that will always be treasured. When we arrived, we fortunately ended up with a house to stay in. Still, spending my nights in a sleeping-bag – albeit on top of a double bed – classifies as camping to me.

When we first drove into town, the memories of my visit ten years previously came flooding back. Nights where we sat around the fire and sang along to the voice and guitar work of Kerrianne Cox and the girls were getting ideas about what they could do with their futures. That week with the ARMtour was extraordinary on many levels, challenging my sense of privilege in a community lacking so much. I knew that my 'luck' was also related to living in an urban environment with access to resources and facilities. But here I was working with students who were so obviously different to those I worked with in and around Sydney. It wasn't so much a culture shock, but a harsh reminder of all the benefits city life brings with it: access to services, libraries, free entertainment, affordable and healthy food, reasonably priced clothes and other necessities. I cried for forty minutes as we pulled out of the community at the end of our stay, because I felt sad for the kids who didn't have the basic resources and infrastructure (local libraries, swimming pools and shaded playgrounds) that city kids had. When I ran a workshop for twelve gifted and talented Koori kids at the National Centre for Indigenous Excellence in August 2011, I was conscious they had three days of focused creative writing time with me, made possible because it was in the city, the facilities are here, there're no airfares involved and these kids are highly literate.

When in 2009 the opportunity to join another ARMtour presented itself, this time to Papunya, I was truly grateful. Since the release of the multi-award-winning *Papunya School Book of Country and History* in 2002, I have wanted to go there. Written and illustrated by Anangu staff and students at the Papunya School, in collaboration with children's author Nadia Wheatley and illustrator Ken Searle, the book was developed as part of the school's curriculum resources. I believe it should be in every Australian home because it is an accessible resource for all Australians to learn the history of such a significant community.

Like many 'children's' books in recent years, *Papunya School Book of Country and History* is not just for kids. It crosses many genres, including history, biography and art. With an estimated 20,000 people going through the stunning Papunya Tula exhibition at the Art Gallery of New South Wales during the 2000 Sydney Olympic Games, it's fair to wonder how many would have understood the history behind the peoples and country that produced those amazing works. The dot paintings of the region are internationally renowned, but how much is actually known about the history, the Tjukurrpa (Dreaming stories) of that place. This book provides an opportunity for us all to learn. It was a bible to me in many ways, even before heading to the community.

Pulling into this remarkable place with so much history excited me. It is also home of the Warumpi Band and, as one who believes the original version of *My Island Home* would make a fantastic national anthem, I was keen to check out their original recording space and enjoy a taste of the local upcoming talent. On tour with me was a deadly young Indigenous graphic designer, Canberra-based Margaret Ross. We'd had a six-degrees-of-separation experience through her flatmate who was working on establishing a glossy Indigenous magazine that I had been in preliminary discussions about. Marg and I had our best conversations preparing dinner while the rest of our crew were at the school doing after-hours activities.

During the ARMtour program, I would wear my tracksuit and jump rope, throw balls and coordinate relays with students, but I wasn't big on kicking footies and getting more dusty after dark. My skills lay in washing up and apparently burning things on the stove. But someone had to cook, and seeing as I couldn't rally the kids excitedly like youth worker Ash Hogan or basketballer Blake Borgia, my options for contributing after-hours were limited to rustling up a high-carb feed and putting on a few loads of washing. The domestic duties were also a gentle reminder that I was perhaps not really cut out for the husband and kids scenario.

In Papunya, six of us shared a two-bedroom house but no-one wanted to use the bedrooms. One team member known as 'Uncle' advised us that he snored and was best kept away from all of us. He slept on a recliner in the lounge room, and the house reverberated with every inhalation. The others – all younger than me, I feel I need to point out – chose to sleep outside around the fire. I wanted to try it as it had been some years since I'd slept under the stars. I lay out there with my swag, beanie, tracksuit, socks and eye mask, which I constantly peeked out of to glimpse the bedroom window not far away where a conformable, empty double bed waited. I froze outside and by the second night, as I looked to the bedroom window that had no curtains, I thought to myself: *I can sleep in a bed and still see the stars – that's good enough for me.*

~

No-one bothers to ask me to go camping anymore. Now we do spa days. In May 2009 Robynne Quiggin and I boarded a Qantas flight to Cairns en route to Port Douglas, where we would hook up with other deadly women to celebrate Robynne's and her cousin Karen Mill's birthdays.

Robynne and I had travelled together before, spending a few days in Paris in 2006 and more recently taking respite at intervals in a small hotel outside of Sydney. We make good roomies because we share the love of laughter and chocolate. We also share a life-coach in Geraldine, which allows us to engage in many in-depth conversations about goalsetting and planning. Robynne and I have often been mistaken for sisters – of the biological kind – and we both love this. Sometimes when I sit across the table at our favourite café, aptly named 'Chaos', in Neutral Bay, I feel like I am looking in a mirror and hearing words that I myself might say if I got them out of my head quick enough.

Robynne and I behaved like teenagers boarding our Cairns flight, taking photos, laughing, being generally excited. But soon after take-off the significance of who we were as mature Black women struck me. I had my Moleskin out making notes on characters for my next novel, a story about five women in their forties living in Brisbane. Robynne had her laptop switched on as she continued to work on a policy document as part of her role with ASIC. While we both worked we also had our headphones over one ear each, half-watching and listening to the film *Invictus*, about Nelson Mandela. We'd both pause and repeat any significant line along the way.

The next day Jake, Robynne and I were lying by a deserted pool at the Sheraton Mirage Port Douglas, no laptops, policy papers or chapter breakdowns in sight. I'll never forget Jake saying, 'Who'd have thought twenty years ago we'd all end up where we are today.' And she didn't mean Port Douglas, although even being there as friends long after our uni days was also something to celebrate. As we quietly reflected on our own personal and joint histories, I recalled a line from *Invictus* where Nelson Mandela reflected on his time in prison: 'I am the master of my fate. I am the captain of my soul.' And so were each of us.

For a period of time when life was somehow less hectic – although our lives have always seemed to be busy – Robynne and I made time to go away with friends for the weekend and eat too much, laugh, lie by the pool, and sometimes hit a golf ball. Well Geraldine, Terry and I hit golf balls, Robynne had the better idea of getting a massage. Now we're so busy we play phone tag most days and when we do connect it's while we're driving to and from work, to and from airports or sitting in airport lounges.

The morning after Terri Janke won the NAIDOC Award for Person of the Year in 2011, Robynne and I spent an hour on the phone dissecting the night, the dresses, the photos, the achievements of our dear friend. In fact, it was such an extraordinary day that among the housework and washing and must-have massages we ended up speaking about four times. Like young teenagers doing a post-mortem on the school dance.

I play a lot of phone tag with Jake too, who lives up in Cairns. Although her day is more structured than mine, she is on country a lot doing Native Title negotiations for her clients. Even when she tells me about the process – minus client details – I am exhausted at the thought of how intellectually and emotionally draining it must be. 'The Commissioner' as I like to refer to her – a hangover from her days as a commissioner of the Land and Environment Court of New South Wales – was once a Maroubra girl, and I often think of her when I take my morning walk to the beach or have breakfast there. Although we never actually went to the beach together, I think we both appreciate the place for the same reasons: peace, memories of younger days, people we love.

Chapter 12

IF YOU ARE A BLACK WOMAN, YOU SHOULD . . .

'PART OF WHAT I WANT TO TURN MY LIFE INTO
IS A TESTIMONY TO THE FACT THAT WE DON'T
HAVE TO BE PUNISHED. THAT WE DON'T HAVE
TO SACRIFICE OUR LIVES WHEN WE INVENT
AND REALISE OUR COMPLEX SELVES.'

BELL HOOKS

I believe that some people think I have failed as a Black woman because I don't *behave* the way a Black woman apparently should. I've often felt that my life is about making others understand that you can't prescribe Aboriginality, and you can't place genetically based stereotypes on individuals.

In July 2010 I was sitting in the American Library in Paris, where I had gone to work on my novel *Paris Dreaming* among other things. It was a bland space and I was grateful that the people were colourful. It's not the place I would normally go when visiting the city of love, but I was waiting to hear Ted Stanger speaking to a largely American audience about his latest offering, *Vacation: A French Obsession, Demystified*, which left me feeling more in sync with the French than the Americans in terms of work and holidays.

Truth is, I wasn't overly interested in hearing what an American thought about Paris: to me it was akin to a white-fella talking about Blackfellas. But I was also researching a travel story on literary Paris for *Women's Health Magazine* so while I sat there waiting I leant over to the shelves on my right. The first book I grabbed without looking was *Notable Black American Women, Book II*. I opened it at random and the page entry was one on feminist and social activist bell hooks, who authored *Ain't I a Woman?: Black Women and Feminism* (1981). I thought it was an omen in terms of my own life experience when I read the previous quote of Hooks's in an interview she'd done with Lisa Jones in the article 'Rebel without a pause', published in *Village Voice Literary Supplement* in 1992.

I know that I should not be punished for the life and person I am, and that I should sacrifice nothing in realising the complex layers of who I am. But the reality is I am sometimes forced into situations, largely through my work, where I am indeed at times questioned not for the Black woman I am, but for the Black woman I am not.

That one quote read in a matter of minutes while sitting in an American library in Paris summed up my own experience as a woman of colour in Australia today. My identity is complex and always open to criticism by others, sometimes not for who I am, but for who I am not. As the guest speaker was introduced I put the book back on the shelf feeling validated. What follows in this chapter is an examination of just some of the stereotypes that go with being an Aboriginal woman today.

IF YOU ARE A BLACK WOMAN, YOU SHOULD ... BE STRONG AND NOT ASK FOR HELP

'CONTRARY TO POPULAR BELIEF, STRONG WOMEN WEAR THIN TOO. QUIT TELLING HER THAT SHE IS STRONG AND SHE CAN TAKE IT. THERE ARE TIMES WHEN SHE DOESN'T WANT TO TAKE IT ... SHE WANTS YOU TO TAKE IT FROM HER'

NAKIA R. LAUSHAUL

I met the poet Nakia R. Laushaul at the Black Writers Reunion and Conference in Atlanta in 2010. I later read her words quoted here in a Facebook status update, and they reminded me of the expectation often imposed upon Black women to be strong and to be 'together'. Lots of Blackfellas ask me how I stay focused and motivated, given I work for myself and could sleep all day, watch television or just go to the beach if I wanted to. It goes back to what Dad told me about loving what I do for work. It has taken me many years to get where I am and reach my career goal of being a full-time writer who makes a living doing writing-related activities. One of the keys to achieving this was signing up with my life-coach, Geraldine Star, in September 2002. At the time I was on a part-time contract at the Australia Council for the Arts, working on the communications strategy for the Aboriginal and Torres Strait Islander Arts Board. I was also on the management committee of the Australian Society of Authors, was a volunteer broadcaster with Koori Radio in Sydney and found it difficult to say no to any request made of me.

Geraldine and I were friends before we assumed a business arrangement, so our coffee and lunches were replaced with coaching sessions instead. This arrangement was the basis of all our contact for the next twelve months, to ensure a separation of the professional and personal. I began fortnightly one-on-one sessions with Geraldine and set short-term and long-term goals. Together, we developed strategies for me to reach them. My primary goals back when I started included my desire to be 100 per cent happy with my work – paid and voluntary. I needed to focus more on a better work/private life balance; I wanted to start dating seriously, and I needed to look at my health. I wanted to 'fit into unworn clothes'. Yes, that's what I wrote down on my official worksheet. Within seven months of starting life-coaching I had in fact lost ten kilos! I'd made a commitment not so much to Geraldine, but to myself. And I'm glad I did that. My secondary goals at the time included having an efficient home office space, organising my superannuation funds, improving my computer skills, reading more and improving my sense of self-image. What people see in the public arena sometimes hides the pain and insecurities of low self-esteem.

At the time I sought out life-coaching because I needed to consolidate all the elements of my life – work, pleasure, relationships, etc. – because I didn't feel I had a balance. I would often sabotage myself by saying I couldn't do something without even trying it – like when asked to speak at the $200-a-head Aboriginal health fundraiser – but at other times I was incapable of saying no without feeling guilty. This was the biggest problem for me, and it took some time to understand that every time I said yes to something I didn't really want to do (which often didn't generate any income), I was pushing to the bottom of the list my own dream of being a writer. I was aware of my own capacity for motivation, I just needed to be more strategic in the work – paid and unpaid – that I did.

These days, I sit down at the end of each year and consider

what I have done well over the past twelve months and what I have achieved and accomplished professionally. I always analyse where I need to put more energy to improve various areas of my life. Then I work out what my focus will be for the year ahead. It may be working on building better professional or personal relationships; it may be focusing on a particular area of writing or an aspect of my health regime. By writing up my list of goals, it becomes more real to me. My desk in Rosebery faces my 2011 Vision Board. On it I have listed three main values for that year, which are:

* *Be passionate*
* *Be positive*
* *Be genuine*

I also have ten goals listed, which are:

* Paris Dreaming – *bestseller, independents*
* On the Couch with the Doc *(to get a broadcaster for my proposed TV chat show)*
* *Complete the memoir* Am I Black Enough For You?
* *Decimate Andrew Bolt in court!*
* *Get a contract for* Tiddas *(my new novel proposal)*
* *Have my birthday in New York (I ended up going to Noumea and spent Christmas and New Year's in New York City instead)*

*   *Meet Mr Wonderful/Kind/Considerate*
*   *Eliminate negatives from my life!*
*   *Be the best woman I can be!*
*   *Increase fitness level!*

Some might say life-coaching and vision boards are not very 'Black' things to do. But they are very 'Anita' things to do. And seeing as I am Black, then it *is* a Black thing to do. I know other high-achieving Aboriginal people who have used or continue to use a life-coach or professional mentor to assist them to reach personal and professional goals.

Lots of people say, 'You're so organised, Anita, you're the last person who needs a life-coach.' I have always been organised with appointments and short-term things, that is true, but only when I got my life-coach did I start to set monthly targets and long-term goals. Many, and I dare say most, Blackfellas who achieve great things through their work for their community don't take the time to stop and recognise their achievements because they're too busy moving onto the next task. I learned through coaching the importance of keeping a check on what I do and how I perform. I need to stop – even if momentarily – to mark each goal reached. It reminds me what I am capable of, where my strengths and weaknesses lie, what more I can do and how and where I need to push myself further.

Coaching has also helped with my anxiety. Few people know that for many years I suffered from the symptoms often attributed to anxiety: feeling tired, muscle tension, inability to fall asleep and stay asleep. It was probably at its peak in 2004–06 when I was teaching at Macquarie and my writing career was on the verge of taking off with my first contract for an adult novel. At that time if I were asked to do a dinner speech, I would have done it and enjoyed myself. But I would've had anxiety about it all day, which would have had physical side effects, including not sleeping the night before with worry. Around the time *Not Meeting Mr Right* was released I had hardly slept for over a year and was always tired.

Now, thanks to the words of my friend and once colleague Michael McDaniel – someone whose views and ideas I respect immensely – and the documentation in my life-coaching files, I ask myself, 'What's your track record, Anita?', and because I keep a check on what I do, I can say, 'Yeah, the track record's pretty good, I've never fallen off the stage or headbutted a microphone, those contracting me have always been happy with what I've delivered and I've generally nailed it.' Feeling success and achievement in my own eyes, and in the eyes of those who have engaged my services, goes a long way to addressing the sense of anxiety that riddled me for years.

IF YOU ARE A BLACK WOMAN, YOU SHOULD … BE ANGRY

Some people think that being Aboriginal equates to being

angry; that you must have a chip on your shoulder when you state truth and facts about Aboriginal existence past and present. But I'm *not* an angry Black woman! I am a motivated Black woman, a positive Black woman, and I think that is the key to the success of my life generally.

The committees and boards, the writing, the travel, the amazing people I meet and the life-changing conversations we have – these make me happy and so I love my life. I never *ever* have to drag myself out of bed. I wake up about 6 am all year round, check emails and my Facebook page, usually on my iPhone while still in bed. At about 7 am I either walk three kilometres to clear my post office box or I go to the gym. On weekends in summer I love walking to Maroubra Beach and back (4.4 kilometres to be exact), hoping the massive Broome Street hill does something wonderful for my butt and legs. I suck in the smells of freshly cut lawns as I pound the pavement and I listen to affirming songs like Helen Reddy's 'I Am Woman', Green Day's 'Minority' and Christina Aguilera's 'Beautiful'. During that time I plan my day and I script conversations that I expect might be unpleasant so the exchange doesn't become emotional. I take note of the environment around me, because I know I'll be staring at a computer for at least five hours later on. I smile at the ocean and breathe in the salt air; I smell the gardenias and I know that I've started the day the best way I can for me. I probably average eight to ten hours of work over the course of a day, and finish up with emails or a blog post on gratefulness late at night.

I keep happy by being aware of my emotional and mental wellbeing. My brother Mark once commented that I'd read enough self-help books to write one. I have read many, but one that stands out is a book that helped shift my view of dealing with 'failure', which is something that people wanting great things often concern themselves with, *Choosing Happiness* by Stephanie Dowrick. Don't think I'm some weirdo: sometimes it takes a complete stranger to say something very basic for us to actually get it.

IF YOU ARE A BLACK WOMAN, YOU SHOULD ... BE MARRIED UP

I know some reading this book are waiting for me to talk about my private life. But this is not *that* kind of memoir; you may want to read some of my adult novels to get a glimpse of the excitement in that part of my life. What is relevant, however, is the way in which Aboriginality has impacted on my personal relationships since my youth.

My first real boyfriend, who I will call Alex, came from a well-to-do Anglo-Australian family in the eastern suburbs of Sydney. We met on my sixteenth birthday at the Randwick Rugby Club – yes, I was underage – and he was nineteen. It was love at first sight for him, he claimed. I vaguely remembered him, but apparently (I don't recall the incident) I threw a drink at him, and then ignored him for the rest of the night.

The 'playing hard to get' and 'treat them mean, keep them keen' mottos of old seemed to have worked, because Alex was persistent and within weeks we were dating for what would turn out to be a tumultuous six-year on-again/off-again relationship.

On one of our first dates out we were with a group of friends from our schools and the lads were talking about football. I wasn't really listening to the conversation because I had and still have no interest in the sport. But my boyfriend's statement, 'I would never take the field against the Redfern All Blacks,' has always remained with me. A schoolfriend at the time laughed and said, 'Haven't you met Anita's mother?' Alex looked at me strangely. 'I'm Aboriginal,' I said, and we simultaneously let go of each other's hand. I mean, what did he think I was?

Don't ask me to explain how we dated for the next six years. It suffices to say that I have always been a fixer, and thought I could fix everything, including his entrenched racism, a product of growing up in a completely white bourgeois cocoon. There is no doubt at all that he loved me and would've done anything to protect me from anyone else harming me; in fact, he swung at an off-duty cop who called me 'abo' once. But for the whole time I was at UNSW, he never entered the Aboriginal Students' Centre when he came to pick me up, just sat in his Volvo outside the window. There are echoes in that of my father waiting outside the dancehalls for my mother thirty years earlier except clearly my dad wasn't racist.

One day, while I was still at school, we argued about

whether or not Australia was a classless society. He was adamant we weren't, and I thought the exact opposite. While we were on the phone, he asked his brother what he thought. The brother responded, 'Yeah, abos are the lowest class.' At the time, Alex neither criticised nor endorsed his brother's statement, but I do think he was probably embarrassed.

One night soon after I was standing at the kitchen sink, crying as I dried the dishes after an argument with Alex. I can't recall what the argument was about exactly, just that Dad was standing on his side of the kitchen table (we all had designated seats), and Alex was on the other side where he usually sat. It sounds like there's some serious role-playing going on here, but Alex did in fact help wash dishes at my place, though at this moment he was at the table. And my father, who was never one to comment on Aboriginal issues or race, said to my boyfriend, 'Anita's mother and I have never argued about race. We just love each other. That is the way it is in this house.' It was an extraordinary moment because of all the arguments ever had in my home, none was ever about racism, and for my dad to get involved in our relationships that way was almost unheard of. Dad didn't want to be 'the bastard', in his words. Years later, he finally told me that he and Mum had hoped that I would figure out for myself that the relationship with Alex was rotten, without them having to dictate what I was or was not to do.

The truth is that Alex loved me. He loved my family, and my family loved him back. He was a likeable, caring and considerate character most of the time, and had flaws like the rest of us. He especially loved my mother's cooking, because he said his own mother couldn't cook – he called her one main dish of silverside 'suicide'. But we were the only interracial experience he ever had and, from what I understand, he married his next girlfriend, a white American girl.

That's not to say that interracial relationships are the only ones to be problematic. The few relationships I've had with urban Indigenous men have been flawed, but there have never been issues about identity. And in terms of the non-Indigenous men I've dated, I have been out with fellas who are pure gentlemen: chivalrous, generous, talented and interested in Indigenous affairs. So interested, in fact, that every date becomes an exercise in cultural awareness training, and I end up explaining everything from Indigenous protocols to community politics. In the past I've had to insist on 'Indigenous-free days' just so I could feel like something other than a personal tutor. I want romance. If I'm going to educate you over dinner and dessert, then I'm going to invoice you in the morning!

It's hard to even maintain friendships with people who not only don't understand Aboriginality but even after years of knowing you, reading your work and hearing you speak *still* don't get it. Comments like, 'But you don't really have a culture,' or 'You don't really look like an Aborigine,' highlight how entrenched ignorance is in the Australian mindset, even amongst those who might know better. It's almost as if they don't want to get it, because understanding the other forces them to try and understand themselves better. It's much easier to put someone else's identity under the microscope for analysis and dissection than your own.

IF YOU ARE A BLACK WOMAN, YOU SHOULD … HAVE KIDS

Just prior to the release of *Manhattan Dreaming* I was reminded of why I write the career-focused characters that I do. At a Christmas party in 2009 a female acquaintance said to me, 'So you never had children?' I said, 'Yes, I've given birth to eight books and don't have a single stretch mark!' The question had made me feel as if everything else I had done in my life was meaningless because at the end of the day I still hadn't done what a woman should do: have children.

I was mortified and angry when she questioned me about children, and I was glad I wasn't drinking when we had our brief exchange because I'm sure my verbal response may have been quite nasty – 'And that's why I look ten years younger and more glamorous than you do', for example. But I wouldn't dare say such a thing; sometimes women age and dress badly without the excuse of children. Either way, I knew the dig was as much about not being Black enough as it was about not being maternal enough. Comments like these are so inconsiderate on so many levels, not least of all because they fail to recognise that some women *can't* have children. And, of course, there are women who don't *want* to have children, or women who haven't met someone they'd *like* to have children with.

I feel that within our own community, Aboriginal women are expected to have kids much more than our non-Indigenous counterparts. We are meant to be matriarchs, to keep the race going and so forth. If anything, have a career but have kids too, you don't have to have a husband, but at least have kids. I know women who have done it well, managed to have beautiful children and successful careers. Women like Jackie Huggins and Terri Janke for example are role models, mentors, strong Black women whom I admire and respect. I'd like to have managed both roles also – mother and career woman.

I could easily have had a child to fulfil the dreams my parents had for me and motherhood, but I was never pressured by either of them to make the decision to do it alone, and just for the sake of it. My parents knew and demonstrated the importance of a stable home, and without that to support me, being a single parent was never an option I would consider. It wouldn't be until writing *Paris Dreaming* that I would contemplate the idea of juggling careers and motherhood.

I used to get sad on Mother's Day. Not for myself, but for those women who desperately wanted to have kids and couldn't. I always felt the day must be a hard day for them. Me? I've never really thought about having children seriously, perhaps because I haven't met the person I want to share my eggs with yet. Will I change my mind down the track? Who knows. Truth is, while not a mother per se, there are children that I love with every fibre of my being.

I'm what is commonly known as 'a good aunty'. I love my nieces and nephews: Ben, Matt, Liesl, Joey, Max, Audrey and Felicity. They are gorgeous and full of love, and easily loved. I like visiting them, seeing them at Mum's, taking them to the movies occasionally or to feed the ducks in Centennial Park. And I like taking them home again. That's what aunties do. I am grateful I am their 'Aunty Anita'. There's something magical about hearing those words from the 'little people' in my family, although the 'little people' are growing up right before my eyes. I can't believe how tall kids get so quickly. See, even the aunty notices these things. I also notice the strength and warmth in their cuddles, and how special a hug is when I don't have to initiate it.

I've been travelling for work for twenty years and I've always missed my family. In recent times – sorry Mum and siblings – I've missed the 'little people' more than anything else. I get so much joy when I see them. Perhaps it's because our meetings are short sessions – a meal at Mum's or Grandma's, or a quick chat when I'm passing through. My time with them is also joyful because I don't have to deal with the tantrums and tears; when those episodes start, I just leave, literally. It doesn't mean I'm only there for the fun and games. I see two of my nephews every day, so we are part of each other's daily grind: the highs and lows, the plateaus, the school and work dramas – the everyday life cycle. I love nothing more than to yarn with them about their day. I'm a nosy bugger at times; much like a parent, I guess, I've got to know every movement! But I don't have to do the 24/7 slog of a parent, and I admire mothers and fathers who manage the hardest job in the world.

But as an Aboriginal woman, I do feel that, in a way, it's my job to keep the race going, to breed more activist kids to continue my vision. This feeling hit me hard when I stood outside the Redfern Community Centre on the Block on 26 January 2011, preparing to march against the Intervention. I realised that I had no-one to pass the activism baton on to and I don't feel that it's up to me to train up my nieces and nephews: they have parents to do that.

But it did leave me wondering: who would carry on *my* legacy? I thought this as I stood in the scorching sun with my tidda Ashlee Donohue from Mudgin-gal Women's Service and her daughter, and as we all marched along Cleveland Street I wondered which Heiss niece or nephew might be the next little activist.

I go through stages of wanting kids, especially when I realise that the moment of being able to physically have them has probably passed. In July 2010, when I was in New York for the launch of *Manhattan Dreaming* and to deliver the NAIDOC lecture at the Australian Consulate, I was walking from my hotel near Central Park to Times Square on an exhaustingly hot summer day, and a wave of *Shit! I forgot to have children!* came over me. I was about to turn forty-two years old. Time was seriously running out, even if I never really heard any ticking clocks. From New York I went to Barcelona via Paris. I called Mum from my friend Julie's place in Barcelona and told her I was thinking of having a baby. She was over the moon. We could both live with her . . . and my sisters and nephews who were just about to move in, which guaranteed instant family and chaos on the cards. I knew then there really wasn't room for another Heiss in the family home and used that as my excuse, although, truth be known, I wasn't really sold on the idea anyway. For me, it has always been about meeting the person I wanted to have kids with.

In any case, I have my chance to pass on my ideas and dreams to the kids that I teach. I was invited to give an address at the New South Wales Department of Education and Training student awards night in 2007. Witnessing over 100 Koori students from the south western Sydney region receive awards for excellence in various fields, not only was I confident that Indigenous Australia had a positive, bright, educated future, but I felt an enormous amount of pride for kids I had not even met. As I drove home along the M5 from Liverpool to Matraville, I felt uplifted by the experience, ful-filled by two parents who had stopped me in the car park afterwards, thanking me for my words. They reminded me of the importance of parental support for our kids in school. Working with students can again sometimes make me con-sider – albeit for a fleeting moment – perhaps squeezing one or two kids out. But there is no guarantee that mine would be so clever or as polite as the students I've met in Deniliquin or La Perouse. And it's not the squeezing that bothers me so much, although I'm not too fond of pain.

Eventually that feeling of 'maybe' is knocked out of me when I enter classrooms where children behave badly and are rude. I understand that individuals have specific home-life circumstances that impact on their ability to concentrate and participate in class, and I make allowances for that when I am forewarned by teachers. But when I visit class after class at the same school where disrespect and bad behaviour is the norm, my capacity to 'like' children and my job is easily diminished. This has happened a couple of times while I've been touring as an invited 'Aboriginal writer'. On those occasions where I am challenged, not only by students but also by teachers who don't instil discipline by separating students or addressing bad behaviour, then the thought of getting my tubes tied kicks in quickly.

IF YOU ARE A BLACK WOMAN, YOU SHOULD ... NOT BIG-NOTE YOURSELF

I don't think we celebrate success enough in our communities, largely because we are busy still working towards equality and equity in the everyday lives of many of our people across the country. To big-note yourself, in Blackfella terms, is 'shameful'. It took me meeting my life-coach Geraldine to understand the importance of recognising milestones – my own and those of my peers. Communally we have events like the NAIDOC Awards and the Deadlys each year. These recognise achievement in various categories of sport, the arts and community, but they can't possibly acknowledge the individual success made by so many of our unsung heroes around the country. We need to reward accomplishment and commitment on a personal level, for ourselves and those in our lives.

IF YOU ARE A BLACK WOMAN, YOU SHOULD ... KNOW ABOUT BLACK STUFF

I am invited to speak at events around the world because I am a writer of many books across many genres and on many topics – but none of my books, I must add, are on Native Title or land rights, Aboriginal health, the legal system, domestic violence or on how to 'close the gap'. It's not that I don't have opinions on these issues or some basic understanding of them, but I am not an expert on these topics or, indeed, anything. I am learning all the time. And I write mostly about what I know and what I am most passionate about. But as is common practice, as an Aboriginal person with a degree, an ability to speak, a platform, and – unfortunately for some – a microphone, I am expected to be the walking, talking encyclopaedia on everything Aboriginal.

To be honest, when I am at a writers' festival, I want to talk about the latest book I've written – to be asked about my characters, my researching methods, my writing process and protocols, my reading habits, all of which include Aboriginal issues, themes and characters. But I don't want to be asked to talk about issues that are unrelated to my field of knowledge or the topic I am there to talk about. As an example of what is common for me, during question time at the 2010 Perth International Arts Festival, while on a panel with authors Professor Larissa Behrendt and Archie Weller, an audience member bravely – or stupidly, depending on which way you read the situation – asked the following question: 'What is the current state of spirituality in the Aboriginal community right now?' There was a communal sigh in the marquee that wasn't caused by the extreme Western Australian heat we were all suffering from. I responded that I had been sitting outside under a tree prior to the panel discussion and I found it a very spiritual moment, but I didn't believe it had anything to do with me being Aboriginal. It had to do with the fact that I, Anita Heiss, find spirituality in various aspects of my everyday life, including the landscape. I didn't attempt to answer what I think is the unanswerable, especially when Aboriginal people today find spirituality in many different forms, and organised religion has replaced or complements personal and communal spirituality for many.

Audiences and, indeed, colleagues both locally and internationally need to be aware that Indigenous 'educators' – those either working in academia or seen to be teachers through their craft such as writing – should not be expected to know more than the average non-Indigenous academic walking into a classroom or onto a stage. I acknowledge that the *Commonwealth Anti-Discrimination Act* legislates that Aboriginality can be a qualification for some jobs, like teaching Indigenous Studies, in the same way that being a woman would be regarded as a qualification for working in a women's refuge. But do people expect every single woman on earth to be an expert on domestic violence or motherhood?

It is true that some of the best educators I have seen are those who teach based on their real experiences living under the Act of Protection, on missions and reserves. In this case, their personal experience as an Aboriginal person certainly qualifies them to teach on the subject of the Stolen Generations. But that doesn't mean that Aboriginality under the law automatically translates to knowing *everything* related to our people, our histories and our diverse cultures. And Aboriginality under the law doesn't mean that we will automatically be 'gifted' a specific job. Just like other job applications, we are required to fill *all* the criteria.

I am never one to try and be the Blackfella others want me to be, especially when it requires me to be the 'exotic other' or impart information to audiences when I have little or no knowledge on the topic. I've been on a few panels at festivals and wondered why I was there. If I am given the opportunity to have a say in programming, I will always pull out of a panel that clearly has me presented as an author with an expertise in all things Aboriginal – or even just one Aboriginal issue.

Some festivals put you on panels without consultation, and I always know that if the topic is not directly related to a book I've written, then it's assumed to be directly related to my Aboriginality and whatever that means to the organisers. With that in mind, I have been placed on panels about a broad range of topics and in the small part of my brain that can be cynical, I imagine that I am expected to *be*, to *say*, to *know* something about these issues that only a Blackfella can! Spirituality is just one of them.

CHAPTER 13

A BLACKFELLA ABROAD

Travelling and speaking internationally on Aboriginal themes associated with my books and writing is a huge privilege, but also a massive responsibility. Being perceived as an 'Aboriginal Ambassador Abroad' requires diplomacy, knowledge and stamina. And I don't always have those qualities switched on simultaneously. What I do require at all times on my trips is the ability to think on my feet.

Some of my most significant learning moments have been when I am on the road. Internationally, I have spoken by invitation in Austria, France, Spain, Mallorca, Germany, the US, the UK, Canada, Tahiti, Aotearoa/New Zealand, Fiji, Japan, China and New Caledonia. At many events I've been confronted by audience members with a question or a blatant attack that I've had to manage. Admittedly, not always well.

I've found my various visits to Paris over time have offered some of the most challenging moments in my professional and personal career. When your work involves talking about your own history and culture, it is always personal. In 2003 I was invited to attend a United Nations Educational, Scientific and Cultural Organisation meeting in Paris focusing on protecting women's cultural heritage. I had tried via email more than once to convince the organisers that someone like Terri Janke or Cathy Craigie (who was then the director of the Aboriginal and Torres Strait Islander Arts Board of the Australia Council) would be a more appropriate, more knowledgeable delegate, although I had worked with Terri as a peer reviewer on the Australia Council protocols on writing about Indigenous Australia. The organisers insisted that it was me they wanted to attend the meeting, and on arrival I was told it was because they'd been advised by colleagues who'd seen me speak elsewhere that I 'would give them drama'! I'm assuming they thought that was a good thing, and I didn't disappoint.

I was one of only two Indigenous women in the room, the other being Tara Browner, a Choctaw academic from the University of California, Los Angeles, specialising in ethnomusicology. Tara and I formed an alliance not only because of our Indigeneity, but because of our respect for 'the researched' in academia – that is, the human subject matter. We sat in a space of about twenty women mainly from Europe (and one man from UNESCO), and listened to French and other academics speak of the rights of the researcher over the rights of the researched. I was completely frustrated by the challenges I faced when trying to bring the discussion back to the *responsibilities* of the researcher.

At one point, one French academic in the room passed

around some photos of a community in Africa she'd been investigating for over twenty years. Only after we had all viewed the images did she tell us that not only did she not have permission to take the photos, but that she had actually been asked *not* to take photos at all. 'But then there would be no documentation of them,' she declared. At that point I was furious that I had been denied the opportunity to respect the community by not viewing the images. My cries for ensuring the rights of women's heritage be protected from overzealous academics fell on deaf ears.

In 2010 I gave the NAIDOC address at the Australian Embassy in Paris. The embassy is a stunning venue overlooking the Eiffel Tower and it is part of the setting of my novel *Paris Dreaming*. The minute I entered the space, I started imagining sex scenes – for the novel, that is, not for my own life. The NAIDOC theme for that year was 'Unsung heroes – closing the gap by leading their way'. It was easy for me to speak on that theme because I believe that most of our Indigenous authors are doing just that, helping to close the gap in terms of improving appalling literacy statistics by creating relevant resources for communities. Our writers also close the gap of ignorance by penning stories that unpack and express the diversity of Aboriginal society in Australia in the twenty-first century, breaking down barriers between our community and others. I explained to the fifty or so guests in the ambassador's residence that Aboriginal literature from Australia serves many purposes: it records our 'truths' about history; it functions as a tool for reconciliation, allowing non-Indigenous Australians to engage with us in non-confrontational ways; it provides a means of self-representation in Australian and world literature and assists understanding of the diversity of our identities; finally, it challenges subjective and often negative media stereotypes and interpretations of our lives.

The audience included the ambassador himself, David Ritchie, as well as embassy staff, French academics, filmmakers, publishers, booklovers and expats, all with varying levels of knowledge and interest in Indigenous Australia. After a forty-five-minute passionate performance on the evolution of Aboriginal writing in the past decade, and while everyone was enjoying the hospitality of the ambassador, I found myself having to exercise extreme diplomacy when I was accosted by a local French (white) academic. A woman in her fifties, she had worked in the Northern Territory twenty years ago and had long since been desperate to write about her own experience of Aboriginality. She felt compelled to undertake a doctorate on the 'Aborigines of the Territory', because no-one else was apparently doing it. She wanted to explain her own assessment of Aboriginal identity. Keen to remove myself from the conversation, and also conscious of the 'Aboriginal Ambassador Abroad' mantle, I advised her that before she wrote a word on her thesis, she would best be served talking to people on the ground in the Territory. I strongly suggested she contact the Aboriginal academics at the relevant institutions in the region. 'I've sent emails but no-one has responded,' she claimed. I ever so gently advised her that sometimes silence is an answer. I thought to myself that her proposal of writing about Aboriginality after visiting Australia twenty years ago might challenge even the most generous of people.

No sooner had she gone than I was attacked by a white expat-Aussie who insisted that Aboriginal literature was only Aboriginal if written in '*the* Aboriginal language'. We nutted this argument out for some minutes before I was rescued, but essentially he argued that, in his opinion, he was a French writer when writing in French, and an Australian writer when writing in English (technically that should make him an English writer, but I digress). His argument was that an Aboriginal writing in English made the work Australian literature and not Aboriginal literature. We do all belong to the Australian literary canon, but I firmly believe that there is a genre that we have created that is distinct within that canon. Our voices, stories and writing styles are different because of the way we have had to forge our place in the industry. But the French/Australian writer (and they think Blackfellas have identity problems!) wouldn't have a bar of it. Essentially his argument was that language equals culture equals identity as a writer – that is, that the whole of someone's identity can be reduced down to the language they speak.

I've also had varying degrees of success working with the French in New Caledonia and Tahiti. I've twice been invited to the (Salon du Livre) Salon International des Littératures Océaniennes (in 2003 and 2006) and had an amazing time with local Kanak writers like Déwé Gorodé and my Tahitian sisters Chantal Spitz and Flora Devatine. I was with Chantal and Flora in Tahiti in 2008 for the Salon Lire en Polynésie following the French release of *Who Am I? The Diary of Mary Talence, Sydney 1937* (translated by Annie Green) and published by Tahitian-based Au Vent des Iles. It was the most extraordinary experience to be in the steamy, Polynesian climate at an outdoor book festival, sitting under palm trees with an English-born French translator talking about the Stolen Generations. I don't know how many people attended that day, but my publisher Christian Robert said he was pleased when someone said they'd run out of chairs. The majority of the audience were local French residents interested in literature and a handful of Tahitians.

As I discussed in lay terms the policies of removal, protection and assimilation, I watched the audience nod and tut-tut at the appalling actions of the white government towards their Indigenous inhabitants. But as soon as I said, 'And of course, the impacts of colonisation were felt as harshly here on the local Indigenous people,' the Tahitians nodded and the French looked shocked. I've always believed that the success of Aboriginal authors – like Alexis Wright, Doris Pilkington, Philip McLaren, Terri Janke, Kim Scott and Sally Morgan – in getting French translations of our works is partly because some French people are quite comfortable and happy to slag off the Brits for their colonial exploits. But to consider their own, well, that's another story.

My experience as an 'Aboriginal writer' was very different in Nagoya, Japan, when I was invited to lecture on Aboriginal literature and the Stolen Generations at Aichi Shukutoku University in 2006. The entire week was filled with interesting yet challenging moments, largely based on my lack of Japanese language skills. The only Japanese I knew was 'konnichiwa', 'sayonara' and 'hai'. Thankfully, before I boarded my plane I'd been prepped with some necessary phrases by my then editor at Random House, Elizabeth Cowell who carefully wrote out phonetically for me: 'Hajeemay-mashte Anita des dozo yorosh-ku', which I hope translated to 'My name is Anita, please be nice to me.' I was also advised to drop into conversation that I thought Japanese rice was the best in the world, and then my audiences would all love me. And it was true, they did love the rice comment, and they were all kind to me. I loved that a nation was so sure they produced the best grain on the planet.

I appreciated the class sessions over the lectures in Japan because the smaller group discussions were enriching and, I must say, fun for me when they asked questions about Australia generally, even though talking about history was serious. The reaction of students in one class in particular was inspiring. They were all reading *Who Am I?* as part of their English lessons, and they tried desperately to grasp the policies of protection as best they could, given their language skills. Their questions were more related to mainstream Australian culture though, and letting me know where I should taste the best eel.

At another university in Nagoya I walked across campus after a lecture and was rushed by a group of young female students squealing as if I were a rock star. I laughed out loud. Who'd believe a writer could elicit such a welcome? Aside from the teaching, my biggest 'Aha!' moment – as Oprah would call it – was walking down a city street in Nagoya one day and realising that it was the first time I had ever considered myself a 'westerner'. It was a while before it dawned on me that in my navy Veronika Maine suit and heels I probably looked like every other business person in town, except that I wasn't Japanese. In fact, I was the only person I'd seen in hours who was not Japanese. Nagoya is not a tourist hub like Tokyo or Kyoto, with Nagoya Castle and Atsuta Shrine its only main sightseeing spots.

Once conscious of my perceived westerner status, I became obsessed with seeing if people were looking at me. Was I being noticed at all? Did they even see me? And if so, did people know where I came from? I wanted them to know that I was from Australia, that I was Aboriginal and not a westerner. But I knew there was probably no way they'd guess I was Koori, even if I was wearing the red, black and yellow flag draped across me. Would they have ever seen the Aboriginal flag? Or a map of Aboriginal Australia? I wanted to scream, 'I'm the other! I'm the one the westerners write about!'

I was so disturbed by my new potential westerner status that I needed a coffee and seat to write out some thoughts. Truth be known, my feet were also killing me. (Another reason I had to get out of academia and back into creative writing: it was a much better option sitting in my nighty and no shoes to write all day than a business suit and heels. But I digress, again.) I headed into the JR Takashimaya department store and sat at the café looking, listening and feeling more of an 'outsider' until another westerner arrived. He spoke in a plum English accent and whined about his piece of cake. I was embarrassed for him: he fulfilled the stereotype of the whingeing Pom in a country that probably didn't know that phrase, but knew the tone of someone who could most likely never be pleased.

He looked towards me and I looked away quickly. *No, I thought. I don't want to be alone in this place, but I don't want people to think I'm like you. You're the coloniser, and you complain too much. That's not me! I'm happy with any cake, especially the one I've got right now.* I got up quickly and headed out to a familiar shop door across the street. Inside I felt happy, warm, at peace, at ease, at home, which some may think weird for a proud Wiradjuri woman, but I had just walked into Tiffany's. I struck up a conversation with a petite salesgirl in all black who had, as coincidence would have it, studied at Macquarie University. The universe then insisted I buy myself a ring in honour of our meeting.

Japan was the first country I'd ever been to where I felt completely intimidated and inadequate as a traveller by not having any language skills, but I was spoiled by being escorted around by native English speakers and there was only one day where I had to get public transport.

My experience in Japan reminded me somewhat of my father's little Austrian village in the Lungau, where everyone was from Österreich and in a sense looked the same – everyone in the Lungau is white. The sense of sameness bound people together in the little Austrian village and in Japan, but it also locked other people, like me, out. On my flight home from Nagoya I was the only 'westerner' on board and – unlike the upgrade to business class I received on the way over – I was herded into cattle class with all the other passengers. I wore an earthy-toned Basque frock with a frill at the hem – which written on the page does not sound all that attractive, but it was slimming. However, I assume it was mistaken for a Qantas uniform, because as I walked down the aisle I was asked by passengers for blankets and pillows. Laughing to myself, I obliged, remembering that in my youth I wanted to grow up and be an airhostess. The job had appeared much more glamorous back in those days, before I knew how much work flight attendants really had to do.

~

While I have enjoyed all my various trips around the world, the country that has given me the most support as a professional writer – as a Black writer, in particular – is the US. It's unfortunate that I can't say Australia has been equally as supportive. There are few coordinated writers' conferences here that provide hands-on practical experience for someone who is at my level (i.e. has published several books) but is still learning. There are workshops at writers' centres and other organisations, and there are writers' festivals that I attend as a participant and a guest, but for concentrated professional development – workshops, tutorials, seminars – my greatest growth has been participating in the Black Writers Reunion and Conference (BWRC) held annually in the US.

Coordinated by the Texas-based freelance editor and event manager Tia Ross, the conference provides a collegial atmosphere that I haven't experienced here. Although many of my friends are writers, editors, illustrators or work within the publishing industry, and we talk books all the time, we don't sit and write together, nor necessarily talk about the practice of writing. My gift to myself each year on a professional level is attending the BWRC. I've been very fortunate to receive financial support to assist my travel from the Copyright Agency Limited and the University of Western Sydney.

I first heard of the BWRC in 2008 through an email from Sam Cook – who designed the cover of my book *Sacred Cows*, then working at the Wilin Centre and now running the Dreaming Festival – via the online Indigenous Writers Group that I monitored for some time. I emailed Tia Ross and asked if the conference was open to Black writers in the US only or to writers of colour internationally. A personal invitation from Tia was then extended, and I ended up giving a keynote address on the Black Words: Aboriginal and Torres Strait Islander Writers and Storytellers research community of the AustLit database, and on the state of Indigenous literature and publishing in Australia at the time.

The night before my address there was a meet-and-greet where I made lasting friendships with writers who had flown themselves in to Tampa, Florida from as far away as Texas,

California, South Carolina, Washington, DC and even France. They had paid their own way, including the registration fees, and were mostly in full-time employment. However, to them hammering the keys and writing manuscripts was a daily exercise, a love, an obligation, a necessity. This new I'm-committed-to-being-a-writer-regardless-of-whether-I'm-funded-to-write attitude inspired me.

I was interested, although saddened, to hear that many at the conference had no knowledge whatsoever of Aboriginal Australia, though some had seen *Rabbit-Proof Fence*. My address was also probably the first time many of the delegates had heard an acknowledgement of country as well, and I remain aware of the distinct divide between Black Americans and Native Americans. It is an interesting space I find myself in as an Aboriginal Australian part of the international First Nations community, but also part of an international Black writing community in the US where I am regarded as a 'Black Australian'. Somehow the two communities in America didn't seem to meet.

For me personally, I see our connection with Black America through the civil rights movement experienced there and here, played out most obviously in Australia with the 1965 Freedom Rides through western New South Wales exposing endemic racism including segregation. Many Aboriginal Australians find motivation in the actions of Black American leaders like Martin Luther King Junior and Malcolm X. And yet our history of dispossession of traditional lands, the representation as savages throughout history and in films, the residential school system and our status as the forgotten First Peoples are what we share as Indigenous peoples with Native Americans. During my keynote address to the conference, I talked about the need for self-representation in literature: how Aboriginal people need the voice to determine how we appear on the page in novels, history books and so on. We need to be documenting who we are and what our lives are like, rather than being considered through the lens of 'the other'. As I spoke, I could see heads nodding in the audience and I knew I'd struck a chord.

In 2009 I went to Las Vegas for my second BWRC, and it was the perfect setting for creative inspiration. I'd been to Las Vegas before, but I was younger and more naïve, and actually too scared to do much by myself. I was excited about heading back, this time with the purpose of professional development but also to do my first international travel story for Brisbane's *Courier-Mail*. By my third day there I was antsy about starting the conference. It's not that I can't entertain myself, it's just that I'm used to working most days, most weekends, and so I was glad when my writing colleagues finally arrived. I'd had enough of shopping and dealing with jetlag by lying by the pool. I was ready to get stuck into some serious writing exercises and discussions. And the minute my feet hit the ground, I was off and running. What do you get when you bring together Black writers from across North America and deposit them in the dusty desert of Nevada, hole them up at one of the oldest casinos in Las Vegas and get them to talk about books and writing? An abundance of stories, laughter and memories that will keep the printing presses busy for the next decade.

Conference delegates participated in workshops on all forms of writing including blogging, self-publishing, epublishing, website development, public speaking and public relations. The program also included book signings, a trade expo and hours of conversations with other writers about everything from how to get motivated, to finding an agent and the need to attend book fairs to promote publications. I presented a workshop on writing memoirs and what emerged during it were stories similar to our own in Australia: segregation, oppression, civil rights and a largely undocumented history of people of colour. Perhaps one of the most memorable conversations I had during the conference centred on one author being told by her white agent, 'You need to blacken up your writing, girlfriend!' There was much gasping and then laughter at our dinner table about the statement, which began a series of ideas for T-shirt slogans.

I was grateful for the enthusiastic and knowledgeable presenters who contributed to my own professional development while there. Patricia Haley from Los Angeles ran a workshop called 'SPEAK' – which in short translates to the need for authors to be SENSATIONAL, POWERFUL, ENGAGING and AUTHORITIVE to unlock the KEYS to their public speaking potential. I also attended a workshop run by novelist Venise Berry on 'Powerful Plots: The Art of Fiction Writing', wherein she advised that one should limit the number of primary characters in a novel. For powerful writing the focus should be on developing three complex characters, rather than having four or more characters that are more superficial. As I listened to Venise tell us that books today have to be visual – this is a media society – I started to think about some of the differences between Black American writing and Black Australian writing. In the US, Black romance and Christian fiction are highly published, whereas fiction is a small list for us and it's mostly in poetry, children's books and life-writing that we find publishers. And I don't know of any Aboriginal 'Christian writers' per se.

At the conference I attended a workshop that would not normally be on my radar in terms of my own writing, but I wanted to support my friend, the presenter Dr Jacqualyn Green. The presentation was titled 'Maximising Your Writing Through Enhanced Spirituality' and in it Dr Green considered how both religion and spirituality can inform our writing. In this session I heard for the first time about 'post-traumatic slave syndrome' – a condition that exists as a consequence of multigenerational oppression of Africans and their descendants resulting from centuries of chattel slavery, and which suggests that African Americans are more vulnerable to some health problems than non-Blacks. It reminded me of health issues such as diabetes and heart disease in our own communities, which are also the consequence of colonisation. Traditional diets high in protein and nutrients had been rapidly replaced with western diets high in sugar and processed fats.

Over the three days of the conference my exchanges with

other attendees were not only about books, though, or all about being women of colour. When I sat with my 'girlfriends', and they with their 'sistagirl', we had plenty in common simply by being 'women' – we loved, we shopped and we got our hair and nails done. Our conversations included which brand of bras were best for the well-endowed, how to use a hair iron, the stigma attached to being forty and single, where the nearest outlet mall was, the phenomenon of 'stepping' – a synchronised dance Patricia Haley told me was popularised in African-American culture and designed to utilise the body as an instrument of sound, which produces a powerful visual and audible rhythmic flow usually accompanied by chants, hand claps, and distinctive 'Step Show' formations by the performing groups. I sat back on our nights out and just watched.

During our chats I also realised my need to brush up on 'Black American lingo'. I loved the language and hoped I could somehow incorporate it into future stories. I practised my Texan drawl by saying 'y'all' a lot, while the more polite local authors practised their Aussie accents in private, letting it slip out mid-conversation on occasion. I loved it. We laughed some more. Laughter, as well as stories of segregation, racism and hard histories, united us during the conference and keeps me in their network. Sometimes I wonder if whitefellas know how much we actually laugh, when you consider the grim stories they read about us in the mainstream media and what they see in many of our more popular films such as *Beneath Clouds* and *Samson and Delilah*.

I wished the Australian public could've seen me in Las Vegas with women from California, Florida and Virginia as we headed to the Elvis Wedding Chapel on 9th Street. We were treated to a twenty-minute tour that apparently took longer than the average wedding ceremony there. Our 'Elvis' was really named Kent, he swivelled his hips, put on his blue suede shoes and gold jacket, gave me some red plastic flowers, planted a kiss on my cheek and 'married me'. I put one of my 'mock wedding photos' on Facebook and sent my friends into a frenzy and my brother Mark into typical protective-brother mode, commenting, 'That bloke had better be fast, cos when I catch him I'm gonna bash the shit out of him.'

That night (officially my wedding night) five of us women hired a car and headed to the Nevada/California border to see the Queen of Soul, Aretha Franklin, perform. The experience of seeing Re-Re (as my sistas called her) in a stunning red frock completely owning the stage was nothing short of one of the most spiritual moments of my life. The workshop earlier that day had helped me understand the nature of spiritual experiences beyond the environmental and community landscape from which I mostly write and live.

On my final night in Vegas, my new bestie Dawn McCoy and I treated ourselves to Chef Joho's Eiffel Tower restaurant as part of my travel story research. I was as much fascinated by Vegas's obsession with re-imagining icons that belong elsewhere – the Eiffel Tower, Luxor, the Chrysler Building – as I was interested in seeing how French cuisine might survive in a city with all-you-can-eat buffets for under ten dollars.

I'm surprised that Vegas doesn't have a hotel in the form of Uluru, especially given the success of Marlo Morgan's fictional *Mutant Message Down Under*. And I cross my fingers as I write this that no-one thinks to build an Uluru hotel in Vegas.

Over dinner, Dawn and I realised the extent of our commonalities as Black women and ability to rise above many of the negatives that keep our own people oppressed. I learned that Dawn had a Masters degree in Public Policy from Georgetown University, that she was about to release her book *Leadership Building Blocks: An Insider's Guide to Success* and that she was among the youngest African-American leaders elected to the Sacramento City Unified School Board in 2002, one of the nation's top fifty largest school systems with 46,000 students. At the time she was also managing the Martin Luther King Junior Centre in Richmond, Virginia. I was impressed beyond belief at not only the achievements of this woman, but her stamina and sense of positivity. I wasn't surprised to learn then that she, like me, had a life-coach. It all fell into place. Setting goals, developing strategies to reach them, being focused on positive outcomes achieved through hard work was something we both valued. Life-coaches weren't just for white people in CEO roles in private industry. They were for Black women writers who want to make change through being leaders within our own communities. Dawn remains one of my greatest inspirations, motivators and friends.

I left Las Vegas with renewed enthusiasm as a writer and as

a strong Black woman with a purpose, and I looked forward to the 2010 conference that was to be held in Atlanta. Always creating writing opportunities wherever I can, I pitched a travel story on Black Atlanta to the *Brisbane News*. The editor responded, 'I do take the occasional freelance travel piece and this would seem a good one so thanks – and yes.' I was excited about the prospect of bringing what I would learn to the readers in urban Brisbane and planned to research the story before the conference proper started.

When locals talk about Atlanta, they brag about their new Georgia Aquarium and its world's largest collection of aquatic animals. Or else they smile about being the birthplace and home of Coca-Cola. And when they talk about the Atlanta Braves, they mean their national baseball team. But to me the attraction of Atlanta was not marine life or fizzy drink, and although the thought of men in tights was appealing – let's face it, there's just not enough of it here in Australia – the 'bravery' I wanted to learn about is that demonstrated through the life of people like Dr Martin Luther King Junior, who was born in Atlanta and was the first Georgian to win the Nobel Peace Prize in 1964 for his role in the civil rights movement; for leading a racial minority in their struggle for equality and organising consistently peaceful demonstrations including the 50,000-men march on Washington in December 1955 when he was only twenty-six years old.

It was stiflingly hot when I arrived at the end of June 2010, and although Atlanta is a city of over 500,000 people, after Sydney it was like a sleepy country town. My first stop was to visit the Martin Luther King Junior National Historic Site, where I began my day at the Sweet Auburn Freedom Walk. I then visited the Ebenezer Baptist church, the location of many meetings and rallies during the civil rights movement era and where King was co-pastor and his funeral service was held in 1968. Across the road the Visitors' Centre moved me to tears with powerful installations, including images, text, original film footage and sound recordings giving the history of segregation and the 'Jim Crow' laws that enforced it. As I tried to absorb the horror of what life in the south was like from the 1880s to the 1960s, someone walked through the centre singing 'We Shall Overcome', and it sent shivers up my spine. At the King Centre I saw Dr King's tomb and the Eternal Flame that burns. At Freedom Hall I strolled through small exhibits that recognised King's relationship with Gandhi – whom he regarded as his mentor – and others on Rosa Parks and Coretta Scott King, Dr King's wife who stepped into the role of community leader immediately following her husband's assassination.

Along Auburn Street, tourists, students and locals visited King's birthplace and the historic Fire Station No. 6, which has exhibitions telling the story of the desegregation of the city's fire department. Further along, the African-American Panoramic Experience (APEX) Museum had movies, installations and timelines showcasing the history of Blacks in Georgian politics as well as musicians from Georgia like Otis Redding, James Brown and Gladys Knight. There's also a series of works on Black American inventors; the automatic stop signal for traffic lights was invented by Garrett Morgan from Kentucky.

As you can imagine, processing such emotional history was exhausting, and I needed to sit and think, and eat. I headed to the Sweet Auburn Curb Market, which has country produce, cheap books and deli counters. Locals had recommended I try the Grindhouse Burger (with lettuce, grilled onions, pickles, gooey American cheese and the special Grindhouse sauce). I devoured their signature burger and fries (I'd walked miles so it was okay) and sat among hospital staff, office workers, lawyers and labourers. I wanted to ask the Grindhouse staff what an Apache Style Burger was, but I didn't have the energy to argue about the commercialisation of Native American culture. That being said, the Atlanta Braves once had mascots named Chief Noc-A-Homa and Princess Win-A-Lotta and other national sports teams also appropriate Native names, like the Cleveland Indians, the Washington Redskins (who have been taken to court about changing the name) and the University of North Dakota's Fighting Sioux.

As a writer I am inspired by the history of literature in all the places I visit internationally, and Atlanta was no different. I took a tour through Margaret Mitchell's house, the birthplace of the Pulitzer Prize-winning epic southern historical romance *Gone with the Wind*. There were mixed views on the novel from locals, both Black and white, I spoke with there. Some hated the stereotypes in the novel, while others were grateful the film version gave Hattie McDaniel the opportunity to be the first African American to win an Academy Award. What many don't know is that while Mitchell may have perpetuated stereotypes in her novel, she fought for international copyright laws for US authors, she funded an emergency room for African Americans at the Grady Hospital in Atlanta and set up a scholarship fund for local Black students to study medicine.

Joe Chandler Harris, author of the Uncle Remus tales – African-American animal stories Chandler recorded and retold with a fictionalised narrator – was another Atlanta author. His home 'Wren's Nest' is the city's oldest house museum and maintains its original furniture and books. The local woman who toured me through the estate told me that as a child she wasn't allowed onto the property by its administrators because she was Black, but she doesn't believe that was something Harris would ever have endorsed.

On my cultural tour of Atlanta's Black artists I was probably most excited about going to Gladys Knight and Ron Winan's Chicken & Waffles restaurant, a local institution.

The conference itself was again a total inspiration, but some of the most important conversations happened outside the workshop rooms. On my last day there, I sat by the pool with Robin Buncamper from Brooklyn, who introduced me to the phrase made famous by comedian Paul Mooney: 'Everyone wants to be Black until the police arrive.' A few weeks after the conference finished I spent two full days writing my Atlanta travel story in a steaming room in Barcelona, home of my friend Julie Wark, a literary translator – English to Catalan and vice versa. I sent the story off to the *Brisbane*

News along with dozens of high resolution photos supplied by organisations in Atlanta. Three months later when I followed the story up, I received an email from the editor: 'We've looked into your Atlanta story and, I'm sorry, but the images you supplied were not suitable and there is very little in our picture library that would hold up the story well enough. Sorry, but I am unable to use the piece after all.'

Needless to say I was furious. I had spent days researching and writing the story. I felt that it had nothing to do with the images because I could've sourced more if they'd wanted me to. In my view, it was about the content being 'too Black' and too political for Brisbane's inner-city whitefellas. Bearing in mind that only 1.7 per cent of Brisbane's population are Indigenous, perhaps the editor thought my article was not relevant to their mostly white middle-class readership. I sent the article on to Kirstie Parker, editor of *The Koori Mail*. They ran the story without any changes and many of the photos I'd offered the *Brisbane News*.

~

Of all the cities in the world, I love New York (and downtown Manhattan) the most – after Sydney, naturally. It is one of the few places I can say I feel truly at home. It is the least conservative city in the US and is a melting pot of cultures, lifestyles and ideas. I felt so at home when I was staying in SoHo in the summer of 2008 that I decided while there I'd write a book set in Manhattan, ergo *Manhattan Dreaming*. When I went back to research the novel in the middle of winter in January 2009, I ended up having one of the most extraordinary days of my life, in the top ten with my Las Vegas wedding and Aretha experience.

I had planned my research trip to coincide with Barack Obama's inauguration. While I had no plans to go to the ceremony proper in Washington, DC, I intended being part of whatever celebrations were going on in New York City, to be part of the historical moment. I began the day with breakfast with Matilde Busana – an expat-Aussie friend – at the Empire Diner in Chelsea, then got the subway to 125th Street where we jumped into a car with a driver who was intrigued to have two Aussie passengers. 'Are there a lot of kangaroos?' he asked. We got out at the 369th Harlem Armory on Martin Luther King Drive and stood in the below-zero temperature, warmed not only by our thermal underwear but by the chanting of hundreds of people – school students, parents, community members, officials, friends and media making their way inside the Armory hall until the crowd was 5000 strong.

We queued with hundreds of others at about 10 am to get into the hall. Behind us in line was Greg Western, the principal of the Democracy Preparatory Charter School who were hosting the event, and his wife Michelle. They were as thrilled and excited as we were to be part of the 'Inauguration of a Dream – A Celebration of Choice, Voice and Democracy in Harlem' – the slogan emblazoned throughout the hall. Busloads of schoolkids arrived excited, dancing on the spot and chanting, 'O-ba-ma.' Shivers made their way up and down my spine seeing them engaging in the political moment and movement, something not seen much in Australia among school students. Inside the hall we watched live footage of the ceremony and numerous school acts drumming and singing. Schoolkids sat at tables working frantically to make posters to hold up as part of the celebration. I also watched a character in front of me who kept shaking his baby in the air whenever he cheered; it made me recall that health campaign back home with the slogan 'Never shake a baby . . . '

It's hard to find the words to explain adequately the emotion that the day evoked in me, an outsider to the community that saw enormous hope and a sense of justice in seeing a brother as president of their country. I saw a strong, capable, articulate, educated Black man become head of a nation that has an incredible influence over the world, especially Australia. The 1960s Freedom Rides and our civil rights action through the FCAATSI and other groups have been directly related to what was happening in the US at the time, and our youth is heavily influenced by the States in terms of music and even gang culture.

My extraordinary 'research day' wasn't over however as Matilde had picked up a ticket to a concert called 'Australia Plays Broadway', running as part of the G'Day USA Tourism Australia campaign. The Australian dollar was so weak at the time that I nearly fell off my wooden chair in my rented Chelsea walk-up apartment when I learned the ticket prices translated to around A$200. I didn't even know who was on the bill, but I did know I'd have to get at least 1000 words out of it for the novel.

Sitting in our box, I felt like Julia Roberts in *Pretty Woman*, and I scanned the space looking for Richard Gere or anyone else that was recognisable. I laughed to myself as all the accents I could hear from the audience were Australian, although the purpose of the campaign was to build relationships with American audiences and potential American tourists. The night included performances by the forty-strong Qantas Kids Choir, the Adelaide Symphony Orchestra, and Jimmy Barnes and son David Campbell. The weirdest moment of the night had to be when Jimmy and David sang 'You've Lost That Loving Feeling' – not really an appropriate father/son duet song, is it? And no-one can ever do it better than Tom Cruise in *Top Gun* anyhow. Now that was entertaining . . . but I digress, again!

These acts weren't anything I could really use in my book. Why would I? These were musos most Australians and some Americans knew. I wanted to showcase Aboriginal artists, our culture, so my $200 was not looking like it was well-spent at all, until . . . William Barton walked down the centre aisle singing in language before taking to the stage and playing the didge. At one point he played some heavy metal on an electric guitar while still playing the didge simultaneously. Soon after, Ursula Yovich graced the stage in a long white gown and sang 'Somewhere over the Rainbow'. The absolute highlight for me was hearing Geoffrey Gurrumul Yunupingu. It was hard to see him on stage though as I cried through the entire performance sung in his Yolngu language while I tried to make notes for the novel and worried about the extent of mascara damage on my face. We still had intermission to get through, and there's nothing elegant about standing in line for a glass of bubbly looking like Alice Cooper!

I was also in New York a week later for Australia Day, which I spent with some Australian friends. I had to 'research' for the novel, and did what my character Lauren would do, which included going to the Australian Hotel because it's owned by ex-footballer Matt Astill and Lauren was in love with a footballer back in Canberra. When we arrived, it was jam-packed with Aussies. I almost felt unpatriotic: I wasn't wearing a green-and-gold headband reading 'Made in Australia'. And I didn't have a rugby union sweatshirt on, nor did I have the Australian flag tied around my neck, á la Pauline Hanson – and I couldn't understand why anyone else would. I was looking for the Aboriginal flag, somewhere, anywhere. I realised I'd have to send one to Matt to put in the bar, but in the novel I made sure there was one there – the joys of writing fiction.

I felt quite embarrassed that day by the drunken Aussie-dom and momentarily felt like I was in Cronulla in December 2005, without the violence or the racism, of course. I was being dramatic. I can be. I am a Leo and I am a writer, and I tend to get away with a lot.

Chapter 14

THE OPRAH INFLUENCE

'THERE ARE STILL A LOT OF BLACK PEOPLE
WHO ARE VERY ANGRY AND BITTER. THEY
WANT ME TO BE JUST AS ANGRY AND BITTER,
AND I WON'T BE. IT JUST BURNS ME. SOME
BLACK PEOPLE SAY I'M NOT BLACK ENOUGH. I
WONDER, HOW BLACK DO YOU HAVE TO BE?
THE DRUMS OF AFRICA STILL BEAT IN MY
HEART, AND THEY WILL NOT REST UNTIL EVERY
BLACK BOY AND GIRL HAS HAD A CHANCE TO
PROVE THEIR WORTH.'

OPRAH

While the greatest personal influences in my life have been Aboriginal women, particularly my mum, I also have major professional mentors and friends in non-Aboriginal women writers – Rosie Scott, Pamela Freeman and Frané Lessac, to name a few – and one of my major international role models and motivators in recent years has been Oprah Winfrey. The previous quote from George Mair's biography, *Oprah Winfrey: The Real Story* (1994), reminds me that you don't have to be angry to be Black. And you don't have to be Black to be my mentor either.

My friend Rosie I met when I joined the management committee of the Australian Society of Authors back in 1998. We became instant friends, some might say allies, through sharing an active interest in social justice. Rosie is from Aotearoa/New Zealand, but has long been involved in rights for refugees and Aboriginal people in Australia. Mum loves Rosie: she was there when Dad died and brought chocolates over. Mum has never forgotten that and neither have I. I admire my friend not just for her writing life (*Faith Singer* is one of my favourite novels), but because of her ongoing and tireless efforts working in the area of social justice via PEN International and Women for Wik. Rosie penned a quote on free speech for me to originally use in my keynote address at the New South Wales Premier's Literary Awards in 2011. She gave me the nod to use it again in my statement following the judgment on the Bolt case, and it was quoted many times in the media and by Ron Merkel on the ABC television show *Q&A*.

Another important writerly friend is Pamela Freeman, and nearly every time Pamela and I meet there is something to celebrate: usually she has a new book out in a trilogy, or there's a publishing deal in the US or UK. Pamela doesn't drink, so our lunches are dry and we toast with what we have named 'the chubby girls' bubbly' – Diet Coke. After having dinner with Rosie or lunch with Pamela I always, without fail, feel inspired and reinvigorated. I am reminded of how fortunate I am to have some caring, kind, generous women in my world.

Frané Lessac, a WA-based illustrator, is someone who supports me via Skype, since she lives on the west coast in Fremantle. Frané is one of those people you can't help but like. She is always up, positive, happy and fun to be around. Frané is non-Aboriginal, but works extensively with kids in remote communities on illustration workshops. Her capacity to make change through her work is an inspiration to me also.

I've always been a big dreamer because it costs nothing but my time – not that I have a lot of that to spare – and what is a life without dreams anyway? When I meet people without aspirations for what they can be, and what the world can be for that matter, I feel a little sad for them. That may sound condescending but, to me, not being able to imagine yourself as a greater human than you already are suggests that there is no room for personal, spiritual or professional improvement and growth. I don't know many who don't need improving on some level, and I'm at the top of the 'need to' list.

Like most of my peers, I am always wanting to be better

at everything: living life, giving back, being there for family and friends, writing well, respecting my body. I want to 'live my best life', as Oprah's famous mantra suggests. I am the queen of clichés when it comes to having a full life – 'This isn't a dress rehearsal!', 'We only go round once,' and 'You're a long time dead!' are just a few of my chosen phrases when justifying behaviour or an activity that some may consider indulgent or unnecessary, like eating chocolate every day or buying that extra pair of shoes.

Part of my 'living life to the fullest' philosophy includes the desire to make change on a global level, if possible, through my work. I have always thought big, wanted big, expected big, behaved big, and sometimes I've delivered big. To me, this is just an extension of my drive to be positive, to be an optimist, to be able to see the brightness in the dark. Working with my life-coach Geraldine over the years has taught me that the cloud needn't have a silver lining when it can have a platinum one.

In fact, the only time I have been accused of being a pessimist was by one of my high school Maths teachers. I was aware then as I am now of my strengths and my weaknesses. I choose to focus on what I am good at, preferring to hone those skills rather than waste time on what does not come naturally to me, what does not inspire me and what does not figure as a priority in my life. I knew enough at sixteen to understand that I wouldn't be using the Pythagorean theorem in any aspect of my future career, and so I didn't beat myself up about mastering it as part of my two-unit Maths course.

But when I failed to stress over not being able to solve a mathematical equation and gave up easily, my Maths teacher would become frustrated. He wrote in my school report not only my miserable C grade, but that I had a pessimistic attitude towards Maths. But really, does *anyone* have an optimistic attitude towards geometry or statistics?

What I did have at the time, and retain as a strength, is a capacity – outside of the classroom – to 'get on with it' in times of dire emotional upheaval, an ability that has nothing to do with numbers. Aside from when my father was diagnosed with terminal cancer and I lost the plot for some days as shock and grieving overwhelmed me, I have always been able to get myself out of bed and to my desk even in my darkest moments. I may have sat there staring at the monitor and cried for hours, but I always met my deadlines, got the job done and continued to do what my life required, especially in areas where others depended on me professionally and personally. I do have down days, and I have had some very dark periods in my life related to personal tragedy, heartbreak, politics and my working environments, but mostly I try to be up. I work at it. I use positive affirmations and mantras and place my trust in the universe and Biami – the creator spirit of the Wiradjuri – like my characters Alice Aigner and Libby Cutmore do. And I have never played the victim, something Oprah Winfrey has never done either.

While I was never professionally diagnosed, I think I battled with a level of depression for many years after my father's passing. I got through it by exercising, working and keeping away from negative individuals and other forces that could easily drag me down. I'm grateful that I have been able to surround myself throughout my life with positive people, that I can draw on my own sense of spirituality and that I have enough going on in my life to remain intellectually stimulated. And I think that mental stimulation was also a key to not falling into a much greater pit of despair. I'm grateful that in those dark moments of my life when I can't breathe from stress or heartache that I have not had to resort to medication or the need to drag other people down with me in order to prop myself up. I have found many moments of extreme happiness in the happiness of those closest to me, like Michelle, Robynne, Terri, Frané, Bernardine and Rosie. Admittedly, though, as I've grown older and seen the impact of my own emotions on those who care about me, I have also retreated in times of absolute sadness to save the domino effect that it can often cause. Such moments have generally centred on the heartache of lost loves, regret around my own foolishness and times of extreme low self-esteem related to both.

I always try to find the positive in every negative, and have learned my ability to laugh in the face of adversity from people like Kerry Reed-Gilbert. Nearly every conversation we have includes her saying at least once, 'You've gotta laugh, babe!' and 'We'll get there!' And she is absolutely right. Laughter has been the tool that has kept Aboriginal people sane over 200 years of oppression. In the anthology *Serious Frolic: Essays on Australian Humour*, edited by Fran De Groen and Peter Kirkpatrick, educator Lillian Holt suggests that Aboriginal humour is 'gentle' and that self-deprecation eases oppression. Her essay is the result of conversations she's had with Blackfellas around Australia on the topic of humour, conversations which determined that our humour is 'spontaneous, part of ordinary life, happening here and now'. She goes on to show that humour can cut the tension between truth and stereotype by reversing such stereotypes. Humour is included in Lillian's list of the five Hs needed for Australia to progress through the thorny terrain of race relations in this country – the other Hs being History, Honesty, Humanity and Hope.

Through watching Oprah's broadcasting and media journey and reading about her life in the past few years (Geraldine gave me a set of books and the twenty-fifth anniversary DVD boxed set for my forty-first birthday), I've come to understand the importance – as Oprah believes – of self-faith and optimism. I am a fan of Oprah for many reasons, one of them because I believe she is a realistic and positive role model for women (particularly of colour) around the world. Born in Kosciusko, Mississippi, she grew up in poverty, began presenting the Nashville news when she was nineteen and moved to Baltimore in 1976, where she was paired with an anchorman who, she says, didn't want a young Black female co-anchor. It was a time when there were very few Black women on American television and certainly none here in Australia.

Oprah recalls in her twenty-fifth anniversary DVD that she walked into the office of program director Dennis Swanson, who gave her her first big break, and said to him as a pre-emptive measure: 'I'm Black and that's not going to change. I'm overweight and that's probably not going to change either.' When I heard and read this story, it dawned on me that it was an important one. Oprah had found her success despite the fact she had a poor childhood riddled with sexual abuse and a professional life full of mainly white males, controlling her career. At no time, however, did she ever let her race, skin colour or her body image interfere with her goals. This is a message that I needed to hear and to adhere to!

Oprah was already breaking new ground through her work when I was still in primary school. The first episode of her own talk show, *People Are Talking*, aired on 14 August 1978, my tenth birthday. When Oprah herself was ten, she watched 'coloured' actor Sidney Poitier win an Academy Award for *Lilies of the Field*. 'I'm coloured, what can I do?' she asked herself. As George Mair writes in *Oprah Winfrey: The Real Story*, by the age of sixteen Oprah 'possessed a driving ambition and a determination to be somebody'.

Years later she had proven to herself what she could in fact do as a woman of colour, and admits that when she finally had Poitier on her show, someone she had admired all her life, it was the toughest thing she'd ever done. After the taping Oprah says she went into the control room and broke down. She couldn't remember what she said in the interview. I imagine that if I were ever to meet Oprah, she would be *my* Poitier moment. As an aside, I watched the interview with Poitier and in it he says that his father believed that the measure of a man is how he cares for his children. It reminded me of the greatness of my own father, who provided tangible necessities (a home, clothes, food and education, etc.) and emotional support as well.

I want to be as successful as Oprah in influencing people, in making the world a more giving, generous, kinder place. When beginning her own show, Oprah asked herself how she could best contribute to change. It is a question that I have asked myself many times. In Oprah's case, she uses her position to tell the stories of other people, to humanise their stories for mass audiences. Although she has strong opinions (as do I), she keeps herself in check, always focused on what her guests have to say. This skill or quality is something I need to work on.

It's the positive energy around Oprah the woman and the brand that I believe attracts so many people to her universe, whether watching her show, reading her magazine or being a member of her book club. Oprah says that you cannot allow yourself to be a vehicle that promotes the energy of hatred in any forum, and this is what sets her apart from those who think they can make change through constantly denigrating others. When I see Blackfellas on social networking sites trashing other Blackfellas, trashing whitefellas, trashing anyone with an opposing opinion, way of life, religion, taste in music, whatever, I realise how damaging their words are, not only to those who read and engage with them, but to themselves. How can you possibly be an agent of positive change in the world when you are full of bitterness and hatred?

I think Oprah's honesty about her own flaws endears her

to many. She doesn't just do stories about others' insecurities, she has also been upfront about her own weight battles and has never let body image stop her being what and who she wants to be. In researching the 'Oprah ingredient for success' for my own career development, I learned a lot from the way she handled difficult shows she taped over the years, particularly those dealing with racism and other forms of prejudice and discrimination. In a show on Forsyth County in Georgia in 1987, where no Black people had lived for over thirty years, Oprah managed an angry, blatantly racist white audience, while Blacks picketed outside the venue and criticised her for not letting them in. Oprah said at the time that living as a minority she felt a responsibility to bring issues of race to her audiences, and that she deals with prejudice by understanding that prejudice is ignorance.

One of the most significant Oprah comments for me personally came at a time when I was preparing for the court case against the Herald and Weekly Times. Oprah was talking about the court case she was part of against Texas cattlemen, who were suing her in relation to her comment about never eating another burger when she did a show on mad cow disease. On reflecting on the court experience where lawyers yelled at her and described her a certain way, she just said to herself, calmly, 'The person he described is not who I am.' When I heard that line it was exactly how I felt about what had been written about me in that column. I was not the person he wrote that I was and it was that simple, and I took comfort in that, just as Oprah did.

~

I went to see Oprah at the Sydney Opera House in December 2010, during the much-publicised filming of her show in Australia. It was an incredible journey just to get to the event on the day. I had been liaising with Austrade staff in New York since the previous July, trying to strategise the best way to get in front of her people and onto her show that was taped in Chicago. I wanted to talk about something I knew she was passionate about: books and literacy.

With support from friends designing campaign flyers, a Facebook page dedicated to getting me on the show and my agent, life-coach and friends sending emails off to producers via the Oprah website, the mere thought of making it onto her show was enough to get the adrenalin pumping. I had never set myself a goal that I hadn't reached – except maybe weight loss – and I was determined that this would be no different. My life-coach Geraldine had registered for the lottery that was being held to allocate audience tickets to the show, and she told me I should as well and I registered my mum too. Never did I imagine that out of the hundreds of thousands of registrants that I would get lucky.

At 5.30 am on Monday, 8 November 2010, I lay in bed contemplating my 6.30 am training session in Bondi Junction. I checked my emails. There, in my inbox, was an email congratulating me on securing my ticket to the 14 December taping. I couldn't believe it. Later that day I would secure a publishing deal for this very book. It was excitement-plus from 5.30 am on as friends and family expressed friendly jealousy at my luck in the draw. My hairdresser, optometrist and mechanic were all thrilled at my win. Aboriginal women from around the country asked if they could be my plus-one, but I had promised that I would take Geraldine. After all, without her pushing I wouldn't have even gone in the draw.

On the day of the taping I was exhausted from nervous energy and lack of sleep before I even sat down in the audience at the Oprah House. I'd been up since 4 am preparing for the 5 am arrival of my friend Felicia Yong, who wanted to do my hair and makeup. Belinda Miller from National Indigenous Television (NITV) and Ming D'Arcy, her cameraman, arrived at 5.30 am to begin interviewing and filming for their new entertainment and lifestyle show *The Gathering*. When the cab arrived nearing 7 am, I donned a black cotton frock, some comfy heals and my all-important good-luck charm: the Australian Society of Authors medal designed by Darrell Sibosado. Aware of the YouTube video done by Bev Manton, chair of the NSW Aboriginal Land Council, on living conditions of Aboriginal people in the Northern Territory, particularly those under the Intervention, I was also aware of the desperate measures many others were using to get information to Oprah, so I stuffed a copy of *This Is What We Said: Australian Aboriginal People Give Their Views on the Northern Territory Intervention* into my purple handbag, hoping I'd get the opportunity to pass it on to one of Oprah's people. Belinda put a copy of my novel *Who Am I? The Diary of Mary Talence, Sydney 1937* in her bag and we were on our way into the city.

It was no surprise that the queue was already flooding Macquarie Street when we arrived after 7 am. Geraldine and I stood alongside 6000 others also antsy to see Oprah live. It was like queuing for a rock concert but without the pushing or the noise. Rather, it was a hushed mass of people moving in an eerie, peaceful silence as we edged closer to the Opera House forecourt. Along the way, I made small talk with the women around me. Many of them had travelled from Melbourne, Perth, Adelaide and Newcastle, all grateful for being there. I spotted a couple of Blackfellas in the distance as well.

Nearing the ticketing area, the crowd erupted as the television icon arrived in her black Audi, waving out the window and thanking us all for coming. It was a surreal moment, only ruined by the bogan anthem, 'Aussie, Aussie, Aussie, Oi, Oi, Oi', chanted by people who needed to be further away from me than they were! Inside the boundary we sat under a perfect Sydney sky at Bennelong Point – the site of the first recorded corroboree, otherwise known as a bush opera, back in 1790 – and waited for the Queen of Television to make her way to the stage. She came out in a hot orange frock with a seed necklace designed by Judy Hosking, an artist based in Wauchope, south of Tennant Creek.

For the next ninety minutes the person who is arguably the world's most influential woman gave her blessing to the country she now loves, we danced in our seats to Bon Jovi and learned of the meeting Oprah had orchestrated between rapper Jay-Z and the students of Canterbury Boys High School (who all received their own laptop). Russell Crowe gave some social and cultural insight into the Aussie psyche (including the 'tall poppy' syndrome), a young father suffering from cancer got a cheque for $250,000 and audience members were treated to a stunning Kailis pearl pendant.

I sat there wondering why so many of the show's guests were American or Hollywood stars. Light bulb: it was a Tourism Australia gig. The US guests talked about how and why they loved Australia because Americans need to hear the plug from their own countrymen that they trust, and the Aussies were those that Americans already knew! Simple. I realised that when the shows would eventually go to air, the world would see the best Tourism Australia advert ever and for a somewhat cheaper price than the production costs of the film *Australia*! I am confident that some of our greatest winners from Oprah's visit will be our own Indigenous tourism industry and tour operators, particularly in the Northern Territory.

As we filed out slowly from the taping, I considered the formula for Oprah's success and how a poor Black girl from Mississippi found herself the most influential woman in the world, now standing at the Sydney Opera House. Oprah's concepts are basic: be genuine, be interested in the stories of others, be positive, be generous and be grateful for the good things in your life. On 30 November 2009 I began keeping a gratefulness blog, similar to the 'gratefulness journal' that

Oprah keeps. It's the blog that Andrew Bolt had pulled the photo of my mother from when I wrote about the tangible items I was grateful for. For almost a year I kept a daily list of five things I am/was grateful for. These could include people, places, emotions, foods, films, books and so on. It was a new and practical way for me to document in writing all that is good in my life, focus on the positives and share the love, so to speak. I found over time that those on my fan page on Facebook also appreciated the blogs and would offer their own gratefuls as well.

During Black History Month 2011, celebrated in February in the US, Canada and the UK to mark and educate people about the achievements and cultures of those of African and Caribbean heritage, I invited my colleagues from the Black Writers Reunion and Conference to guest blog about things they were grateful for. The blog posts from Bryan-Keyth Wilson, Nakia R. Laushaul, Dawn McCoy, Patricia Haley, Bonita Penn Lee, Sherrice Thomas and Alicia Williams were moving. Through their words on my blog, a cross-fertilisation began in terms of blog visitors to my space and my own visitors venturing to the sites of these amazing Black writers.

I find similar food for the soul at major events where Blackfellas gather. The annual Survival concerts that began on 26 January 1992 at La Perouse have become one of the most significant gatherings not only for Blackfellas in the inner city, but for Kooris who travel from around the state to share the meaning of 26 January – the tragedy of Invasion Day and the survival of our people and cultures. Over time, the festival has changed names from Survival to Yabun (a Gadigal word meaning 'song with a beat') and has changed venues from La Perouse, to Waverley Oval, to Redfern Park to Victoria Park. Its most recent location caters for larger audiences, is accessible, is near a local pool and has more shade than was ever provided previously. Even Blackfellas need to get out of the sun. I've always relished the opportunity to catch up with friends and family at Survival/Yabun – some who live within close proximity to me, some whom I only see at this festival and family funerals. This reunion of sorts is what drives me most years to go to the event.

I was particularly moved in 2008 when dance groups from the four corners of New South Wales welcomed crowds to Victoria Park through corroboree. I stood alongside then minister for Local Government, Aboriginal Affairs and Mental Health Paul Lynch and I smiled. The sun was streaming down upon us as the sounds of the didgeridoo and clap sticks echoed across the park. I even felt momentarily maternal as I watched a young Koori boy of no more than five years of age dancing for the crowds. He was so cute. And he was the future of our people in front of us. We had survived the past 220 years since the point of first contact, and we would survive another.

Collectively, our non-Indigenous friends, international visitors and officials such as the Lord Mayor, Clover Moore, councillor Marcelle Hoff, the governor of New South Wales, Her Excellency Marie Bashir, and federal MP Tanya Plibersek, validated what we already knew: that 26 January marks a significant moment for Aboriginal peoples in recognising the consequences of invasion and colonisation, and how these acts continue to impact upon us as Australian citizens.

That day in 2008 was also the first time I ever made a blog post and marked the 70th anniversary of the 1938 Day of Mourning Protest and Conference in Sydney – a landmark moment in the civil rights movement in Australia. So I wanted to make it clear in my blog post that it was important that while celebrating we not only focused on acknowledging those warriors who had fought for human rights for our people until now, but also took the opportunity to discuss the current state of affairs for our people, including the Northern Territory legislation, the issue of an apology, the road to reconciliation and so on.

Over 12,000 festival goers that day made it clear that we weren't on this journey alone, and as I strolled the park in my capacity as chair of Gadigal Information Services, I knew that the tide had turned, that 2008 was going to be a positive year on many fronts for Aboriginal Australia. I knew this because I'd just heard award-winning authors Tara June Winch and Romaine Moreton talking about their books and I saw Kutcha Edwards, Shelley Morris and the band Whitehouse among other top quality musicians on stage. I knew we were going to thrive because I watched people in the AIATSIS tent talking about their family histories, and I saw a visual display of photographer Mervyn Bishop documenting the history of Yabun festivals to date.

I joked with the minister and offered to pay the two dollars so he could have his face painted. He declined. I shared stories with the governor about The Black Arm Band's performance at the Sydney Opera House earlier in the week. I don't know one person who wasn't in awe of their show. For what it's worth, I believe that performance was one of the best of any kind that I had ever seen, and I had *never* seen the Concert Hall so rocking.

Back to Yabun 2008. After lunch, I sat under a tree with Kerry Reed-Gilbert, who was there to launch her sister Minmia's book *Under the Quandong Tree*. We caught up as people do when they go to Yabun. I yahooed (because I can't whistle) as I watched young kids on the dance stage learning to breakdance. I had a helmet, tracksuit pants and a piece of cardboard myself ready to go, but didn't think the then thirty-nine-year-old chair should embarrass herself. I spent most of the day with a dreadful headache because I didn't drink enough water (because, to be honest, I hate portaloos and so was trying to lessen the need to go!). But I was filled with the spirit of unity that marks every Yabun Festival, and I felt so much alive. The sense of unity that most Kooris feel at Yabun comes not only from all the Blackfellas that travel across country to be part of the day, but from all our supporters. What I saw was a diverse crowd that spoke volumes about the way in which Australians think about and choose to celebrate 26 January in our country today.

~

Another monumental day that I was grateful for in my life was Wednesday 13 February. I was in Canberra for the official government apology to the Stolen Generations, but the day before there had been a national rally to get the Intervention troops out of the Northern Territory. The rally saw people travel across the country specifically to declare their disgust at the racist legislation. I met one young Nyungah woman who had travelled from Perth. We met as the crowds gathered at the site of the Tent Embassy on the lawns of Old Parliament House. We stood there after Ngambri elder Matilda House had welcomed politicians to the forty-second sitting of Parliament – a groundbreaking moment in Australian political history – as our government was recognising in its formalities, prior and continual land ownership by Aboriginal people.

After we were given a welcome by the Tent Embassy mob at the ceremonial fire, we marched, led by our brothers and sisters from the Northern Territory. I marched alongside friends from the Australian National University, others I went to university with twenty years ago, supporters of Residents for Reconciliation in Western Sydney I'd met ten years previously, family members I was meeting for the first time, local school students in full uniform, and many others (Black and white) who were united under the banner: 'STOP THE INTERVENTION – HUMAN RIGHTS NOW'. Also supporting us was federal Greens leader Bob Brown.

There were many familiar faces there on the day, some locally from Sydney and others from across the country. Activist Sam Watson Senior and daughter, lawyer Nicole were there. The band Street Warriors and poets Kerry Reed-Gilbert and Elizabeth Hodgson were there. It truly was a convergence of Blackfellas on Canberra all fighting for the rights of our brothers and sisters in the Northern Territory. I noticed that even though I'd rallied in four different states in the past fifteen years on issues such as land rights, Black deaths in custody, budget cuts to Aboriginal affairs, the Stolen Generations and the Intervention, this was the first rally I had ever participated in that didn't have police lining the streets or watching our moves. There was not *one* cop to be seen, until we arrived at Parliament House and saw they formed a protective coating to the building.

The wide range of media present spoke volumes about how the convergence on Canberra was being regarded generally. Apart from the expected Indigenous print, television and radio media, there was mainstream media from every medium. I won't 'out' any of the normally right-wing stations that employ the shock jocks I never listen to, but these outlets were covering the rally and interviewing key members of the Northern Territory representatives on-site. I was heartened by that because it meant that our issues, Australian issues, were getting mainstream coverage.

I spent much of my day with Aunty Eileen Cummings from the Northern Territory, whom I'd met at a Sydney gathering of Women for Wik (WFW) in 2007. Aunty Eileen was part of the WFW project to keep a check on what is happening in the Northern Territory in lieu of any formal accountability processes being put in place by the government. As a collective,

WFW supported the rally as a statement to the Rudd government that we demanded to see Aboriginal rights as a priority on their agenda. We wanted to see an end to the lack of respect for the First Nations peoples of this country, a lack of respect that had allowed racist legislation to be enacted and the human rights of Aboriginal Australians to be denied. We believed that an apology would be the first symbolic step in a process that would require actions and resources to ensure Aboriginal Australians retained control over our own lives.

When I listened and watched Aunty Eileen being interviewed by filmmaker and friend Richard Frankland, she made it perfectly clear what needed (and still needs) to be done in the Northern Territory: the government needs to start talking to communities, the Community Development Employment Program needs to be restored so that people can work and the quarantining of wages needs to end. She said, 'Our people need to get back the power to control what's happening in our communities. We're now reliving what happened to us as children when the Native Police came in. Right now in the Territory, I'm reminded of growing up on a mission settlement.'

The next day marked one of the pivotal moments in Australian history with the Apology. I headed to the parliamentary lawns with cousin Carol and met up with many friends and family. For me, there were so many emotional moments, especially when messages of 'Sorry' and support started flooding in via SMS and email on Monday. They reached a peak as the speeches ended and I stood among thousands on Parliament Hill, breathing in fresh air that was filled with hope, history, forgiveness and unity. Every time my phone rang or beeped, the lump in my throat grew. I was taking messages and calls from people all around the country. Some were ex-students of mine, others were people I'd been to primary school with. One message came from someone I met on the Gold Coast at schoolies in 1986!

I was just one of many Blackfellas who received an outpouring of love and support that day. While many of the people who contacted me didn't know each other, they generally had several things in common. Firstly, they were mainly non-Aboriginal. Secondly, they shared a common language that included terms like 'sorry', 'healing', 'relief', 'justice', 'hope', 'peace', 'solidarity', 'renewed hope', 'there in spirit' and 'moving forwards together'. These words were accompanied, I'm told, by a lot of emotion, many tears and boxes of tissues.

On the ground, I shared the joy of Kevin Rudd's words with my family and friends, but also with thousands of complete strangers standing around me. There were hugs and tears and sighs of relief. The applause that echoed around Parliament House came from Australians (and some tourists) who'd taken leave from their work and their normal daily lives to be part of one of the most pivotal moments in this nation's history.

To me, the Apology was about finding some peace for those stolen and our families, and there were many levels of relief experienced when Rudd finally said 'Sorry' – six times!

His carefully crafted and sincere words finally provided Australians of all denominations the opportunity to heal and share what was in their hearts. An apology from the national Parliament also legitimised what many had felt for a long time. I heard many non-Aboriginal Australians say that day that, 'I am so proud now to be Australian.' It seems to me that Kevin Rudd gave our nation a new sense of identity and perhaps a new sense of patriotism with his words.

The leader of the Opposition, Brendan Nelson, channelled John Howard through his speech, stating, 'Our generation does not own these actions, nor should it feel guilt for what was done in many, but certainly not all cases, with the best intentions.' I was one of the thousands on the day who turned their backs. I was disturbed by the sobbing of an elder next to me who cried out during Nelson's speech, 'Why? Why? Why?' Indeed, why did he have to take such a significant moment for our country, a healing moment, and turn it into a spiteful moment? The Liberal Party was left behind that day as the rest of Parliament and Australia made history for the betterment of our nation.

I remain emotional about what happened that day, because it filled me with hope and expectation for what we can do now to ensure real social equity and sovereignty for the First Peoples of Australia. I recognise, though, that not all Blackfellas had the same response to the symbolic gesture that I did, some seeing it as nothing more than lip-service, with no real change to the standard of living of Indigenous people. And although former Prime Minister Kevin Rudd and the Opposition Leader signed the Close the Gap Statement of Intent in March 2008, only weeks after the Apology, given the ongoing appalling issues of black deaths in custody and the government's Stronger Futures in the Northern Territory policy – which extends the Intervention – it's easy to be cynical about how much has really changed for our people on the ground, out there in the wider community. I am always conscious of our community's many issues and remind myself and others of them when we tend to whine about the mundane things in life. I am so incredibly fortunate on every level, and I make a point of celebrating this and choosing positivity over negativity.

THE TRIAL: JUDGMENT DAY

woke up early on Wednesday, 28 September 2011. I was anxious and wanted the day to pass quickly. In normal circumstances I may have been seedy, as it was the morning after the annual Deadly Awards for Aboriginal and Torres Strait Islander achievement, held at the Sydney Opera House. It's one of the few nights of the year when I go to bed after midnight. But the 2011 awards were difficult to enjoy, even though I took home the gong for Outstanding Achievement in Literature for *Paris Dreaming*. My night was tainted by the cloud that had been hovering over me for more than two years. I just wanted to get home, get a good night's sleep and be prepared for the outcome of the court case the next day.

I had always believed we would win. From the moment I decided to go in the case, through the months of preparation with video conferences, teleconferences, preparing my witness statement, numerous phone calls with Joel Zyngier and Natalie Dalpethado from Holding Redlich and conversations with Blackfellas at events across the country, my day sitting in court and then months of waiting for the verdict. I always had faith in justice being served. To contemplate the alternative was too emotionally disturbing for me. I knew that no-one in the article had been portrayed honestly. We all knew who we were and where we were from, and why we did the work we did. We were right, Bolt was so terribly wrong, and for that the law must protect us and those like us in the community. But I also knew how naïve I was being: the law had failed so many times before, like the case of Cameron Doomadgee and his death in police custody in 2004.

By the time judgment day arrived, this case was no longer simply about Blacks, it was a case about all those oppressed by opinion columnists. For me, this case had become about fighting for a better society, one where individuals could feel safe from abuse by ignorant powerbrokers. I wanted a better media. I wanted those who got paid to be writers to feel compelled to do their job properly (check facts, cite sources, not engage in racial discrimination and cause venomous comments by readers, write ethically), just like I had done since I published my first piece of journalism back in 1992.

I had always planned on going to Melbourne, where the trial was taking place, to hear the judge hand down his judgment. I wanted to have the say that I was denied the day I went to court back in March and wasn't called up to give evidence. I wanted to clear my name and reinstate the integrity that is attached to it, personally and professionally. But when my solicitor, Joel Zyngier, called me to advise the date of judgment I suddenly panicked. What if the judge condemned Bolt for his writing, but found he hadn't actually broken the law?

After all, at the end of the day the question for the judge was whether or not a law had been broken.

I was already fragile from the trial, from having to read media commentators, mainly whitefellas, argue the case for 'free speech', with little comment on or respect for the responsibilities that came with such rights. I had watched media professionals I had long respected remain silent in the debate, and so too some high-profile Aboriginal people. My own union, the Australian Society of Authors, had failed to make a statement, when I believed they should have been leading the discussion on the topic. This led me to revoke my membership shortly after the case closed.

After talking to my lawyer Joel Zyngier, my agent Tara Wynne and my life-coach Geraldine Star, and Martin Flanagan, who remained a staunch supporter throughout the trial, I decided that in my own best interests I would stay in Sydney. Mum was overseas at the time and my siblings had to work that day, so I went into Redfern to be among those who supported me, not only during the case, but over the years as friends and colleagues. I sat in the boardroom of the National Aboriginal Sporting Chance Academy at the National Centre for Indigenous Excellence in Redfern. I had been appointed a board member (unpaid) in 2010. I had my laptop plugged in as I fielded media inquiries on my phone before the courtroom had even opened. Three friends were attending court to represent me in my absence: Michelle Evans, Belinda Collins and Michelle Nicol. Belinda texted me to describe the atmosphere of the courtroom before the hearing had commenced. Within twenty minutes Michelle Nicol texted me to say we'd won.

I was shaking. I hadn't heard from the lawyer, and I didn't want to jump the gun. Michelle texted me again with more details: we'd won, and the judge was reading the orders. It certainly sounded like victory. I was torn between wanting to scream and wanting to cry and hug someone. I rang Larissa Behrendt, friend and co-plaintiff, immediately and while I was on the phone to her, the confirmation victory text came through from Joel Zyngier. By 11 am the news was reporting that the federal court had found Andrew Bolt and the Herald and Weekly Times had engaged in unlawful racial discrimination. Judge Bromberg had said:

> *I am satisfied that fair-skinned Aboriginal people (or some of them) were reasonably likely, in all the circumstances, to have been offended, insulted, humiliated or intimidated by the imputations conveyed by the newspaper articles . . . On the basis of my findings, I am satisfied that each of Mr Bolt and the Herald and Weekly Times engaged in conduct which contravened section 18C of the* Racial Discrimination Act.

His Honour Justice Bromberg went on to say that as well as being offensive in tone, the article had contained 'errors of fact, distortions of the truth and inflammatory and provocative language'.

While the judgment was a significant win for our own right

to self-identification, self-representation and determination, victory did not remove the trauma of the previous two years, or undo the damage done to race relations in Australia. But for a fleeting moment that day, we were able to celebrate. It was a victory for Blackfellas in the federal court and that was something to stop and acknowledge. I spent five hours at a bistro in Redfern taking calls and emails and being congratulated in person by staff members of Australians for Native Title and Reconciliation, the National Congress of Australia's First Peoples, Koori Radio and strangers who were eating at the same bistro. It was an extraordinary moment of solidarity; everyone knew the win was for all of us.

Over the next few days I was overwhelmed by the level of support and messages of congratulations I received from friends, peers, strangers. They were youth workers, public servants, policy makers, lawyers, writers, publishers, academics, filmmakers, health workers, Australians living overseas, local councillors, Blackfellas from across the country, Aboriginal parents and artists. The most common words were 'justice', 'congrats' and 'thank you!' Many of those messages also came from non-Indigenous Australians, who had not only been following the case but were also fed up with the state of opinion journalism published in Australia.

~

As the debate on free speech continued for months after the case, few acknowledged that Part IIA of the *Racial*

Discrimination Act deals with finding a balance between freedom of expression and racial discrimination, as acknowledged by Justice Bromberg in his decision. In his findings, Justice Bromberg made it clear that it was not that the media was banned from discussing racial identification or challenging the genuineness of people's identification, but rather that they needed to take responsibility for 'the manner in which that subject matter was dealt with'. People were not being silenced – they were being asked to act reasonably and in good faith.

While journos and other media types continued to talk about their rights to free speech, few managed to unpack the crux of the case and discuss in depth the issue of racial vilification. After the appeal period had passed (the Herald and Weekly Times accepted the judgment), Ron Merkel clarified the issue in his article 'Freedom to vilify must be checked by freedom from racial vilification', which appeared in the News Limited *The Australian* newspaper on 21 November 2011.

> *Justice Bromberg explained the harm caused by stereotyping that leads to racial vilification. The disparagement of the 'others' in society, because they belong to a racial group, stigmatises the group's members, leading to racial prejudice, discrimination, social exclusion, even violence.*

And that's where Andrew Bolt had come undone. He had allowed his work to be the breeding ground for racial vilification. And now, after all his years of writing – challenging the status of Blacks, criticising government refugee policies and 'illegal immigrants' and making offensive comments about women (he took out the 2011 Ernie Award for misogynistic remarks for an article he wrote suggesting male soldiers would be turned from warriors into escorts if women were allowed to serve on the frontline) – someone had finally had the courage to stand up to him. When he targeted myself and my co-plaintiffs, he took on an educated and articulate group of people who were supported by a legal team who also felt *enough was enough*!

I don't intend to give a literary review of who said what and, trust me, I've read most of what's been written. But among the many columns penned, I was grateful for Mike Carlton's 'Nuts come out after the truth has bolted' (published in *The Sydney Morning Herald*, 1 October 2011), in which he simply stated: 'The judge did not smother free speech. He skewered dud journalism.' There was also the column by anti-censorship advocate and president of Watch on Censorship David Marr, who acknowledged in his piece 'In black and white, Andrew Bolt trifled with the facts', (*The Sydney Morning Herald*, 29 September 2011) that, 'Freedom of speech is not at stake here. Judge Mordecai Bromberg is not telling the media what we can say or where we can poke our noses. He's attacking lousy journalism. He's saying that if Andrew Bolt of the *Herald Sun* wants to accuse people of appalling motives, he should start by getting his facts right.'

I haven't talked to those who chose not to be in the case as to why they opted out. Everyone has their own reasons. And, until it was all over, I couldn't understand why people kept telling me I was brave. What was so brave about clearing your name and fighting for your right to self-identity? Only when I read anonymous blog comments and received emails from strangers filled with hatred did I realise how powerful the Bolt brand is in the media and in stirring up hatred in readers, and only then did I come to understand that the so-called bravery to some, was also crazy to others.

I wrote to a friend recently and said, 'The case was traumatic, but it will remain the most important thing I will ever do in my lifetime.' As Joel Zyngier stated in a media release on judgment day, 'The court recognised that you can have a debate about racial identity, but you must conduct the debate in an appropriate way. There is a balance between freedom of expression and freedom of identity.'

Writing my memoir on identity has been a significant and challenging personal process, but as someone who sees the need for resources in the classroom I also felt a responsibility to provide answers to inquiring minds. As it turned out, the work has also managed to set the record straight between what's been said about me in recent years and what is actually true.

I am a writer, and so my life is about words and the impact they have on individuals, communities and whole societies. I know only too well the power of language and role of books in educating, informing and bringing different communities together, just as the power of the word in any medium – the press, book, poem, play or song – can be someone's salvation or nemesis.

I hope that by unravelling my own forty-plus years of life as an Aboriginal person that the general Australian reading public and students in our schools and colleges come to appreciate without criticism or concern, the diversity and complexity of Aboriginal identity in the twenty-first century, and that the power of self-identity and representation is a right we should all enjoy.

GLOSSARY OF TERMS AND ACRONYMS

General note on the use of 'Indigenous' and 'Aboriginal' in this book

In the Australian context, 'Indigenous' is a collective term used when referring to both Aboriginal and Torres Strait Islander people. 'Aboriginal' is another collective term, but is used to specifically refer to those First Peoples within Australia who are not traditionally from the Torres Strait Islands.

Terms

Barangaroo
Barangaroo was a Cammeraygal woman of the Lower North Shore region of Sydney and an important figure in Sydney's early colonial years. She was the second wife of Bennelong,

who often resided within the colony and advised the governor. Unlike her husband, Barangaroo actively resisted the adoption of European culture and disapproved of her husband's association with the colonial Europeans. Barangaroo died in 1791 shortly after giving birth to a baby girl named Dilboong. Bennelong buried Barangaroo's cremation ashes in the garden of Government House. Sadly Dilboong died shortly thereafter and was laid to rest with her mother.

Bennelong

Bennelong belonged to the Wangal clan. In 1789 he was kidnapped under the orders of Governor Arthur Phillip so that the governor could learn more about Sydney's Aboriginal people. Bennelong escaped that year but remade contact with the colony shortly afterward. Through subsequent interactions Bennelong rose to a respected position within the colony and became an advisor to Governor Phillip. Bennelong travelled with Phillip to England in 1792 and upon his return to Sydney commenced advising Governor Hunter. Bennelong died on 3 January 1813 and was buried in a location provided by his friend, brewer James Squire.

Biami

Biami is a father-like creator spirit of particular traditional importance to south-east Australian nations such as the Wiradjuri, Kamilaroi, Darkinjung and Eora. Biami resides in the sky and descended to form much of the land and laws of south-east Australia.

Bundjalung

Bundjalung are the people of the Bundjalung nation spanning across north-east New South Wales and south-east Queensland. The term 'Bundjalung' can also be used when referring to the language the Bundjalung people traditionally shared. The approximate border of Bundjalung country covers Grafton to the south, Warwick to the north-west, the Logan River to the north and to the coastline between Yamba and Surfers Paradise to the east.

Cammeraygal

The Cammeraygal people are a clan whose traditional land covers much of Sydney's Lower North Shore. There's some discrepancy in sources as to what nation they belonged to. Some sources say they existed within the Eora nation while others state they existed within the Kurrin-gai nation.

Dharawal

Dharawal are the people of the Dharawal nation south of Sydney. The term 'Dharawal' can also be used when referring to the language that the Dharawal people traditionally shared. The approximate border of Dharawal country covers the south-side of Botany Bay to the north, the Shoalhaven River to the south, and to the west inland from the coastline as far as Bowral and Camden.

First Peoples

First Peoples is a broad collective term used to describe the original people of a post-colonial land and their descendants.

Gadigal

The Gadigal people are one of twenty-nine clan groups who traditionally resided within Sydney. Gadigal land lies approximately between the suburb of Petersham in the west, the Cooks River to the south, and the South Head of Sydney Harbour in the north-east.

Haudenosaunee

The Haudenosaunee is a pre-colonial confederacy of the Mohawk, Oneida, Onondaga, Cayuga, and Seneca nations spanning across the border of Canada and America. The Haudenosaunee operates as a participatory democracy and unites each of the individual nations with the common goal of living in peace and harmony.

Iwi and Hapu

'Iwi' and 'Hapu' are terms commonly used today by Maori to specifically define where they belong within Maori-dom. A Maori 'Iwi' is a tribe whilst a 'Hapu' is a sub-group found within that Iwi.

Koori

A generic term primarily used by Aboriginal people of New South Wales and Victoria (Koorie) to identify as traditionally belonging to the south-east of the Australian mainland.

Noongars

Noongars are Aboriginal people traditionally belonging to the south-west corner of Western Australia. Variations of the term include Nyungar, Nyoongar, Nyoongah, Nyungah, Nyugah and Noonga.

Stolen Generations

A term used to refer to the Aboriginal children removed from their family over the space of many generations by state and federal government agencies, as well as church missions. This practice was undertaken for a number of reasons. One reason was a desire to protect Aboriginal children from what was considered by white Australians to be unsuitable Aboriginal parenting. Another reason was to stop the practice of Aboriginal culture by preventing Aboriginal parents from passing their oral traditions to their children by removing them and 'assimilating' them into white Australia instead.

Terra Nullius

'Terra Nullius' is a Latin term meaning 'land belonging to no-one' and a legal doctrine derived from Roman law. The doctrine Terra Nullius exists in international law and essentially allows a foreign nation to claim sovereignty over any land that is either unoccupied, or has people but they are deemed to be too 'uncivilised' to possess sovereignty.

The Apology

'The Apology' was a motion moved in Parliament on

13 February 2008 by then Prime Minister, the Hon Kevin Rudd MP. This address received bipartisan support and was delivered with respect to the historical mistreatment of Indigenous Australia, and particularly to those who were Stolen Generations.

The Northern Territory Intervention

The Northern Territory National Emergency Response, or 'the Intervention' as it has come to be known, was announced by the Howard government in August 2007. It was proposed as a plan for addressing child abuse in Aboriginal communities of the Northern Territory, following its existence being highlighted by the Little Children are Sacred Report. In order for the Intervention and its controversial features to be implemented the Howard government suspended the *Racial Discrimination Act*. Such controversial features include the government's compulsory acquisition of townships held under the *Native Title Act* without being required to provide compensation on just terms, the removal of a permit system that allowed Aboriginal control over who accessed their land, imposed restrictions on alcohol and kava, pornography filters on publicly funded computers, the partial quarantining of welfare benefits to all recipients in designated communities and the quarantining of all welfare benefits for those who were deemed to be neglecting their children.

Truganini

A Tasmanian Aboriginal woman who lived from approximately

1812 to 8 May 1876. Non-Indigenous Tasmanians of her time widely considered her to be the 'last full-blood' Aboriginal person of Tasmania. This led them to declare upon her death that the Aboriginal people of Tasmania had become extinct.

Wiradjuri

Wiradjuri are the people of the Wiradjuri nation of central New South Wales. The term 'Wiradjuri' can also be used when referring to the language the Wiradjuri people traditionally shared. Wiradjuri country is geographically the largest in New South Wales and loosely consists of the land between Nyngan to the north, Albury to the south, Bathurst to the east and Hay to the west. The Lachlan, Murray and Murrumbidgee rivers run through Wiradjuri country and are of particular cultural significance to Wiradjuri people.

Acronyms

ACM
Aboriginal Catholic Ministry

AIATSIS
Australian Institute of Aboriginal and Torres Strait Islander Studies

AIDAB (now AusAID)
Australian International Development Assistance Bureau

AMMS
Aboriginal Multi-Media Society

ASA
Australian Society of Authors

ASIC
Australian Securities and Investments Commission

ATSIAB
Aboriginal and Torres Strait Islander Arts Board

BWRC
Black Writers Reunion and Conference

CAR
Council for Aboriginal Reconciliation

CCDB
Community Cultural Development Board

DEET
Department of Employment, Education and Training

FCAATSI
Federal Council for the Advancement of Aborigines and Torres Strait Islanders

ILF
Indigenous Literacy Foundation

NAIDOC
National Aborigines and Islanders Day Observance Committee

NAPLAN
National Assessment Program – Literacy and Numeracy

NASCA
National Aboriginal Sporting Chance Academy

NMAI
National Museum of the American Indian

UNESCO
United Nations Educational, Scientific and Cultural Organisation

WFW
Women for Wik

(Glossary was prepared by Lachlan McDaniel.)

ACKNOWLEDGEMENTS

I wrote this book to honour my family. I am thankful every day for their love, support and caring.

To my friends, mentors and colleagues of all cultural persuasions who have been part of my journey, this work is a way of acknowledging the contribution you have made to my life and the woman I am.

I want to specifically acknowledge Lawrence and Mavis Bamblett for reading drafts and providing significant and valuable information about the history of Erambie and Cowra. I remain forever grateful. To my cousins Buster, John, Sharon and Naomi Williams for supporting me in writing our family's story, thank you.

To Lachlan McDaniel for preparing the glossary for this book, many thanks. To Tara Wynne at Curtis Brown, the team at Random House and Geraldine Star for having my back always, I am indebted.

To Martin Flanagan who I admire for his conviction and ethics – thank you for the inspiration and support.

To my tiddas as mentioned here, the meaning in my life comes from being able to share it with you.

To you reading this, I hope that my journey adds something to your own. Much peace.